B+T
AP 21 '82
$2 3.50

Corruption
A Study in Political Economy

Corruption
A Study in Political Economy

SUSAN ROSE-ACKERMAN

Department of Economics and
Institution for Social and Policy Studies
Yale University
New Haven, Connecticut

Academic Press   NEW YORK   SAN FRANCISCO   LONDON

A Subsidiary of Harcourt Brace Jovanovich, Publishers

ACADEMIC PRESS, INC.
111 Fifth Avenue, New York, New York 10003

United Kingdom Edition published by
ACADEMIC PRESS, INC. (LONDON) LTD.
24/28 Oval Road, London NW1   7DX

Library of Congress Cataloging in Publication Data

Rose—Ackerman, Susan.
    Corruption : a study in political economy.

    Bibliography : p.
    1. Corruption (in politics)——Economic aspects.
I. Title.
JF1081.R67   320.4   78—6170
ISBN 0—12—596350—5

To Sybil and John

CONTENTS

Bureaucratic Corruption

Conclusion

ACKNOWLEDGMENTS

Since I have drawn from a variety of intellectual traditions in both political science and economics, many different people have been helpful at various points in my work, and I cannot acknowledge all of their contributions individually. I would, however, particularly like to thank Charles E. Lindblom, J. Michael Montias, Sharon Oster, Merton J. Peck, and Burton Weisbrod for reading portions of the manuscript. I owe special debts to both Richard Nelson, and my husband, Bruce A. Ackerman. Richard Nelson read and commented on the entire manuscript, and Bruce Ackerman was a persistent and invaluable critic and a constant source of encouragement at all stages in the preparation of this book.

Three students: Arthur Slepian, Bruce Chapman, and Henry Chappell, helped to check sources. Henry Chappell also prepared the index and made many useful suggestions after reading the draft manuscript. Over the years, several secretaries have patiently borne with my numerous revisions, but Amy Yu Chen-Kung deserves special thanks for her excellent work in preparing the final round of drafts before publication. I am also extremely grateful to Susan Siemionko for taking care of my children over the past 3 years. She made it possible for me to combine career and family with the assurance that my children were loved and well cared for when I was not at home.

My research was partially supported by the Institution for Social and Policy Studies at Yale University. In addition to financial support, ISPS and its director Charles E. Lindblom provided me with a hospitable environment in which to pursue interdisciplinary studies and made it easy for me to talk with both political scientists and economists about my work. After the book was begun, the National Institute for Law Enforcement and Criminal Justice, Law Enforcement Assistance Administration, U.S. Department of Justice, also supplied research support under Grant No. 75N1-99-0127. Of course, the points of view or opinions presented in this book are those of the author and do not represent the official position or policies of the U.S. Department of Justice.

Introduction

1

CORRUPTION AS A PROBLEM IN POLITICAL ECONOMY

1. CORRUPTION AND THE MIXED ECONOMY

Although the corruption of public and private officials is constantly exposed by the popular press, the interest of the public seldom goes beyond the details of particular scandals. Yet as the episodes accumulate, it becomes clear that there is more at stake than the set of disjointed stories implies. For the study of corruption requires a confrontation with the most fundamental questions of political economy in a modern society. Whatever else is problematic, societies obviously do not use a single, consistent method to make allocative decisions. A good or service may be allocated through a market system in which wide inequalities of income are taken for granted; dispensed through a democratic political system that grants a formal equality to each citizen's vote, assigned by administrative rule, by random selection, or on the basis of some standard of "worthiness." Mixed systems are common, and many allocative mechanisms do not easily fit under one or another simple rubric. While there is, of course, much dispute about the precise normative line where the price system should leave off and other methods take over, *both* market and nonmarket mechanisms clearly have important allocative roles to play. Assuming that society has drawn a line *somewhere* in the vast middle range of mixed alternatives, this

1

book explores the way in which wealth and market forces can under-mine whatever dividing line has been fixed. Thus, political decisions that are made on the basis of majority preferences may be undermined by wide use of an illegal market as the method of allocation. Legislative decisions may themselves be "for sale" to the highest bidder. The more persistent are market forces, the less likely is the survival of a mixed system. A central question is whether democratic government can withstand the pressures of market forces: To what extent does the stable operation of a mixed system *require* political participants to dedicate themselves to democratic ideals, even when this is not otherwise in their self-interest?

Corruption not only reveals a basic tension between market mecha-nisms and voting processes but also forces the political economist to deal with allocative problems raised by the presence of large organiza-tions in both the public and private sectors.[1] In both complex modern societies and underdeveloped states, the delegation of decision-making authority is a fundamental organizational technique. Whenever an agent is given discretionary authority, corruption provides a way for the objectives of the higher authority to be undermined. The central question here is whether organizational incentives can substitute for personal honesty in maintaining hierarchical control: Does a realistic model of a stable modern economy require agents who value honesty even when high personal scruples are not rewarded by superiors?

By raising these questions, I plan to do more than explore substantive issues central to modern economic and political life.[2] I also hope to suggest the possibility of building on different theoretical traditions in economics and political science to develop a more comprehensive form of political economy. Unless we draw from both disciplines, we will fail to develop a framework adequate for our subject. While the economist's concern with profit-maximizing behavior is of obvious relevance to the study of corruption, it is equally plain that the standard techniques used to analyze private markets are not adequate to the problem. Neither the

---

[1] In taking large organizations as given I do not mean to imply that they are necessarily desirable. See Lindblom (1977) for a critical assessment of the role of the modern corporation.

[2] The analysis is not, however, limited to a consideration of modern, industrialized democracies. Corruption is pervasive in undemocratic planned economies (see Berliner, 1959; Smith, 1976), in underdeveloped countries (for examples, see Heidenheimer, 1970, Chapters 4, 7, 10, and 11; V. T. LeVine, 1975; Scott, 1972), and has been endemic in previous historical epochs (for examples, see Heidenheimer, 1970, Chapters 2 and 8; and Wraith and Simkins, 1963). Much of the discussion of corruption applies to certain features of these politicoeconomic systems as well.

decision by a politician to trade votes for bribes nor the corrupt bureaucrat's dealings with politicians and interest groups can be treated as simple extensions of the profit-maximizing calculus of the private entrepreneur. Since both politician and bureaucrat operate in distinctive institutional frameworks different from those of competitive theory, a simplistic application of market analysis is not sufficient.

Standard political science approaches are equally unsatisfactory. On the one hand, formal efforts to model political behavior typically assume that politicians singlemindedly seek to maximize their likelihood of reelection;[3] this simple view is not very helpful, however, for an analysis of the politician's tradeoff between dollars and votes. On the other hand, while less formal theories recognize that politicians have a multitude of objectives, they fail to develop a general theory describing the way tradeoffs between competing goals are made.[4]

There is, in short, no body of theory ready made for application to the problem at hand. To make progress, one must develop a set of analytic techniques that combine an economist's concern with modeling self-interested behavior with a political scientist's recognition that political

[3] Schumpeter (1950) hypothesizes that the dominant motive of political candidates is winning elections. Ben-Zion and Eytan (1974), Brock and Magee (1975), and Welch (1974) also assume that the probability of reelection is the politician's maximand. While agreeing that winning elections is the primary motive, Shepsle (1972) asserts that vote maximization is a convenient secondary motivation to consider. Bartlett (1973), Downs (1957), Kramer (1975), Niskanen (1975), Nordhaus (1975), Page (1976), and Riker and Ordeshook (1973, Chapters 11, 12) all employ the simplifying vote maximization hypothesis. A slightly different approach is used by Frey (1974) who assumes that politicians manipulate macroeconomic policy with the objective of maximizing their length of stay in office. In his model, short-run vote maximization may be sacrificed for long-run security. Barro (1973) has developed an alternative model in which politicians are only interested in public and private consumption goods and seek election as a means of increasing their consumption possibilities. Many of the issues raised by other authors are irrelevant to his analysis, however, since he assumes that voters have equal incomes and tastes.

[4] Excellent studies in this tradition are Fenno (1973, 1977), and Mayhew (1974). The same dichotomy between very simple formal theorizing and comprehensive, informal, and largely descriptive work is also found in work on bureaucracy. Compare Niskanen (1971), on the one hand, with most of the work surveyed in Nadel and Rourke (1975) and Warwick (1975, Chapter 10) on the other. Both Niskanen (1971) and Breton (1974) set up formal models that include both politicians and bureaucrats. Breton's politicians maximize a utility function that includes the probability of reelection, income, power, ideals, and other variables. Bureaucracies maximize the number of employees in the agency. Breton recognizes the interaction among clients, bureaus, and politicians, and discusses the fact that low-level officials may have different objectives than superiors. Neither he nor Niskanen considers the possibility of bribery, however.

and bureaucratic institutions provide incentive structures far different from those presupposed by the competitive market paradigm.[5] While this unification of disparate scholarly concerns is the book's central methodological task, it represents only a part of the larger work of theoretical construction necessary to provide a full, positive theory of political economy. For the offer of a bribe represents only one way in which individuals try to influence government behavior. There are at least six other types of interactions. First, the relationship may be wholly "legalistic." Individuals follow the rules as spelled out by the law without trying to obtain preference or change the rules, that is, they wait their turns, fill out forms, obey traffic signals, pay entrance fees, and supply goods at prices set by the government. Second, friendship, family ties, or personal loyalty can determine an agent's actions. Third, individuals might try to persuade or inform government officials. Fourth, citizens may work through the legal system by bringing lawsuits or seeking injunctions. Fifth, if the government is democratic, individuals could try to influence the outcome of the next election or sponsor referenda on important issues. Finally, citizens may use threats to make officials do what they wish.

These seven types of relationships between government agents and citizens all coexist in a single political system, and any individual whether within or outside government is likely to use or be the subject of several. Moreover, many actual situations involve more than one of the seven categories. A threat of forceful arrest by the police may be countered by attempts to persuade or bribe them. Alternatively, if citizens attempt to obtain favors through appeals to family ties or by bribes, officials may present arguments demonstrating why the favor is not justified.

Nonetheless, in considering this complicated reality, I shall always keep bribery in the analytic foreground. It is true, of course, that gifts of time, personal favors, family ties, lobbying, and threats are all forms of influence similar to bribery. The analysis, however, does not attempt to do justice to the distinctive character of these alternatives. It leaves to one side the interesting social–psychological question of why norms differ across professions, government agencies and political jurisdictions. While I do not wish to minimize the importance of variations in

[5] The analysis draws from past work on corruption in political science and economics. In political science the basic sources are Banfield (1975), Gardiner (1970), Key (1936), Scott (1972), and the articles in Gardiner and Olson (1974) and Heidenheimer (1970). Work in economics is especially scanty, but see Becker and Stigler (1974), Johnson (1975), Krueger (1974), Pashigian (1975), and Schmidt (1969) for treatments of particular aspects of the problem.

individual scruples and accepted practices, the analysis will concentrate on structural incentives. Similarly, while the argument emphasizes the politician's desire for reelection, it slights the role of ideology, logrolling, and "rational" argument in explaining government behavior. I shall, however, consider one form of monetary payment which is not always illegal—campaign contributions from special interest groups. Given the relative ineffectiveness of legal sanctions as a deterrent to legislators and the strength of the reelection motive, it seems useful to expand the analysis to include these contributions.[6] In short, the book focuses on the dimensions of political life where the professional economist's training can provide useful insights if tempered by a concern for the structure of government institutions. In a study of corruption, one can make substantial progress with models that take tastes and values as given and perceive individuals as rational beings attempting to further their own self-interest in a world of scarce resources. Information may be imperfect; risks may abound; but individuals are assumed to do the best they can within the constraints imposed by a finite world.

Although a political economic approach has a special relevance to the study of corruption, I do not claim that it completely illuminates the subject. Indeed, the analysis leads one to emphasize the importance of personal morality in explaining the viability of democratic government in a market economy; similarly, the widespread delegation of authority to agents in large organizations presupposes that most economic actors are unwilling to milk their positions to the limits of possibility. Some political and organizational structures, however, *are* less corruption-prone than others; in fact, it will be one of my major objectives to isolate the critical structural variables. Nevertheless, the continuing operation of familiar institutions would be inexplicable in the absence of wide-spread personal commitments to honesty and democratic ideals. Thus, the professional economist looking at political phenomena must steer a middle way between the extreme claim that "no other approach of remotely comparable generality and power is available [Stigler and Becker, 1977:77]" and the narrow view that economics is concerned mainly with the determination of such macroeconomic variables as the level of income, employment, and prices.[7] Although an economic

---

[6] Another justification for considering campaign financing is the availability of data. Chapter 3 raises some issues that can be tested empirically using information from the Federal Elections Commission.

[7] See, for example, the view of Scott (1972) that an economist who finds "that the ruling party of a new nation through its minister of public work exacts 5 to 10 percent in graft on each contract it awards, might want to know how this affects the society's rate of savings, its investment decisions, its pattern of income distribution, or its ability to carry out a five-year development plan [p. 2]."

approach to politics can accomplish a good deal, it cannot explain the origination and transmission of the democratic and personal ideals required to preserve a functioning mixed economy.

2. AGENCY RELATIONSHIPS AND FUNCTIONAL BRIBERY

The "agency" relationship is the basic unit of analysis. The relationship links at least two actors. On the one hand, the superior expresses a set of preferences which specify desired outcomes. On the other hand, there is the agent, whom the superior has directed to achieve these outcomes. Thus democratic legislators are the agents of voters; agency heads, of legislators; and bureaucrats, of agency heads. A similar pattern of delegation is characteristic of the private firm as well.

While superiors would like agents always to fulfill the superior's objectives, monitoring is costly, and agents will generally have some freedom to put their own interests ahead of their principals'. Here is where money enters. Some third person, who can benefit by the agent's action, seeks to influence the agent's decision by offering him a monetary payment which is not passed on to the principal.[8] The existence of such a payment does not necessarily imply that the principal's goals have been subverted—indeed the payment may even increase the principal's satisfaction with the agent's performance.[9] Both tips to waiters and bribes to low-level officials may often improve service beyond the level attained by employees paid only a regular

[8] In the legislator's case, the "third party" might be a member of the legislator's district who wants a benefit which will impose costs on a majority of the legislator's constituents.

[9] This essay is therefore quite different in emphasis from work on the economics of agency relationships. None of this past work considers active outsiders who try to influence agents' behavior. Instead, the research is concerned with a principal who can set a fee schedule for the agent. The fee paid depends upon the agent's behavior and upon the state of world. Ross (1973, 1974) and Wilson (1968) find fee schedules which induce the agent to maximize the expected utility of the principal. Bonin (1975), Bonin and Marcus (1976), Groves (1973), and Weitzman (1976) are all concerned with inducing the agent to provide correct information to the principal.

All this work seeks efficient fee schedules but does not deal with broader questions of institutional design. In my work, Pareto optimality is not always used as a benchmark, and fees cannot always be used to control agents. Elected representatives are not, for example, paid by voters. Several chapters do, however, explore the way in which expected penalties affect bureaucratic agents. In addition, I go beyond previous work and analyze a richer variety of institutional alternatives including some where competitive pressures substitute for hierarchical control.

salary. Thus my focus is not limited to payments that conflict with the principal's goals. Nor is it limited to payments that have been formally declared illegal. Rather it embraces all payments to agents that are not passed on to superiors. Nevertheless, many third-party payments *are* illegal, and it is only these which I shall call "corrupt." [10] Although the analysis concentrates on these illegal payments, it can often be easily extended to legal activities with similar public policy consequences. For example, the discussion of campaign contributions and lobbying in Chapter 3 makes this extension explicit in one important case.

Although corruption is thus a legal category, it does have consequences for the economic analysis of agent behavior. Branding a transfer as criminal means that expected legal penalties will lower an agent's willingness to accept, and a third person's willingness to offer, money payments. Similarly, the moral costs of breaking the law will affect the behavior of the actors. [11] The formal similarity between legal and illegal payments is important, however, in order to assess the desirability of converting "bribes" to "payments" by a change in the law. This possibility is often ignored by those social scientists who emphasize the "functional" characteristics of bribery. [12] Yet if a payment system is

[10] This definition should be compared with Nye's (1970). He and Scott (1972) define corruption as "behavior which deviates from the formal duties of a public role because of private-regarding . . . pecuniary or status gains: or violates rules against the exercise of certain types of private-regarding influence [Nye, 1970:566–567]."

Both Nye's definitions and mine exclude any mention of the public interest, but I also include as corrupt, actions which, even though illegal, further the principal's goals. Since I essentially equate corruption with bribery, my definition is narrower than Nye's, which includes "nepotism (bestowal of patronage by reason of ascriptive relationship rather than merit) and misappropriation (illegal appropriation of public resources for private-regarding uses [p. 567]." In some of the analysis, however, I discuss the distinction between conflicts of interest and corruption, as I have defined it, but I do not analyze the simple theft or embezzlement of public funds.

Nye avoids mentioning the legal status of corrupt behavior and instead speaks of formal duties and rules. This difference is unimportant to my analysis since I assume that there is no wide divergence between *formally* acceptable practice and the law. Governments where there is, in fact, a wide divergence will present complicated moral dilemmas to most citizens, businessmen, and foreign visitors. For an exploration of this issue in the case of Thailand see Von Roy (1970). It is not the aim of this book, however, to resolve these vexing questions. Instead the main focus is on the relationship between institutional form and corrupt incentives.

[11] When anticorruption statutes are never enforced, the analytic distinction between corruption and legal payments reduces to these moral costs alone. Moral costs may be relatively small, however, if individuals interpret lax enforcement as evidence that bribe paying is not really very "evil."

[12] Social scientists emphasize the fact that corruption may be efficient or stress its role in holding shaky political systems together. See Bayley (1966), Huntington (1967), Leff (1964), Merton (1968:126–136), Nye (1967), and Scott (1972).

truly functional, it seems better to legalize it. Corruption is never more than a second-best solution. Its very illegality produces inefficiencies since resources are wasted in keeping transactions secret and in enforcing antibribery statutes. Moreover, a corrupt system of government services has the distributional disadvantage of benefiting unscrupulous people at the expense of law-abiding citizens who would be willing to purchase the services legally. Corruption may also be impossible to limit to "desirable" situations. A system which overlooks corruption in areas where it is "economically justifiable" may find in time that corruption has spread to all aspects of the government structure. If trust, honesty, and altruism are valuable traits in some areas of life, they may be impossible to preserve if dishonesty is openly tolerated elsewhere.

Legalization has its own difficulties, however. Even with a legal price system, the "public marketplace" is generally only a pale copy of the competitive market of economic theory: Buyers and sellers may be few, the product is often highly differentiated and hard to evaluate, entry and exit may be blocked, and externalities are likely to be of major importance. Furthermore, distributional goals can prevent the use of prices—it hardly seems equitable, for example, to allocate apartments in a public housing project by selling them off to the highest bidders. Nevertheless, even an imperfect and inequitable legal pricing system seems preferable, on both allocational and distributional grounds, to a corrupt administrative mechanism.[13]

Yet even a demonstration that a legalized payment system is better than corruption often fails to shake those who recommend the "sophisticated" acceptance of corruption. For their views are often grounded in a more fundamental conflict between cost–benefit analysis and the democratic political process. Those economists who use the maximization of the dollar value of consumers' and producers' surplus as their measure of benefit will inevitably find that their recommendations conflict with many of the policy decisions of a representative democracy. If costs are broadly diffused, while benefits are narrowly concentrated, projects which produce large benefit–cost ratios may be defeated if subjected either to a popular referendum or a vote in the legislature. Similarly, a majority of the legislature can easily pass laws with negative net benefits.[14] This dissatisfaction with political choices may lead committed

---

[13] Of course, legal payments will often also have the advantage of entering the government treasury. This benefit will be relatively unimportant, however, if the expectation of corrupt receipts implies that the government can pay low salaries to bureaucrats (Barzel, 1974).

[14] Buchanan and Tullock (1962, Chapters 10–12) are especially concerned with this latter possibility.

cost–benefit analysts to favor the corruption of existing laws as an alternative to obtaining the power to impose their own favored policies. The incompatibility of cost–benefit analysis and majority rule, however, does not provide a sound justification for corruption. Not only is bribery seldom a surplus maximizing procedure, but also the maximization of the dollar value of surplus is not a self-evidently appealing maxim: It neglects distributional objectives and weighs outcomes in favor of the wealthy.

Some economists' critiques of politics are, however, even more sweeping than the complaint that governments do not make decisions on the basis of cost–benefit analysis. Social scientists may view corruption tolerantly because they believe that the political sphere is "too large" relative to the private market sector and that, even in those areas of justifiable state action, government is likely to bungle the implementation of policies. Hence, corruption is taken as a signal that government has overextended itself. This argument, however, muddles normative and empirical issues together in an unacceptable way. Although drawing the line between market and democratic methods represents one of the fundamental, unresolved questions of *normative* theory, it does not follow that the existence of corruption necessarily implies that the government has overstepped itself.[15] Instead, corrupt incentives are the nearly inevitable consequence of *all* government attempts to control market forces—even the "minimal" state (Nozick, 1974) has a coercive police force whose agents will often have discretionary power. Since *some* level of corruption will be associated with every mix of market and democratic mechanisms, its existence cannot be taken as an indictment of any particular system.

Normative statements about corruption, therefore, require a point of view, a standard of "goodness," and a model of how corruption works in particular instances. Those economists who look favorably upon corruption generally have a limited point of view, a narrow definition of goodness and an oversimplified model of the corrupt marketplace. This is not to say, however, that bribery is never justified as an adaptation to an unpleasant reality. An individual, unable to affect overall government policy, may in some situations, pay a bribe without moral opprobrium. One does not condemn a Jew for bribing his way out of a concentration camp. I have, however, argued that one cannot judge corruption without

---

[15] High levels of corruption may also be associated with extremely low levels of public services. For example, see Gardiner (1970:13) on Wincanton and Robinson's (1977) discussion of the low service levels provided by the O'Connell machine in Albany, New York. Furthermore, as Chapter 10 demonstrates, corruption can occur in the private sector without the involvement of any government agent.

a theory of the state and that the case for corruption often presupposes a strikingly undemocratic standard for government action.

3. AN OVERVIEW OF THE ARGUMENT

While leaving the broad task of normative political economic analysis to others, I shall try to develop a positive theory of corruption that can aid those concerned with the practical application of political ideals. This theoretical task is approached on two different levels. The first half of the book models the sources of high level corruption in a democratic political process; the second half considers the incentives for low-level bureaucratic corruption in the administration of laws.

Chapters 2 and 3 analyze corruption in the most fundamental of democratic relationships—that between citizen and elected official.[16] Politicians tradeoff gains in personal income against reelection probabilities and may use special–interest money for personal enrichment or for campaign spending.[17] Once one admits that maximizing the probability

[16] These chapters do not discuss the simpler case of a direct democracy since in that system no one acts as an agent of anyone else, and corruption—as defined here—is impossible. Economists, however, commonly use the term *bribery* to describe payoffs made in simple political systems where all citizens vote on all issues. Bribes of this kind are simply payments to individuals to silence their opposition to programs they would otherwise have voted against. If *all* opponents must be bought off, these bribes permit changes to be made that make all voters at least as well off as they would have been without the change. Of course, if majority rule rather than unanimity is used to decide issues, then side payments need only be made to a subgroup of opponents and results which are not Pareto efficient are possible. See Buchanan and Tullock (1962) for an attempt to justify unanimity as the ideal voting rule in a direct democracy without transactions costs.

[17] The politicians in this model have no personal ideology and never vote on principle. I therefore do not analyze cases where a legislator's principles conflict with the wishes of most constituents, and ignore the possibility that a bribe might cause a representative to forsake principle and follow the preferences of the majority. Pitkin (1967:144–167) discusses the conflict between alternative normative theories of a representative's role. She writes that "the representative's duty, his role as representative, is generally not to get reelected, but to do what is best for those he represents. In a democracy, the voters pass the final judgment on their representative by reelecting him or refusing to do so. But it does not follow that whatever will get him reelected is what he is obligated to do, or is equivalent to 'true' representation. [pp. 164–165]."

My model of legislative motivation accords with current American attitudes. Thus, recent Harris polls show that Americans' belief in the idealism of politicians has eroded rapidly over the last few years. Only 38% believe that "most men go into elected office to help others." (A fall from 80% in 1971.) Furthermore, in 1976, only 9% said they had a "great deal of confidence" in Congress (down from 42% in 1966). The data are from the Harris survey and are reproduced in Fischer (1976:46,64).

of reelection is not a politician's only goal, the analysis can make headway only by carefully specifying the motives and opportunities available to other participants in a democratic political system. Thus, if one assumes an ideal electorate, well informed about legislators' voting behavior, corruption is possible; but bribes must be large enough to compensate the incumbents for voting against the interests of their constituents. Indeed, there can be more corruption in this "ideal" case of an informed and concerned electorate than in a more realistic model where citizens have poor information. For in the case where voters are poorly informed, most of the money received from special interest groups may be legally spent on campaign propaganda rather than used for personal enrichment. Such results as these will seem paradoxical only when one fails to move beyond vague labels like *democracy* to specify the relationships between the major political participants.

Given politicians who are "willing to be bought" through illegal bribes or legal campaign contributions, organizational factors will play a role in determining the volume of money which changes hands. Politicians may be able to extort payments higher than their minimum willingness to accept, and interest groups, in competition over some piece of legislation, may up the ante by bidding against each other. Any feature of the institutional environment which centralizes authority—be it strong party discipline, charismatic opinion leaders, or legislative committees—may permit influential legislators to make extortionary demands. Anything that makes it easier for groups to organize and collect funds may increase the willingness to pay of those affected by public actions. The possibility of extortion is clearly a cost that reformers must consider when they propose tighter party discipline, less overlap in committee business, or other changes that presuppose that legislators are so committed to democratic ideology that they will never put their own personal interests ahead of the wishes of the majority of their constituents.

While Chapters 2 and 3 concentrate upon the relationship among voters, legislators, and interest groups, Chapter 4 deals with the role of the government bureaucracy in shaping legislative choices. Corruption can influence this relationship in three ways. First, the corruption of low-level officials may lead to skewed data on the cost of agency actions. The legislature may then appropriate larger or smaller amounts of money than they would have chosen if the bureau had operated honestly. Second, corrupt top bureaucrats can estimate how their peculation will affect the legislature's choices and will modify their corrupt demands accordingly. Third, when legislators solicit illegal bribes or legal campaign contributions, bureaucrats may be able to provide favors to a legislator's benefactors or constituents. In return for these favors, e.g., government contracts or a beneficial regulatory decision, the representative votes for large budgets or an expansion in an agency's power.

Thus, one can build a model of democratic government in which legislators' needs for campaign funds, bureaucrats' desires for power and influence, as well as simple greed, all interact to skew public choices away from those preferred by a majority of the population. These tendencies can, however, be checked by a combination of structural and motivational factors. If voters are both well informed and issue oriented; if elections are closely contested; and if politicians and bureaucrats are personally committed to majoritarian ideals, then corruption can be restrained. The first half of the book may thus be read as an economic argument on behalf of the traditional democratic virtues of an informed and interested citizenry represented by legislators committed to following the electorate's wishes.

The second half of the book takes a more concretely reformist position. It assumes that the policymaking organs of government, working in a reasonably honest fashion, have drawn a line indicating those areas where nonmarket allocations are appropriate. The basic problem, then, is to prevent legislative mandates from being undermined by corrupt administration. To understand how corrupt incentives can arise in the administration of laws, four factors are of critical importance. First, the structure of legal and administrative sanctions must be specified both for those who pay and those who receive bribes. Second, bureaucratic allocation rules and organizational forms must be modeled. Third and fourth, the nature of the bureaucratic task and the market structure of potential bribers can both influence the volume and incidence of corruption. Policy responses can take two basic forms: On the one hand, the criminal law or administrative sanctions may be used to discipline both bribers and bribees; on the other hand, bureaucratic structures may be reformed to lower the expected benefits of paying or accepting bribes. When neither organizational reform nor sanctions are efficacious, the system must rely on personal morality. What emerges from the analysis is a set of conclusions about the impact of structure on performance which echoes the market organization literature (Bain, 1968) and complements the work of political scientists.

In making this attempt, however, I have neither tried to build another vague, but "comprehensive," theory of bureaucracy nor focused on the solution of a narrow set of formal mathematical problems. I have chosen instead to defend an awkward middle ground between theoretical proof and common-sense intuitions which nonetheless promises some progress in understanding. Thus, while some bureaucratic situations, are formally modeled, the analysis frequently moves beyond these abstractions to consider more complex but realistic problems. Chapter 5, illustrates the basic relationships with an analysis of a monopolistic government official charged with allocating a benefit through a queuing system. It shows that bribe prices will generally be less efficient than a legal pricing system—even when the sanctions imposed by the legal system or bureaucratic superiors are easy to avoid. Indeed, even a *legal* pricing system will operate efficiently only under very special institutional conditions.

Chapter 6 retains the assumption of a single official with monopoly power but moves beyond the queuing model to consider alternative sanctioning strategies, a wider variety of bureaucratic tasks, and bribers who may be competitively or monopolisticly organized. When superiors issue vague guidelines to those beneath them, this chapter explores the way in which legal and administrative sanctions may be used to constrain both bribers and bribees. The analysis concludes that much current law in this area is misguided. Even if existing laws were vigorously enforced, penalties are often not associated with the briber's benefits and frequently deter only petty corruption.

Bureaucratic reorganization may, at least sometimes, be a powerful complement to the threat of criminal and administrative sanctions. The next three chapters explore the potential of a variety of structural remedies. Chapters 7 and 8 consider a somewhat disorderly administrative structure which nonetheless may help check corruption. In contrast to the usual bureaucracy, where each low-level official is given exclusive authority over a particular phase of agency business, these chapters explore the potential of a system where officials are permitted to compete with one another in processing applications for governmental benefits. Under this system, an individual or firm rejected by one official can seek the benefit from other bureaucrats. Of course, this reform is not applicable to governmental functions where interbureaucratic competition will undermine the basic purposes of the program. If superiors only want 1 ton of cement, it is unwise to give 10 different contracting officials authority to purchase a ton apiece. The option of using overlapping jurisdictions, however, can help check corruption in many familiar regulatory and social programs.

Chapter 9 introduces a final administrative variable into the analysis. In the preceding chapters bureaucratic superiors did not attempt to review the activities going on beneath them. Reforming this oversight function, however, is one of the standard remedies prescribed for corrupt practices although traditional reform efforts proceed without an analysis of the ways in which oversight may be organized and the limits of each possibility. This will be the purpose of the study in Chapter 9 of four forms of internal bureaucratic organization: the *fragmented*, the *sequential*, the *hierarchical* and the *disorganized*.

The final two chapters place the study in a broader political–economic context. Chapter 10 extends the discussion of governmental corruption to analogous corrupt activities entirely within the private sector. Chapter 11 elaborates the broader themes raised here: the relation between corruption and democratic theory, the possibility of reforming corrupt bureaucracies, and the link between economics and morality.

Legislative Corruption

2

CORRUPTION AND THE LEGISLATIVE PROCESS: THE COST OF INFLUENCE IN AN INDIVIDUALISTIC LEGISLATURE

1. INTRODUCTION

The corruption of democratic legislators has occurred at all levels of government, and in a wide variety of cultural and historical contexts. This chapter, however, abstracts from the infinite variety of factual detail to develop an analytic framework which reveals how individual preferences and organizational opportunities can interact to produce corrupt behavior. Although the analysis emphasizes the incentives for bribery, I do not wish to suggest that everyone has a price. Many legislators do not accept bribes or illegal contributions, and many special interests refuse to pay them, not because of the political or legal costs involved, but because of strong scruples against law breaking. This difference between bribes and legal campaign contributions helps to explain why special interests are likely to be more powerful in states with few restrictions on political contributions. The distinction should be kept in mind in reading Chapters 3 and 4, which move beyond the stylized models of politics developed in this chapter to more realistic political systems where legal campaign contributions are feasible.

In modern representative democracies the preferences of three groups combine with the organizational context to generate incentives for corrupt legislative transactions. The preferences of citizens, legislative representatives, and potential bribers must all be specified. Since representatives are assumed to seek reelection as one of their goals, the preferences of voters influence the behavior of representatives through their impact on the probability of reelection. The willingness of representatives either to tradeoff political support for private monetary gain or to use money to purchase constituents' votes will then interact with the organization of the legislature to generate opportunities for corruption. The preferences of those willing to pay bribes combined with their organization costs will determine the maximum bribe offers of various interest groups.

While legislators may be corrupted in return for a wide variety of special favors, this chapter will only consider bribery designed to affect their *voting* behavior. The use of legislators to procure administrative benefits is, however, a common practice and will be analyzed in Chapter 4. The focus here, however, is on the central democratic conflict between a legislator's personal interest and the wishes of his constituents.[1]

Corrupt opportunities may exist even in a political system where citizens know and care about political issues and where information about legislative actions is so complete that incumbents must run on their records. To simplify further, assume that the legislature is "individualistic"—there are no political parties or legislative committees, and each representative is equally powerful. Wealthy interests can organize, however, and may be able to induce representatives to tradeoff popular support against an increase in income. The aim of this chapter, then, is to present a simple model in which a study of corruption highlights basic tensions between interest-group activity and majority rule. Section 2 analyzes corrupt incentives that will arise even in a system so idealized that politicians have perfect information about constituents' preferences. The bulk of the analysis, in Sections 3 and 4, however, begins the long process of exploring the opportunities for corruption under increasingly realistic assumptions by dropping the assumption that politicians have perfect knowledge.

---

[1] Although it concentrates on the tradeoff between money and votes, the analysis could be generalized to take account of more complex preference structures. See Buchanan (1977:13) for a similar perspective. He hypothesizes that politicians tradeoff reelection against a catchall category called "political income." While there is little doubt that reelection is *one* goal of legislators (Fenno 1977:889, Mayhew 1974), the way in which this goal is traded off against others such as high income or power within the legislature has not been empirically estimated. Fenno (1977:916) notes the constant tension faced by U.S. Representatives between attaining influence in the Congress and serving the interests of constituents.

2. CORRUPTION IN A PERFECT DEMOCRATIC STATE

Imagine, then, a perfectly functioning representative democracy where legislators pass laws by majority vote and are chosen, in turn, from single member districts by a majority vote of their constituents. Representatives all act independently in deciding how to vote on issues—thus no collusive behavior or logrolling occurs within the legislature. Representatives care both about the proportion of the popular vote they receive and about their income.[2] Legislators, however, are quite amoral: They neither have qualms about accepting bribes nor independent ideological positions on any issues they are called upon to decide. Finally, in calculating the tradeoff between money and votes, legislators have perfect information about the preferences of their constituents on the issues that come before the legislature.

Voters in turn are knowledgeable, issue-oriented individuals who have preferences on every issue, which do not change over time, and who also know how their representative votes on every piece of legislation. They have no reliable information, however, on the income of legislators or on the tastes of their fellow constituents. Citizens care only about the positions taken by their representatives, not whether they are on the winning side. They are more likely to vote for incumbents the greater the volume of benefits they would have generated had they been in the majority on every issue.[3]

[2] This model should be compared with the other formulations listed in Chapter 1, note 3, and with Pitkin (1967).

[3] For evidence that this assumption accords with reality, see Mayhew (1974). Alternatively, voters may prefer legislators who bargain away their positions on some issues in return for the votes of other legislators on issues constituents care strongly about. Introducing this possibility may imply that logrolling is a worthwhile strategy. Internal legislative bargaining can be a substitute for corruption by outsiders, but interest groups who would not have needed to engage in corruption in the absence of logrolling may now find that bribes are needed to counteract the internal bargaining of legislators. Buchanan and Tullock (1962), Fenno (1973), and Ferejohn (1974) emphasize the importance of logrolling in legislative processes, and Ritt (1976) found that tangible benefits accruing to the home district are important for a politician's popularity.

Logrolling coalitions are, however, difficult to establish because constituents care about their representatives' votes on particular issues. For example, urban and rural Congressmen voted for increased farm supports and an overhaul of the food stamp programs. Charles Rose, Democrat of North Carolina wrote about the difficulties of establishing the coalition in an open letter to Edward Koch, Democrat of New York, published in June 1977 in the *Congressional Record*. "Many hurdles face our coalition hopes, principally because the interests of our districts tend to override most other considerations, whatever the issue. But I think that men and women of good will can come to an accommodation [quoted in the *New York Times*, July 30, 1977]."

Given such a state of perfection, what opportunities remain for corrupt deals frustrating the majority's will? To make the prospect for bribery unattractive, it is necessary to posit even more restrictive assumptions about the political process. Thus, in addition, the issues voted on by the legislature remain constant from period to period, and politicians announce their position on each issue during the campaign. Under those conditions, I assume that it is possible for incumbents to take a set of positions on legislative issues which assure them of reelection. In other words, voters' preferences are constituted in a way that prevents challengers from finding a platform capable of defeating incumbents.[4] The political process is then as corruption proof as it is possible to imagine, since corruption can be inferred from the public conduct of the representatives themselves. To uncover bribery, it will not be necessary to rely upon prosecutors to locate hard evidence of illicit activity. To see why, one need only recognize that politicians seeking reelection, rather than private gain, must—in this model— always keep their campaign promises if they are to succeed in their objective. Since the only way politicians could beat their opponents initially was to design a set of campaign promises that was capable of generating support, and since voter preferences and public issues remain constant from period to period, the only way they can win the next election is to vote their promises. Otherwise, challengers will predictably emerge at the next election who will match the incumbents' promises and exploit the fact that they have not (yet) shown themselves to be untrustworthy.[5] Given the assumption that legislators have no personal preferences on political issues, a representative who breaks a promise must have done so for private gain. This does not mean, of course, that no corruption will occur in the model. A legislator may be willing to lose the next election if corrupt returns are high enough. But at least here votes motivated by corruption would be so obvious that political influence cannot be expected to cover up corruption—thereby eliminat-

---

[4] For a discussion of the restrictions on voter preferences sufficient to guarantee a stable majority winner and prevent voting paradoxes, see Sen (1970:166–186) and Sen and Pattainaik (1969). Slutsky (1977) finds necessary and sufficient conditions for consistent majority choice by restricting the *number* of individuals holding particular preference orderings. In multidimensional policy spaces, Tullock (1967) ensures consistent majority choice by making assumptions about the spatial distribution of voters' optima. However, Kramer (1973) and Plott (1967) have shown that for multidimensional policy spaces, the assumption of a stable majority winner is not realistic. Thus the model in this section essentially assumes that the legislature votes on the level of single public good where tax shares are fixed.

[5] For a similar discussion, see Downs (1957, Chapter 4).

ing one of the features distinguishing high-level bribery from more humble sorts.

But this is a very special case. Consider, for example, the consequences of changing only one restrictive assumption: that voter preferences assure the existence of a stable majority winner. When this condition is violated, all legislators expect to be defeated in the next election—since they must run on their records in the last session and there exists at least one set of campaign promises that dominates their own. It follows that myopic legislators have little incentive to turn down bribes in exchange for votes since they will leave politics at the end of their terms in any event. While a professional politician—who expects to stand for reelection after an initial loss—would have an incentive to keep promises, a system with cyclic majorities does not encourage professionalism, since no one can have a stable career in politics.[6]

Thus, despite the knowledgeability of voters, the political system imposes few constraints on corruption. Instead, reliance must be placed upon prosecutors to gather evidence showing that bribe payments rather than mere whim were the cause of broken promises. Without aggressive prosecution, corruption can flourish and the political system be discredited as a means of fulfilling the majority's preferences even under a model which assumes clear information channels between legislators and their knowledgeable constituents.[7]

---

[6] Barro's (1973:28), work also recognizes the difficulty of controlling politicians who do not expect to be reelected, but does not deal with cycles since he assumes that all voters are identical. Kramer's (1975) model of political equilibrium assumes professionalism in the presence of cycles. A political party carries out its promises even though it knows that in general it will be defeated by the opposition in the next election. His paper is especially interesting for its characterization of the behavior of a Downsian two-party system acting over a multidimensional policy space. Assuming that parties seek to maximize the number of votes received in a given election, Kramer shows that, if certain restrictions are placed on citizen's preferences, the policy platforms of the parties will converge to the "minmax set." Kramer defines this term formally, but essentially it is the set of policies where the maximum number of votes that challengers can obtain is minimized. In short, even if a single, stable majority winner does not exist, the system will avoid wide swings in political choices if citizen's tastes are not too "far apart." The difference between one half and the fraction of votes obtained by challengers in equilibrium is a measure of "how close" the society is to having a majority winner. Kramer does not, however, model the case in which political parties will accept a reduction in their reelection percentage in return for an increase in politicians' incomes.

[7] Knowing that voters will not trust them, politicians may refuse to state any positions at election time. In that case, even if voters are very knowledgeable and issue oriented, they have no reason to vote. Elections might then depend upon the purchase of votes by competing candidates.

3. POLITICIANS WITH IMPERFECT INFORMATION

The cause of realism will be served, however, by concentrating on a less rarified model, which nevertheless retains the central democratic assumption of knowledgeable, issue-oriented voters. The new model is identical to the previous one in basic outline—majority voting is used both to choose representatives and to pass laws in the legislature. Representatives are independent and care about both income and reelection,[8] and voters judge incumbents on the basis of their voting records. However, in addition to assuming that citizens do not know the preferences of other citizens, I now assume that *politicians* have only imperfect knowledge of the present and future preferences of their constituents.[9] While politicians have access to various indicators of constituent opinion, special interest groups are unable to supplement these data in a credible way—representatives discounting interest group presentations as nothing more than self-serving compilations. As in the previous model, election campaigns are simple affairs—incumbents' platforms are determined by their votes in the preceding legislative session, while challengers simply announce their positions to the ideal democratic electorate. Thus there is no room in the model for incumbents to seek money from special interests either to gain more information about voter preferences or to finance their election campaigns.

In short, interest groups are only able to provide direct monetary payments to legislators, and legislators can only use these payments to raise their personal income, not to generate votes. Furthermore, I abstract from the prosecutorial side of the problem and assume that legislators are sure that their political influence is strong enough to

[8] This model is similar in perspective to Barro (1973), who assumes that reelection is only desirable because of the increased consumption opportunities it brings. Barro is especially concerned with the tradeoff between current consumption and future consumption. Politicians who are too greedy in the present will be defeated at the next election.

[9] In particular, politicians do not know whether or not a stable winning platform exists. Even if challengers did believe that winning platforms could be constructed, they would not know for sure which policy positions to espouse. Thus, the incumbents' vote-maximizing strategies will depend upon their prediction of the campaign platforms their opponents will choose for each set of votes cast by incumbents. Fenno's (1977) interviews with congressmen confirms their uncertainty about constituents' preferences. He writes that "the process by which [an incumbent's] desire for reelection gets translated into his perception of a reelection constituency is filled with uncertainty. . . . They rarely feel certain just who it did vote for them last time. And even if they do feel fairly sure about that, they may perceive population shifts that threaten established calculation [p. 886]."

prevent others from publicizing or prosecuting their illicit activity.[10] This condition permits me to concentrate upon the expected loss in voter support that undetected corruption entails.[11]

Since voters use their legislators' voting records to decide whether

---

[10] While allegations of corrupt practices or conflicts of interest may lead to the defeat or retirement of a politician, they seldom lead to strong disciplinary action by the United States Congress itself. Thus the House Ethics Committee only recommended that Representative Robert Sikes be reprimanded for two of three complaints of conflict of interest. The third complaint was mooted because Sikes' actions occurred before the committee was founded. Not only did the committee take the lightest action possible short of clearing Sikes, but this case was the first action taken by the committee since its founding in 1968 (New York Times, July 27, 1976). Other evidence on Congress' unwillingness to discipline members is found in Beard and Horn (1975) and Crawford (1939).

The judicial system does, however, prosecute some allegations of bribery and conflict of interest. Recent examples involved Senator Edward Gurney, who was acquitted of all charges of improper conduct (New York Times, July 11, 1974, August 8, 1975, October 28, 1976); Representative Frank Brasco, found guilty of taking bribes (New York Times, October 24, 1973, July 20, 1974); and Representative Bertram Podell, who pled guilty under a conflict of interest statute (New York Times, October 2, 1974).

[11] In order to incorporate the risk of detection, let α be the probability of detection, where α depends upon the size of the bribe and upon the issue involved. Legislators are then essentially purchasing lottery tickets that provide a low return with probability α and some combination of income and proportion of the popular vote with probability $1 - \alpha$. In other words, if their corruption is discovered, then their reelection probabilities fall to a low level, and they must relinquish the bribes to law enforcement authorities and suffer punishment. (One could also construct a more complex model in which bribers accept some of the risk of detection by promising employment to politicians if their corruption leads them to lose the election.) Legislators would then have utility functions defined over these lottery tickets. However, because an explicit consideration of law enforcement is left to later chapters, I have assumed here that the existence of corruption is unknown to the electorate, who react only to the *votes* of their representatives.

To assess the impact of a scandal on a politician's career requires information on how the public views corruption. The meager evidence available suggests that attitudes vary widely over time and space and depend upon the effect of the corruption on government behavior. Gardiner (1970:46–56) shows that the citizens of Wincanton had strong negative feelings about corruption, even when they did not care very much about the decisions that were influenced by bribery. In Japan, discovery of Lockheed's payoffs to government officials caused the government to fall (New York Times, February 11, 1976). In Georgia in the late eighteenth century, almost the whole state legislature was bribed. When this peculation was uncovered, all were defeated in the next election (Deakin, 1966). In some societies and at some levels of government, however, bribery is so acceptable to the participants that its formal illegality plays little role as a deterrent. See Waterbury (1973) for a discussion of the Moroccan case. A recent experimental study (Rundquist, Strom and Peters, 1977) indicates that U.S. voters tradeoff evidence of corruption against information on candidates' positions on issues.

their positions are superior to those of their opponents, incumbents guess which position will maximize their share of the vote in the next election, but they cannot be sure that they have made the correct choice. Constituents are aware not only of one another's imperfect knowledge about voter preferences, but also of their representative's need to predict the tastes of future voters. Thus while they are aware of instances when their representative does not follow campaign promises, they do not conclude from this behavior that corruption has occurred.[12] The introduction of legislator uncertainty implies, therefore, that corruption cannot be inferred from a broken campaign promise, even in situations where the underlying preference structure will produce a stable majority winner. Undetected corruption can become a part of a functioning democratic system. The political incentives for corruption, however, will still be maximized if incumbents believe that they are certain to lose the next election regardless of their voting behavior—as in cases where the voting paradox arises. Nonetheless, imperfect information will make it unlikely that legislators will believe that their defeat is certain.

Having sketched the basic relationships between legislators and their constituency, let $U(\hat{p}, y)$ be a legislator's preference relationship between income y and the expected proportion of the total vote, $\hat{p}$. The expected proportion of the vote is a simple means of summarizing the incumbent's knowledge of reelection possibilities and is a proxy for the probability of winning the election. For simplicity, assume that there are no primaries and that the incumbent faces only a single challenger, so the incumbent's probability of winning can be expressed as the probability of obtaining more than 50% of the vote.[13] Furthermore, the level of $\hat{p}$ can be taken as a rough measure of the long-run political staying power of the representative. The legislator believes that the higher the actual margin of victory, the more likely is reelection in subsequent periods

[12] Since voters believe that legislators are trying to maximize their shares of the vote, they interpret a broken promise not as a breach of trust but as an attempt to follow changes in constituent tastes. At election time they are myopic, however, and believe that the candidate's campaign promises will be carried out. Without this last assumption, no one would know how to cast his ballot.

[13] Both the expected proportion of the vote, $\hat{p}$ and the incumbent's estimate of the variance around $\hat{p}$ are important. Using $\hat{p}$ instead of both the mean and variance implies that the mean and variance have a one-to-one relationship to each other and that the higher (lower) is $\hat{p}$ the lower (higher) the chance of actually losing the election. For a more detailed discussion of the relationship between vote maximization and maximization of the probability of election, see Aranson, Hinich, and Ordeshook (1974).

and the easier it will be to seek higher office.[14] Similarly, the larger the margin of defeat the less likely it is that he or she can return to challenge the incumbent in subsequent elections. If legislators must obtain just over 50% of the vote of their constituents in order to be reelected, then $\hat{p}$ has a point of inflection at $\hat{p} = .5$ with the marginal rate of substitution between $\hat{p}$ and y declining for $\hat{p} > .5$ and rising for $\hat{p} < .5$. The reason for this shape, illustrated in Figure 2.1, is that when $\hat{p}$ is close to .5, small increases in $\hat{p}$ are valuable because they increase the probability of actually winning the election (i.e., $\Pr[p > .5]$, where p is the actual proportion of the vote obtained by the candidate). When $\hat{p}$ is much larger than .5, the chance of actual $p < .5$ is relatively small and the marginal value of an increase in $\hat{p}$ mainly reflects the long-run benefits of high levels of p. Similarly, when $\hat{p}$ is small, marginal increases in $\hat{p}$ do little to improve the politician's meager chances of success in the next election.

To be more specific about the derivation of these utility surfaces, consider a representative with a utility function defined over income and the probability of winning. The legislator has no direct information about this probability but can estimate the proportion of the vote expected $\hat{p}$ and infer a probability of winning, $\Pr(p > .5)$, from this information. The critical issue, then, is the assumptions the politician makes about the probability distribution of p. Appendix 2.1 works through a case with

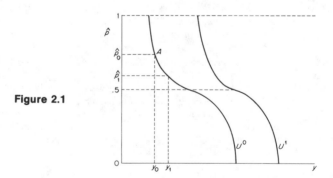

Figure 2.1

---

[14] Compare Peltzman (1976) who argues that the politician "seeks to maximize net votes or a majority in his favor. There is no presumption that the marginal utility of a majority vanishes at one. Greater majorities are assumed to imply greater security of tenure, more logrolling possibilities, greater deference from legislative budget committees, and so on [p. 214]." Stigler (1972), in writing about political parties rather than individuals, assumes that a party's influence $I(s)$ is a monotonically increasing function of its share of legislative seats s. He believes that $I''(s) < 0$ beyond some point.

assumptions sufficient to generate utility surfaces like those shown in Figure 2.1. These conditions are by no means necessary, however. A range of probability distributions and underlying utility functions imply utility surfaces like those shown in Figure 2.1 even ignoring the long-run considerations raised in the preceding paragraph.

Suppose that point A in Figure 2.1 with $\hat{p}_0$, y_0 is the $\hat{p}$ maximizing position for a particular legislator,[15] and that citizens or firms can form coalitions to influence legislative outcomes through payoffs. If A is one legislator's initial position, then the minimum payoff needed to cause that legislator to change his or her vote on a particular issue[16] can be easily illustrated in Figure 2.1. Let $\Delta p = \hat{p}_0 - \hat{p}_1$ be the fall in $\hat{p}$ that will result if the legislator changes his or her vote on a particular issue. Then, since the politician has no personal interest in the policy, the minimum bribe is $y_1 - y_0$. The minimum acceptable bribe is larger the more important the issue is to the legislator's constituents (the larger is Δp),[17] and the lower the marginal utility of income to the legislator. Notice that the minimum bribe depends upon legislators' initial positions. It is lower the *more* secure they are so long as $\hat{p}_0 > .5$, but is also lower the *less* secure they are if $\hat{p}_0 < .5$.[18]

---

[15] The expected proportion of the total vote obtained by the legislator, $\hat{p}$, depends upon the probability of obtaining any constituent's vote, $\hat{p}_i$, $i = 1, \ldots, n$, where n is the total number of constituents, i.e., $\hat{p} = (1/n) \sum_{i=1}^{n} \hat{p}_i$. For each constituent, i, the congressman's voting behavior translates into some potential gain x_i, i.e., if the representative had been in the majority on every vote, i's actual gain would have been x_i. Assume that $\hat{p}_i = 0$ if $x_i \leq 0$ and that $\hat{p}_i$ is an increasing function of x_i, approaching one as x_i becomes infinitely large. Legislators will often follow the preferences of the majority of their constituents on a particular issue. However, they will sometimes support minorities who strongly favor a bill which the majority weakly opposes.

[16] The analysis is a partial equilibrium one since y can only be changed by bribery and is unaffected by the implementation of the policy (cf. Barro, 1973). To prevent voting paradoxes on particular issues, proposed laws are presented as bills with fixed provisions which must be either approved or disapproved.

[17] A striking example of a situation where wealth could not be used to override the legislators' Δp occurred in Mississippi in 1899. When the legislature sought to end the tax privileges of the Illinois Central Railroad, this proposed policy was so popular with voters that no politician was able to favor the railroad. As owner of large amounts of fixed capital, the railroad could not credibly threaten to leave the state. Legislators ran successfully on a platform of collecting taxes from the railroad since the tradeoff between taxing individuals and taxing the railroad was obvious to all voters (Brandfon, 1965).

[18] The behavior described here is similar to that postulated by Riker (1962) in deriving his "size principle." Riker observed that the desire to share the spoils of victory among as few as possible will cause victorious coalitions of voters to approach the minimal winning size. In my model, each politician reduces the size of his or her winning coalition by trading away policy and accumulating corrupt payments.

If issues are independent so far as voters are concerned, then a further conclusion is possible. By independence, I mean that any citizen's preferences with respect to a particular bill are independent of the bill's position on the agenda, that is, preferences are independent of the outcome of votes on other bills, and, more strongly, that the dollar value of the benefits or costs of a particular bill's passage to any individual is independent of the outcome of votes on other bills. If this condition holds and if corrupt coalitions of citizens can be formed on several issues, the order in which bribe offers are made to an individual legislator will determine the minimum size of the required bribe. For $\hat{p}_0 > .5$ the initial offers are "cheaper" per unit of $\hat{p}$ than subsequent offers until the $\hat{p} = .5$ threshold is reached. Then "prices" fall once again.[19]

4. THE STRUCTURE OF INTEREST GROUP ORGANIZATION

Given the utility functions of legislators, I can now show how the structure of interest group organization will affect the volume and incidence of corruption. There are two basic situations. In the first, supporters of only one side of an issue are organized into a pressure group capable of collecting a slush fund.[20] Here the analysis is straightforward. If the group can command the honest support of only a minority of the legislators on some issue, it merely calculates the minimum bribe required to influence each of the legislators who favor the majority. So long as the group's funds are sufficient, it can then bribe enough of the cheapest members of the majority to change the outcome of the vote.

[19] Of course, as pointed out in note 4, a stable majority winner is very unlikely in multidimensional policy space. The assumption of separable utility functions does not change this conclusion. The possibility of cycles is not a critical determinant of legislative behavior in this model, however, because neither incumbents nor challengers have good information about constituents' preferences. There is always some chance, however small, that even a very corrupt incumbent may be reelected.

[20] Legislation affecting a particular industry often falls in this category. For example, in Italy 12 drug manufacturers joined together to back a bill allowing nonprescription drugs to be sold in supermarkets where the drugs would not be subject to price control. Although it is unclear whether the money was actually paid, each firm was assessed $80,000 to be contributed to the Christian Democratic party (*New York Times,* March 21, 1976). Similarly, land development decisions are frequently uncontested by organized opposition groups, and zoning boards and city councils have frequently been the object of payoff attempts by land developers (Amick, 1976:76–97).

The second case, however, requires somewhat more discussion. Here, organized groups support the majority as well as the minority. In this situation, bribers whose preferences agree with the legislator's "honest" choice have an inherent advantage. To see this, imagine that an interest group attempts to change legislators' votes by offering them "minimum" bribes just sufficient to compensate them for their reduction in $\hat{p}$. Then any positive bribe offered by the other side would induce them to return to their "honest" position. Thus in order for corruption successfully to alter the outcome of a legislative vote in a majority rule regime, the group that wishes to change the outcome, the "initiators," must be able to pay bribes that cannot be overridden by their opponents, the "majority." Otherwise, competitive bribe offers will be made[21] and the final result will depend upon both the financial resources of each side and the portions of the utility surface occupied by different legislators.[22] Essentially, the initiators seek to minimize their expenditure of funds subject to the condition that the majority be unable to override the initiators' offers. If no such winning strategy exists, the group will pay no bribes at all. The initiators can make bribery costly for the group with majority support either by purchasing considerably more than 50% of the assembly or by paying individual supporters bribes which are far above their reservation prices. The group's choice of strategy then depends upon the marginal "productivity" of money in these alternatives, where productivity is measured by the additional outlays required of their opponents (see Appendix 2.2 for a formal statement of these ideas).

[21] The text assumes that the majority has no recourse other than the competitive bribery of legislators. If, however, they have evidence of the initiator's bribe offers, they may be able to expose that group's corruption and win the legislative vote without any expenditure of bribes.

[22] Competition to obtain a contract, franchise, or other exclusive benefit illustrates situations similar to those described in the text. One costly fight, for example, was the competition between the Union Pacific and the Central Pacific railroads to obtain track building rights from the Congress (Farnham, 1963:672). Amick (1976:101–103) also describes the competition among 13 firms in Trenton for city council approval of Cable Television licenses. TelePrompter contended that it paid $117,000 over 3 years to four members of the Trenton City Council to obtain approval of a license.

In my model, legislators can bargain with both sides but can actually take money from only one group. In New York State in the 1860s, however, the assembly was asked to approve legislation which would legalize stock issues by the Erie Railroad designed to frustrate a takeover bid by Cornelius Vanderbilt. In this case, the competitive bribery of legislators has been documented, but this assumption was violated. One important legislator accepted $75,000 from Vanderbilt and $100,000 from the Erie, voted for the Erie, but kept Vanderbilt's money (Smith, 1958:316).

The most favorable situation for the initiators occurs if their legislative supporters are all close to $\hat{p} = .5$, making it expensive for the majority to bid them away, and if their legislative opponents have either very secure seats or very insecure ones so that they are relatively inexpensive to influence. Similarly, if legislators who support the minority position have constituents who care intensely about their representatives' votes on this issue while representatives favoring the majority have relatively indifferent constituents, then a corrupt outcome favoring the initiators is also more likely. For example, a bill authorizing a dam that will promote economic development in one state may be strongly supported by the state's residents and business interests and weakly opposed by everyone else. In this case, even a very unfavorable distribution of positive and negative votes may be reversed through corruption.[23]

5. CONCLUSIONS

Even these highly stylized models are sufficient to demonstrate the close ties between the personal venality of legislators,[24] the political situation in each legislative district, and the organizational ability of competing interest groups. These models do not necessarily imply a presumption in favor of the independently wealthy. While people may value additions to income less highly the greater their wealth, the value of holding office may fall as well. Wealth may give people so much status and independent power that they care little about reelection. In economic jargon, although an individual's marginal utility of income will generally fall as wealth increases, the marginal rate of substitution between $\hat{p}$ and y may be unaffected.

The political climate in individual legislative districts is important for two reasons. First, when campaign spending plays no role, representatives will, in general, be costly to corrupt if $\hat{p}$ is close to .5. Hence, an active opposition within each election district that can produce candi-

---

[23] Although excluded from the model in the text, this example illustrates a common logrolling situation. For an analysis of logrolling in public works projects see Ferejohn (1974) and Fenno (1973).

[24] Organized groups may also be able to influence the type of individuals who seek office. If the structure of the legislature or the bases of representation can be changed, business groups will generally favor a redistricting policy biased toward conservative citizens and may wish to keep legislative pay low. For evidence on lobbyists' opposition to redistricting and legislative pay raises see Allen (1949).

dates able to take advantage of any of the incumbent's weaknesses may be a crucial check on corruption.[25] When opposition of this type does not exist or when most legislators have already lost the support of their constituents through past behavior, more issues may be decided corruptly because the reservation prices of representatives will generally be low. Second, given any initial level of $\hat{p}$, issues that have an important impact on the $\hat{p}$ of those who must be bribed will be harder to corrupt than others.

Just as closely fought elections may be a potent check on corruption, legislative struggles where both sides of the issue are backed by organized interests may also discourage bribery.[26] Indeed, public support for a group's position may encourage it to organize since holding on to a base of support will be cheaper than inducing representatives to change their votes.[27] Thus, if only groups with minority support are organized, the *incidence* of bribery may be high in the sense that many legislative outcomes are influenced by payoffs but the actual dollar *volume* of bribes may be close to the minimum necessary to generate the bribers' desired outcome.[28] Alternatively, if both sides of an issue are organized, the incidence may be low, but when corruption does occur, the volume of payments will be high.

In short, these results permit a reassessment of conventional demo-

---

[25] Wealthy groups may sometimes be able to pay challengers as well as purchase incumbents. With both sides in the pay of the interest group, the incumbent's support of a group's positions cannot be used to defeat him.

Crain (1977) discusses the possibility that incumbents will try to structure the electoral system to make it difficult for challengers to defeat those already in office. According to him, incumbents have incentives for restricting electoral competition similar to those implied by my model. "For example, the ability to extract rents from those seeking favorable regulatory legislation would be a function of a politician's expected tenure in office. In addition, the politician's influence over legislative outcomes is generally related to his length of service (because of seniority rules) and hence his ability to back promised political benefits to specific interest groups [p. 830]."

[26] Key (1936) writes that "when there are well-organized pressure groups possessed by equal or nearly equal power, the legislative decision on an issue between them is not likely to be influenced by bribery on behalf of one of the parties [p. 403]." He is not very clear, however, about the meaning of the term *power*. Observers of interest group activity have concluded that competition between lobbyists produces a situation where the legislators are free to exercise their own judgment or follow their own perception of constituent wishes. For example, see Milbrath (1963:345) and H. Lowe's discussion of the Pennsylvania Legislature in Allen (1949:99).

[27] Milbrath (1963:276) reports that lobbyists in the United States Congress are deterred from bribery by the belief that corruption will be costly because a legislator who can be bought by one side, can also be bought by the other.

[28] Broadus (1976) makes this distinction in his studies of corruption in the New York City Police Department and in the administration of strip mining legislation in Kentucky.

cratic theory. I have shown that an informed electorate is certainly not a sufficient condition for the proper functioning of a representative democracy. Nor is it true—as the interest group theorists believed[29]—that the existence of a comprehensive set of interest groups would be a sufficient condition for effective democracy. It is only when *both* of these conditions are combined with a political system generating closely contested elections that one can devise a model with strong—if not perfect—protections against corrupt activity.[30]

In addition to examining the viability of classic democratic theory, I also wish to understand the relationship between wealth and political outcomes in real political systems which fail to fulfill many of my idealized assumptions. Of particular importance is the role of an apathetic or poorly informed electorate in facilitating the influence of wealthy, organized groups on politics. As we shall see in Chapter 3, the impact of voter ignorance on corruption is not straightforward: While sometimes it makes bribery more likely than in the idealized models with which I have been dealing, it is also quite possible that it will lead to a less corrupt political system.

APPENDIX 2.1. AN EXAMPLE THAT GENERATES THE UTILITY SURFACES IN FIGURE 2.1

In this example politicians try to guess the true level of p by questioning a sample of constituents to obtain an estimate, $\hat{p}$. If voters must either be for them or against them, then each politician can use the normal approximation to the binomial distribution to estimate p (Mood and Graybill, 1963:262–264). Uncertainty about the actual level of p is introduced by assuming that the politician only questions a sample. (Alternatively, voters may either lie or change their minds. Then, even if all constituents could be polled, politicians would still be uncertain about their probability of actually winning the election.) It is now possible to associate a level of $Z = \Pr(p > .5)$ with each level of $\hat{p}$.

$$Z \simeq f(\hat{p}) \simeq \int_x^\infty \phi(t)\, dt, \qquad \hat{p} \le .5,$$

$$Z \simeq f(\hat{p}) \simeq .5 + \int_x^{.5} \phi(t)\, dt, \qquad \hat{p} > .5,$$

[29] See, for example, Bentley (1908) and Truman (1951).

[30] The mere organization of all relevant interests, of course, may not be sufficient to check corruption even in this context if those who support minority interests are much more wealthy than those with the support of the legislative majority.

where

$$x = \frac{|\hat{p} - .5|}{\{[\hat{p}(1 - \hat{p})]/n\}^{1/2}}, \qquad \phi(t) = (2\pi)^{-1/2}e^{-t^2/2}, \qquad n = \text{sample size}.$$

Assume that $n = 10$. Since this is a rather small sample, the normal approximation will be quite inaccurate but will suffice for illustrative purposes. The graph of Z as a function of $\hat{p}$, when $n = 10$, is shown in quadrant I of Figure 2.2. Assume that the politician has a simple linear utility function in Z and y: $U = 11y + 1000Z$. One indifference curve, $1100 = 11y + 1000Z$, is illustrated in quadrant II. Substituting $f(\hat{p})$ for Z in $1100 = 11y + 1000Z$, yields the function illustrated in quadrant IV. This is a curve with the shape of the indifference curves in Figure 2.1. Larger samples would produce curves in quadrant IV which become parallel to the $\hat{p}$ axis at levels of $\hat{p}$ close to .5 and have long midsections parallel to the y axis. A utility function with a diminishing marginal rate

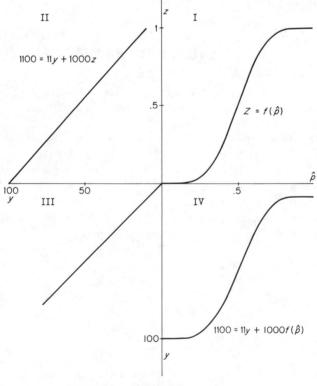

Figure 2.2

of substitution between Z and y would still produce a curve in quadrant IV that is consistent with Figure 2.1.

The analysis could be extended by replacing the simple binomial distribution with a model in which a representatives' behavior could affect both $\hat{p}$ and the variance. One could also explore the implications of changes in the utility function and in the sources of uncertainty about p on the form of the relationship between y and $\hat{p}$.

APPENDIX 2.2. COMPETITIVE BRIBERY IN AN INDIVIDUALISTIC LEGISLATURE

In order to be more precise about the process of competitive bribery, consider a simple stylized model of the bargaining process. Assume that the content of a piece of proposed legislation is fixed and that in the absence of corruption, the measure would fail to pass. Thus if the legislature contains m members, and if n representatives support the bill, then $n < m/2$. To avoid worrying about tie votes, assume that m is odd and that abstention is impossible. Assume that there are organized interest groups on both sides of the issue and that each group has an exogenously determined maximum willingness to pay. Thus the initiators have W dollars, and the majority V dollars. The actual bargaining process is similarly simplified. Each side makes offers and counteroffers, but no money actually changes hands until a final settlement is reached. Both interest groups know what offers their opponents have made to each legislator and know how much must be offered to sway any legislator's vote. Legislators can bargain with both sides but cannot ultimately accept money from more than one interest group. Legislators are assumed to be unable either to blackmail interest groups by reporting their corruption or to collude to present a united front to those who wish to corrupt them.

In order to win the vote, group I (the initiators) needs to influence a minimum of $(m + 1)/2 - n$ votes. Assume that I can rank the $m - n$ opponents of the bill in terms of the minimum cost of purchase, $b_1^0 < \cdots < b_{m-n}^0$. If group M (the majority) is unorganized, the cost to I is simply $\Sigma_{i=1}^r b_i^0$ where $r = (m + 1)/2 - n$. So long as $\Sigma_{i=1}^r b_i^0 \leq W$, corruption will succeed. When the majority is also organized, Group I must offer more than $\Sigma_{i=1}^r b_i^0$, since these r legislators can all be repurchased by M for a minimal sum. The "initiators" must now associate each bribe they make, b_i, with the bribe, c_i, that M must pay to buy back the legislator. Furthermore, if some of the initiators' legislative supporters have not received bribes, group I must also be concerned with the cost of changing the votes of these legislators. Thus group I minimizes $\Sigma_i b_i$ subject to $\Sigma_{i \in J(\{b_j\})} c_i > V$ where $J(\{b_i\})$ is the set of voters that is cheapest for M to buy in order to achieve defeat of the legislative proposal given any set of bribes paid by I. In other words, the initiators seek to pay bribes just large enough so that they cannot be overridden by the majority interest group. If the initiator's minimum successful bribe, $\Sigma_i b_i$, is less than or equal to their maximum willingness to pay, W, then the bill's supporters can pass the legislation.

In the face of an organized majority interest group, the initiators have two ways of solidifying their position. They can purchase a larger majority, and they can pay any of their present supporters a larger amount. Consider, for example, a group of initiators who at some point in the bargaining process offer bribes of b_i^1 to their s supporters when $s \geq (m + 1)/2$. Some of the b_i^1 may, of course, equal zero. With competitive bribery, the ranking of the b_i^1 in dollar terms is relatively unimportant. Instead associate with each b_i, the appropriate level of c_i and rank the s legislators so $c_1^1 < c_2^1 < \cdots < c_s^1$. The initiator's choice of b_i^1 is not an equilibrium solution if $\Sigma_{i=1}^t c_i^1 \leq V$, where $t = s - [(m - 1)/2]$. So long as group I is within its budget constraint, it can attempt to increase the majority's minimum counteroffer. On the one hand, it can purchase an additional vote k by paying $b_k > b_k^0$. Corresponding to b_k is an amount, c_k, that will fit somewhere into the ranking of the c_i^1. The cost to I is thus b_k, and the resulting increase in V is $\min[c_k, c_{t+1}^1]$. On the other hand, I can increase b_i^1 to b_i^2 for any $i = 1, \ldots, s$. Group M can respond to this increase by either offering to pay the new higher level c_i^2 or by substituting individual $t + 1$ for individual i. Thus the cost to I is $b_i^2 - b_i^1$, and increase in V is $min[c_{t+1}^1 - c_i^1, c_i^2 - c_i^1]$. The initiators can then weigh the productivity of various methods of increasing their bribe payments in terms of the effect on $\Sigma_{i \in J} c_i$. In a world with the high degree of information assumed by this model, the initiators will only pay bribes if they are certain to succeed. Because of the lack of parallelism between Is and Ms, the initiators will need $W > V + \Sigma_{i=1}^r b_i^0$. Depending upon the form of individual utility functions, the actual level of W required for successful bribery may be considerably above the minimum.

3

INTEREST GROUP ACTIVITY AND THE LEGISLATURE: CORRUPTION, CAMPAIGN CONTRIBUTIONS, AND LOBBYING

1. INTRODUCTION

In an effort to establish basic relationships among voters, politicians, and interest groups, the introductory models in Chapter 2 characterized the relevant actors in very simple ways. Thus voters were assumed to be perfectly informed about the voting records of incumbents; representatives were not organized into political parties or legislative committees; and the factors determining the wealth and organizing ability of different groups were omitted from the analysis—interest groups with given resource endowments were simply "there." Equally important, the political activity of government bureaucracies was entirely ignored. The next two chapters attempt to remedy these deficiencies and, in doing so, go beyond a study of bribery to consider other ways in which money can help determine political outcomes.

This chapter begins by showing in Section 2 how changing the assumptions about voters' knowledge and concern for politics will make it sensible for wealthy groups to pursue their interests by making campaign contributions and engaging in lobbying and educational campaigns instead of paying illegal bribes. The rest of the chapter further complicates the picture of the political process. Section 3 considers the extortionary possibilities raised by the presence of especially powerful parties, committees, or individuals. Section 4 relates previous work on interest-group organization to my discussion of corruption and campaign contributions.

2. IGNORANCE, APATHY, AND THE ROLE OF WEALTH

A. Introduction

Voters may fall short of the knowledgeable, issue-oriented ideal in any number of ways. First, although they may remain ready and willing to monitor legislative voting behavior closely, it may not be possible to use this information at election time as a perfect predictor of the incumbent's future voting pattern—this case will be discussed in Part B. Part C, in turn, will consider a more serious departure from the "ideal." Here, while "apathetic" voters may have information about legislators' positions on the issues, these data are unimportant to them since their votes are determined exclusively by personal favors or payoffs provided by the candidates. In contrast, Part D considers voters who are poorly informed rather than apathetic.[1] All these cases require modifications of the earlier analysis in which legislators faced a stark tradeoff between personal income and the likelihood of victory in the next election. Instead, it will often be possible for interest groups to substitute legal activities for corrupt payments in an effort to influence legislative

---

[1] This case seems closest to the American reality. Campbell *et al.* (1964) found voters uninformed on most issues, although followup studies of the 1972 elections by the same group indicated a greater awareness of issues (Miller *et al.*, 1976). Popkin *et al.* (1976) interpret these results not as a change in voter attitudes but as a change in the political situation. They see voters as rationally trying to make choices in the face of imperfect and costly information. In their interpretation of the data they are close to Key (1966) who also believes that the electorate, although not well informed, is basically "responsible."

Furthermore, other work indicates that many politicians believe that their positions on issues are important to their election. In particular, a study of candidates for office in Wisconsin in 1964 concluded that on the average, both successful candidates for higher office and marginal winners believed that issues were more important than did "safe" winners, losers, and candidates for the state legislature (Kingdon, 1966:25–30). Fenno (1977) found that congressmen stress the importance of explaining votes. "House members believe that they can win and lose constituent support through their explanations as well as through their votes [p. 910]." He writes that "on the vast majority of votes, a congressman can do as he wishes—provided only that he can, if and when he needs to, explain his vote to the satisfaction of interested constituents [p. 911]."

decisions. This process is viewed from a slightly different perspective in Part E, dealing with lobbyists' efforts to influence legislators who themselves are ignorant of voter preferences.

B. Issues Not Predetermined

Chapter 2, assumed, unrealistically, that the legislature's agenda remained constant from session to session. This fact permitted perfectly knowledgeable constituents to use incumbents' voting records in the past session as an indicator of their votes in the next session in the absence of corruption. If, however, issues change over time, an incumbent's voting record will be an imperfect guide, even for well-informed voters.

The variability of issues over time has two consequences. First, if issues are not fully specified in advance, legislators may avoid taking positions on specific issues at election time (the *specificity* effect). Corruption can then occur without voters perceiving that any promises have been broken. Second, instead of making corrupt payoffs, interest groups can provide campaign monies[2] to neutralize the effect of the representative's past votes in their favor (the *neutralization* effect).[3] Thus, rather than paying opponents to change their votes, interest groups may contribute to friends who have done their bidding in the past. While these contributions to known supporters may appear to be a waste of the group's resources, friendly legislators' votes may, in fact, be conditional upon continued support of their reelection campaigns.

---

[2] Although I do not analyze them separately, contributions need not take the form of monetary payments. Labor unions often supply gifts of members' time, and firms contribute advertisements, services, and the time of employees (Alexander, 1972, Chapter 10; Fenno, 1973, discusses the political services provided by postal unions). These in-kind services are analytically similar to money payments except that they may limit the candidates' freedom to channel spending in particular directions. Thus, the economists' general argument in favor of the superior efficiency of monetary over in-kind transfers applies to this case as well.

[3] An incumbent's vote in favor of an interest group may also be neutralized by contributions to the incumbent's challengers. North (1953) discusses the use of this technique by insurance companies. Shannon (in Allen, 1949:44) reports on the activities of the two Pappas brothers in Massachusetts. In order to protect their dog track, horse racing, and wholesale liquor business, one was an active Democrat, the other an active Republican. The diversified campaign contributions of the Associated Milk Producers, Inc., came to light during the Watergate investigations in 1974. Over time the association has contributed to both Republican and Democratic candidates in presidential races and in key House and Senate contests (*New York Times,* July 2, 6, 20, 27, 31, and August 1, 1974).

Moreover, the interest group may wish to be sure that supporters return to help them out in the next legislative session. Unlike corrupt payments campaign contributions will be positively correlated with the closeness of the legislative contest.[4] These contributions might also demonstrate to other, more uncertain legislators that the group can be counted on to aid its "friends."

When money has broader political uses than bribe paying, however, the relatively simple analysis of the politician's tradeoff between money and votes bumps into the complexities of the legal status of various types of payments. Some payments are legally defined as bribery, others are illegal but do not fall under the corruption statute, and still others are formally legal but could lower one's reelection probability if made public. If there were no legal restraints on payments to politicians, they would always prefer untied cash transfers to other forms of payment which give them less freedom of disposal. Legal restrictions complicate their lives in various ways. Candidates must spend campaign contributions on their election bid or else find costly and risky ways of transferring the money to private use. Politicians may try to protect themselves by arranging for "bribes" to be paid to aides, spouses, or business associates; and if they do accept money directly, must spend it discreetly to avoid arousing suspicions.[5] The illegality of bribery and the legality of certain campaign contributions implies that interest groups may now find that politicians in close races are cheaper to influence, ceteris paribus, than either lame ducks or safe seats. Even in the absence of legal restraints, these candidates would choose to spend contributions on campaign expenses. This conclusion would not follow,

---

[4] Jacobson (1977) has stressed this aspect in his research on campaign finance. Since incumbents' campaign contributions are highly correlated with spending by their opponents, he believes that incumbents have little difficulty raising funds. They can always match an opponents' campaign contribution by exerting a small amount of additional effort.

[5] For example, Korean attempts to influence American politicians seldom took the form of direct bribes. The Koreans established a Washington club, gave money to the wife of a member of Congress, entered into business deals with a congressman and provided parties, free gifts, and other favors (*New York Times*, October 28 and December 19, 1976; March 28, June 15, and June 23, 1977).
   One of the most common types of benefit is the employment of legislators by interest groups (see Allen, 1949; Milbrath, 1963:279; Margolis, 1974; *New York Times*, July 25, 1975). Alternatively, interest groups have attempted to cut off business to unfriendly legislators (Shannon, in Allen, 1949:47). In the nineteenth century, these indirect methods were less necessary since the notion of conflict of interest was not well developed. Business did not simply try to influence politicians; they often *were* politicians (see Cochran, 1953; Rhodes, 1906; Smith, 1958). Legislators could be influenced by one other without the need for outside business representatives.

however, if voters are deeply opposed to policies favored by wealthy groups or if, in fact, money could be used to benefit the politician personally with little risk—for example, the offer of a high paying sinecure to a lame duck legislator.

In this complicated legal environment, the proportion of issues decided on the basis of corrupt payments is determined by the relative strength of the *specificity* and *neutralization* effects. The first implies that, because of the uncertain agenda, corruption will be more difficult to infer from a legislator's behavior and so may have less effect on p. The second implies that legal campaign payments may be a substitute for bribes. Thus, the ultimate impact of a more realistic view of the legislative agenda is uncertain, depending upon the *productivity* of campaign spending, the way in which incumbents value personal income gains, and the possibility of using legal campaign contributions for personal expenses.[6]

[6] The productivity of campaign spending has been studied by Jacobson (1977), Welch (1974) and Palda (1975) for congressional elections; Alexander (1971, 1976) and Dunn (1972) for presidential races; and Adamany (1969, 1972) for races in Wisconsin and Connecticut. Adamany (1977:294–295) summarizes several previous studies of the efficacy of money in deciding elections, but he does not draw any firm general conclusions. Jacobson, Welch, and Palda have estimated production functions for votes, and each study has found that campaign expenditures are significant in explaining the percentage of votes received. Welch notes that the elasticity of the vote share with respect to expenditure is small, which in the context of his model's specification also implies that the marginal productivity curve for campaign expenditure is downward sloping. Jacobson does not constrain the effects of expenditure to be equal for incumbents and nonincumbents. He finds that increasing incumbents' expenditures does not increase their chances of reelection. This may be attributed to a low marginal productivity of money for incumbents, who are already well known and hence cannot purchase much additional exposure. Challengers, however, may increase their expected vote share by increasing campaign expenditures. In summary, the empirical work shows that the marginal productivity of money in producing votes may vary, and depends upon the context of particular campaigns.

Beyond a certain point, campaign contributions may be of little value to a politician unless they can be converted to private payments. However, those legislators with little interest in campaign funds may hold powerful positions that make them valuable to special interest groups. Thus, Federal Elections Commission data indicate that many members of Congress who run without opposition in either the primary or the general election, nevertheless accumulate large "campaign funds." Others who are typically reelected by wide margins also raise large amounts of money (Common Cause, 1974a). Under current law, these funds, if not expended in the incumbent's reelection bid, may be used "to defray any ordinary and necessary expenses incurred by him in connection with his duties as a holder of Federal office, may be contributed to any organization [fulfilling certain standards] or may be used for any other lawful purpose [2U.S.C.§439a]." While formally legal, these excess funds are clearly much closer to direct bribes than money used in waging a closely fought reelection campaign.

C. Apathetic Voters

I turn next to analyze a political environment where the electorate is dominated by personal or family concerns and wants "help" from its political representatives, not general legislation. In this model, the actual issues voted on by the legislature are irrelevant to the vast majority of the population. Instead, their votes for candidates are determined by the value of personal election-time benefits handed out by the highest bidder. This model of politics accords with the situation in much of the underdeveloped world and in the machine-dominated cities at the turn of the century in America.[7] The best contemporary example is, perhaps, the Philippines: Direct per capita campaign expenditures are the highest in the world and, in addition, 10–20% of the electorate is reported to sell its vote; wealthy elites provide most of the campaign funds in the hope that individualized benefits distributed at election time will prevent the poor from organizing to dislodge the wealthy from power.[8]

The existence of vote buying completely eliminates the tradeoff between reelection and interest group payments that was central to the analysis in Chapter 2. A politician will remain in power because of these payments rather than in spite of them. Instead of trading votes off against private income, politicians now trade self-enrichment off against payoffs to constituents. Figure 3.1 illustrates this situation using the simplifying assumption that the cost of a 1% improvement in the probability of reelection is a constant. Assume that, with no vote buying, the legislator's income is y_A, and the expected fraction of the vote $\hat{p}$, is .5. Interest groups pay a bribe of $y_{BA} - y_A$ placing the legislator at B. If the cost of buying improvements in $\hat{p}$ is given by L_0 (i.e., minus the inverse of L_0's slope), then the politician will spend $y_B - y_C$ buying votes and will keep $y_C - y_A$. The expected proportion of the vote is then $\hat{p}_C$. If instead votes are very expensive, so that L_1 represents postcorruption opportunities, the legislator will retain all of the bribes. If the marginal cost of votes remains constant or increases as $\hat{p}$ increases, then the more confident the legislator is of reelection in the absence of vote buying, the less likely he is to spend payments to buy additional votes.

[7] For conventional models of machine politics see Banfield and Wilson (1963, Chapter 9), Merton (1968:126–136), and Scott (1972, Chapters 6 and 7).

[8] See Scott (1972:96–97). A recent example of the presumed "purchase" of a seat in a legislature occurred in the 1977 Israeli election. A millionaire, seeking to avoid extradition to France where he was wanted on embezzlement charges, ran for the Israeli parliment, since if elected, he would be difficult to return to France. He spent a large sum on his campaign, and despite an inability to speak Hebrew, won two seats under Israel's proportional representation rule (*New York Times* May 19, 1977).

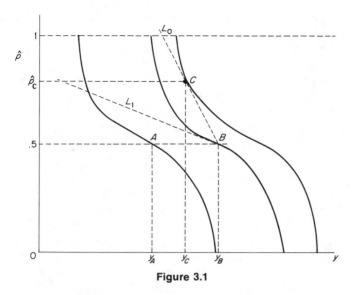

Figure 3.1

Politicians facing either weak opposition or voters who are expensive to buy are likely to enrich themselves rather than their constituents.[9]

Having analyzed the legislator's tradeoff, interest group behavior is easy to model. In contrast to an "idealized" political system with issue-oriented voters, legislators in the present model will never support an interest group's position on an issue for free. Instead, the group will always have to purchase at least a majority of the representatives. If only one side of the issue is organized, however, the per capita bribes can be very small since, without party organization, no one in the legislature has the power to extort high payments. The bribe-minimizing strategy can be specified further if the interest group has a long-run perspective and there are certain fixed costs of establishing corrupt relationships with politicians. Under these conditions, interest groups will, ceteris paribus, prefer to bribe legislators who are relatively likely to win the next election so as to continue the corrupt course of dealing. Thus interest groups will favor those incumbents who plan to spend their bribe money on vote purchases rather than self-enrichment or who otherwise have a high $\hat{p}$. In terms of Figure 3.1, an interest group would

[9] In some contexts, politicians may be able to structure the political system to improve the position of incumbents and reduce the need for campaign spending (Crain, 1977). In a more general case Johnson (1975) analyzes how a corrupt government may change its institutions and laws to reduce the need to pass on receipts to citizens.

rather spend $y_B - y_A$ on a legislator with opportunity locus L_0 than on one with L_1.

When both sides of an issue are organized, neither group has any inherent advantage because no legislator has any prior position on any issue. Thus a comparison of total financial resources is more relevant in this case than in the model of Chapter 2. Evenly matched groups will be unable to dominate each other. A winning coalition established by one group can always be disbanded by the other.

In short, simply by changing voters from issue oriented to politically apathetic actors, I have constructed a model of a "democratic" political system that contrasts starkly with the idealized situations described in Chapter 2. Moreover, it is easy to hypothesize dynamic systems where the presence of some corrupt payoffs or even legal campaign contributions convert issue-oriented voters into citizens indifferent to their representative's voting record in the previous legislative session. For example, suppose that issue-oriented voters elect representatives on the basis of their positions on policy questions. Once in the legislature, however, these politicians accept money in return for voting to favor special interest groups. In the next electoral campaign challengers arise who promise to follow citizens' preferences and overturn legislation passed by their predecessors. Voters, while unhappy with the incumbents, now assume that no politicians can be trusted to vote as promised. Therefore, citizens ignore the policy positions of candidates and instead seek personalized benefits. This possibility is, of course, overlooked by those social scientists who emphasize the favorable consequences of monetary contributions from special interest groups.

D. Voter Ignorance

Ignorant voters are analytically equivalent to indifferent voters if their ignorance cannot be changed by the intervention of either legislators or interest groups. When ignorance is remediable, however, the interest group can choose between bribing a legislator or expending funds on voter education, so that a legislator's constituents come to favor the interest group's position.[10] Voter education may in turn be supported in two different ways. On the one hand, the interest group may conduct the

[10] See, for example, a discussion of the public relations activities of railroads in trying to prevent an increase in truck weight limits in Hacker (1962).

advertising activity itself;[11] on the other, it may provide campaign contributions to the incumbent. This second approach will be favored if the incumbents' vote-maximizing strategies involve public relations campaigns which downplay their votes on special interest legislation and emphasize their positions on issues of particular concern to the voters.[12] Recent work in political science, in fact, stresses the ability of candidates to affect the "salience" of issues.[13] Even if we accept current scholarship which views voters as rational "investors,"[14] the uncertainty and ignorance surrounding political choices gives candidates substantial freedom to conceal certain actions and emphasize others. While the media and one's opponents prevent complete concealment, it is nevertheless reasonable to suppose that money can be spent to help neutralize both promises to major campaign contributors and unpopular votes on special interest legislation.[15]

[11] When an issue is to be voted on in a public referendum, interest groups must concentrate on obtaining the support of voters. Billboards which misrepresented the purpose of a referendum were used in California in 1925 to gain voter approval of a proposal to designate buses as public utilities (Richard Hyer, "California: The First Hundred Years", in Allen, 1949:390). Massachusetts racing interests sought public support by pointing out that gambling taxes aided the aged. Simultaneously, they lobbied in the legislature to keep taxes low (Shannon, in Allen, 1949:46).

[12] Of course, large contributors will often have other motives besides neutralizing the electoral impact of legislative decisions favoring special interests. See Alexander (1972:141) and Adamany (1969:203–229, 1972:126–178).

[13] Page (1976). In fact, the decision to present blurred, ambiguous positions may have nothing to do with the attempt to raise campaign funds. Downs (1957), Page (1976) and Shepsle (1972) all argue that ambiguity may be a way to attract votes. Therefore, if incumbents are willing and able to present ambiguous faces to the voters, special interest money may have little cost for candidates in terms of electoral support. Since they do not, by hypothesis, wish to run on their legislative records, they can vote to favor wealthy interest groups, use this record to obtain contributions, and then spend these funds on a campaign which emphasizes a few popular issues.

[14] For example, Popkin et al. (1976) and Magee and Brock (1976).

[15] Ben-Zion and Eytan (1974), Brock and Magee (1975), Magee and Brock (1976), and Welch (1974) have developed similar models in which policy and campaign expenditures are inputs in a production function for votes. Politicians deviate from the median voter's policy optimum in order to gain money from interest groups; this money is then used to produce votes. Politicians choose an equilibrium policy where the marginal vote loss from undesirable policy equals the marginal vote gain from the added campaign expenditure. These models assume that neither voters nor interest groups require incumbents to "run on their record." Instead, politicians make promises at election time and do not renege. Their work also assumes that information is costly and partially under the control of candidates. A politician's promises depend upon both voter and interest group preferences, upon opponent's behavior (this variable is held fixed in the formal model of Ben-Zion and Eytan), and upon the productivity of money.

(Continued on next page)

An interest group may also travel both the high road of voter education and the low road of legislative corruption simultaneously. Bribery insures that the details of the legislation benefit the company or interest group, while advertising minimizes the legislator's political risks. Thus in Massachusetts in 1918 the head of the Boston Elevated Company both attempted to persuade the public of the importance of continued transit and also showed legislators how they could buy shares of Boston Elevated stock inexpensively and benefit from the price rise caused by a state guarantee of dividends.[16]

Indeed, if an interest group believes that the political productivity of an advertising campaign is low, it may make a conscious attempt to hide from the public legislation favorable to its interest, using bribes or campaign contributions to enlist the collaboration of legislators in these efforts. For instance, business interests have opposed reforming state constitutions to lengthen sessions since a pile-up of bills in the last few days is beneficial to those who favor legislation that would be opposed by knowledgeable voters.[17] Hence, omnibus bills bestowing benefits on a multitude of special interests are a common feature of the closing days of many legislatures, and particularized benefits may be added as riders to general legislation.[18] Similarly, if issues are neither predetermined nor well defined, interest groups may try either to frame issues so that they

---

Hard evidence on the tie between contributions and legislative outcomes is, however, unavailable. Tullock (1972), assuming that the return on campaign contributions will approximate the return on other investments, argues that policy distortions caused by the influence of contributors will be small because a very small fraction of national income is devoted to campaign contributions. This argument ignores the external costs that a group of contributors can impose on unorganized citizens. Dunn (1972) reports that contributions at the very least supply access to officeholders and contends that "solicitation [of campaign funds] by either the office seeker or his staff implicitly promises a sympathetic response to matters of interest to the giver [pp. 19–21]." Senator Mike Gravel of Alaska told the *New York Times* (July 19, 1976) that all campaign support guarantees is access. "I would pick up the telephone for a supporter before I would pick it up for someone else." The article, however, documents several instances where special tax breaks were provided to groups or individuals who contributed to the campaigns of key members of the Senate Finance Committee. The ties between legislative outcomes and contributions are also fairly clear in some of the incidents reported by Alexander (1972:1976) and Harris (1971).

[16] See W. Shannon on Massachusetts (Allen, 1949:64).

[17] For example, a bill regulating entry and rates in the Chicago taxi industry was hidden in an omnibus bill passed at the end of a city council session (Kitch, Isaacson, and Kasper, 1971). See also the introduction and many of the individual articles in Allen (1949).

[18] In 1937 a bill permitting the drug and liquor industries to fix the minimum retail sales price of branded goods was attached as a rider to a District of Columbia appropriation bill (Crawford, 1939:21).

appear to be complicated or else influence the specific provisions of bills in a way which leaves most citizens undecided or indifferent while the interest group benefits.[19]

In short, the role of money in affecting legislative outcomes is extremely sensitive to our model of voter behavior. While in the case of apathetic voters, money was critically important, as soon as education becomes a possible strategy, predicting the relative power of groups on the basis of their monetary resources is unwarranted.[20] The productivity of money in buying effective persuasion is not a simple linear function of the number of dollars expended. Not only must each group choose between bribery, issue-oriented public relations, and general campaign contributions, but relatively impecunious groups may succeed in persuading citizens to favor their positions even though the opposing interests have many times more resources to expend on persuasion.[21]

E. Legislator Ignorance

Up to the present point, I have failed to consider a political figure who bulks large in discussions of legislation. There, lobbyists are often depicted as educating legislators,[22] rather than the general public, as to the merits of special interest groups' positions. To make this function credible, it is necessary to modify the model in one of two ways. On the one hand, one might change the fundamental assumption concerning the politician's motivation. Rather than considering only y and $\hat{p}$, one could assume that the legislator is public spirited with an open mind as to the nature of the public interest. Changing the assumptions in this way,

---

[19] For some evidence on these points see Kagen (1975) and Scott (1972).

[20] Although little is known about the effects of advertising on public policy outcomes, a comprehensive study of the effects of advertising on product sales has been undertaken by Lambin (1976). Lambin found that brand advertising has a significant effect on current and long-term brand sales and market shares, subject to decreasing returns. Perhaps his methodology could be applied to the study of public policy outcomes as well.

[21] Nadel (1971) and Wilson (1974) cite examples.

[22] See Deakin (1966:14) and Lindblom (1968). Lindblom explains the impact of lobbying as follows:

> In short, the proximate policy maker has an underlying set of dispositions. He is faced with policy choices. He has a good deal of freedom or discretion to act as he sees fit. He does not know which policies best match with his basic attitudes or principles. He needs help. Interest groups are important instruments for helping him by showing him with fact and analysis how to reach a decision [p. 66].

while descriptive of some legislative behavior, obviously limits the role of economic analysis dramatically. On the other hand, one might take the less drastic step of modifying the earlier assumption that legislators completely discount as biased information concerning voter preferences provided by lobbyists. Thus, one might assume a somewhat more gullible legislative body or perhaps one where uncertainty about voter preferences is so great that any crumb of information, however meager, is gladly accepted. So long as this is so, educational activity aimed solely at legislators makes sense. Nonetheless, given the nature of the required assumptions, it may be that the prominence of these lobbying campaigns in the political science literature is a consequence of the fact that this form of activity is quite easy to observe. Instead, lobbyist–legislator interaction may only be part of a larger strategy to generate increased public support for interest group positions.[23] In this model, if a lobbyist cannot successfully claim to represent constituent sentiment, legislators would refuse to be educated and would seek to have the cost of the proffered information converted into a direct payment. There is some impressionistic evidence supporting this conclusion. Thus Milbrath (1963), in his study of Washington lobbyists, concludes that "the smart lobbyist tries to demonstrate to a member that following a particular course of action will help him in his constituency [p. 335]."[24] Unfortunately, however, political scientists have not systematically considered the relationship between lobbying activity and broader based industry efforts to shape voter preferences.

---

[23] Analysts have not entirely neglected this connection. Bauer, de Sola Pool, and Dexter (1962), for example, emphasize the importance of lobbyists as sources of information to both legislators and outside business interests. Deakin (1966:194–207) discusses the successful effort by savings and loan associations in 1961 to kill a proposed federal withholding tax on interest and dividends. The associations sent letters to their depositers urging them to write letters against the withholding proposal and implying that the law would mean a new tax on savings.

[24] Deakin (1966) makes the same point. Lobbyists for foreign countries would thus appear to be especially disadvantaged if legislators will not accept bribes or campaign funds. However, powerful legislators may be able to trade legislative decisions for foreign country decisions which favor their districts' interests. Thus, in 1955 the chairman of the House Agriculture Committee reportedly tried to associate the size of the Philippines' sugar import quota with a Philippine decision to purchase United States tobacco. The chairman's district was in the heart of the North Carolina tobacco country (Deakin, 1966:84–85). Edwin Edwards from Louisiana stated that while he was a member of the House of Representatives, a Korean businessman and lobbyist helped him sell Louisiana rice to Korea. It is not clear from the newspaper report, however, whether Edwards provided any services in return for this help (*New York Times*, June 15, 1977).

F. Conclusions

The relationship between the characteristics of voters and the incidence of corruption is not the simple one to be deduced from the lessons of high school civics class. When voters conform to the knowledgeable, issue-oriented ideal, outright corruption is, in my model, the only possible way in which a legislative vote can be changed through interest group activity. When voters are poorly informed, a wide variety of other techniques, from educational programs, to lobbying, to the payment of campaign contributions, can be substituted for bribery. Thus, while voters may be less likely to vote corrupt incumbents out of office, alternative legal forms of influence may be more productive. It is only in the case of apathetic voters, discussed in Part C, where a high incidence of corruption is likely. Interest groups purchase politicians who in turn purchase voters. Thus, while voter ignorance has an uncertain (though important) relationship to the preservation of an honest democratic process, an electorate that does not even care about its politicians' stands on the issues is incapable of maintaining governmental integrity.

3. MONOPOLY POWER AND LEGISLATIVE CORRUPTION

A. Political Parties

Thus far, I have assumed that legislators are "price takers" in the market for corrupt services or campaign funds. In many legislatures, however, strong political parties are capable of controlling the votes of members and so may have considerable market power.[25] A system with strong parties may be particularly susceptible to the influence of wealthy groups for several reasons. First, instead of dealing with legislators individually, the group can simply approach the party hierarchy. Thus, the party organization may represent a scale economy. Second, while a party will be concerned about its probability of returning to power after

---

[25] The best examples here come from outside the United States in legislatures where party discipline is high. See Palmier's (1975) discussion of India, and reports of contributions to Italian political parties by Exxon (*New York Times*, July 7, 1975) and by a group of drug companies (*New York Times*, March 21, 1976).

Even in the absence of party discipline, some legislatures are small enough to be organized as a unit. The entire five-member city council of Lackawanna, New York, was indicted for extorting kickbacks in return for contracts to build and furnish a city hall annex (*New York Times*, June 29, 1975).

the next election, it may be willing to sacrifice the political careers of legislators in marginal seats if the party's position is strong. Furthermore, so long as the party itself remains in control of the government, it can appoint defeated politicians to government posts. These political rewards, unavailable to private interest groups dealing with individual politicians, increase the likelihood of a successful deal since the support of some legislators can be "bought" by the party without an expenditure of money by the interest group. Third, parties may last longer than politicians. Hence an interest group whose members are affected by a wide range of actions in every session of the legislature may be willing to back a party financially, even though it may lose the next election, since a party has a greater chance of returning to power next period than a defeated politician.[26]

The existence of a strong party organization may increase not only the incidence of corruption and campaign contributions from special interests but also the volume of money changing hands. A majority party is in a very strong bargaining position and can extort high payoffs from interest groups. Payments equal to a group's maximum willingness to pay are possible even without the competitive organization of interest groups.[27] When only one side of an issue is represented by an effective interest group, the existence of a party with majority control converts the situation into a case of bilateral monopoly. Indeed, it is possible to imagine political situations where firms fear expropriation, either if an opposition party wins or if the present governing party is reelected without the firm's aid. This, for example, was the dilemma which Gulf Oil confronted in both South Korea and Bolivia—if its efforts to justify its large payoffs are to be believed (*New York Times*, May 17, 1975; November 26, 1975).

Since interest groups will wish to blunt the extortionary power of political parties, individuals and firms may refuse to organize politically

[26] In the American system—where no single party is clearly dominant and where party discipline is weak—one study concluded that most interest groups would rather contribute campaign funds to individuals than to political parties (Milbrath, 1963:284). This preference seems to have a dual explanation. First, to reduce the risk of "extortion," groups did not want to strengthen the power of the party relative to the individual legislator. Second, given that parties do have some long-term influence, groups might fear too close an association with a single party, believing that they would have to bear the expense of supporting both sides if they supported either.

[27] A strategy of extracting high payoffs from those willing to offer them, however, may not be in the long-run best interest of the party leadership. Organizations who might have made offers had the stakes been lower may not even try to influence policy. International firms, for example, may seek alternative investment opportunities where political payoffs are less expensive.

in the face of a strong party. They may fear that if they form pressure groups, this will simply make it easier for representatives to propose unfavorable legislation as a device for generating bribes or campaign contributions.[28] Indeed, insurance companies at the turn of the century kept the fact of their political organization hidden to prevent "hold-ups" by corrupt legislatures (North, 1953). Similarly, established interest groups will wish to appear as weak amalgams of business firms that are likely to disintegrate if pressed too assidously for corrupt payments or compaign contributions.[29] Or the agents of an interest group may state that the payments they make are not sanctioned by the members of the group. The tactic of appearing poor and honest will not succeed, however, if the other side of the issue is also organized. In that case, outright competition for votes may occur here, just as it did in the case of an individualistic legislature.

While it is important to emphasize the way in which a dominant party may be transformed into a powerful extortionary force, even here complications arise. Even a party "dictator" must still consider the impact of the party's voting behavior on its success in the next election. To focus only on *corrupt* payments for a moment, it is possible to construct situations in which the presence of a dominant political party reduces the incidence and volume of corruption compared to what would occur in an individualistic legislature. For example, imagine that 51% of legislators have safe seats and that the other 49% have $\hat{p} \sim .5$. Suppose that only the supporters of a particular bill are organized to pay bribes, and that voters are so knowledgeable that no campaign money is needed by incumbents. All payoffs will increase y and lower $\hat{p}$. In an individualistic legislature, if fewer than 51% support the bill, the bribers will clearly concentrate their bribe money among those in secure seats. Now suppose that the dominant party consists of all of those in insecure seats as well as enough secure members to provide control of the legislature. Assume further that many of those with $\hat{p} \sim .5$ have constituents who strongly oppose the legislation. A party vote in favor of the bill may thus substantially increase the chance that it will lose legislative control in the next election. Thus the party leadership may demand a very high bribe, while a decisive corrupt coalition of individualistic legislators would have been relatively cheap to organize.

---

[28] Crawford (1939:92) states that the well-known wealth of a motion picture lobbying group in the 1930s led state legislatures to introduce rigorous censorship and regulation bills as a way of collecting payoffs.

[29] Compare Schelling's (1963) argument about the bargaining power of weakness and irrationality.

When a multiplicity of political parties makes it possible to form alternative majority coalitions, competition for the privilege of being bought may reduce the costs of corruption and campaign contributions to interest groups. While much of the analysis of the individualistic legislature can be applied here, one distinctive feature of a parliamentary multiparty system may make both corruption and campaign contributions more prevalent than they would be in either an individualistic legislature or one with a single dominant party. Where several different party coalitions could produce a majority, the relationship between citizens' votes and government policy may be very thin (Swaan, 1973). Parties may profess particular positions on issues at election time only to modify them later in an effort to form a coalition government. If this behavior is prevalent, voters may attach little importance to the positions taken legislators, leading to the payoff-prone case of an apathetic electorate discussed previously.

B. Influential Individuals

Thus far, the political party was taken as the paradigmatic mechanism through which legislators attain monopoly power over special interests. Even without parties, however, the interaction between legislative voting rules and the preferences of legislators can produce situations in which a small group of individual legislators have considerable monopoly power. Clearly, if unanimity is required for the passage of new legislation, then every legislator has a bargaining advantage over groups which want a change, and no one has any monopoly power over groups which wish to retain the status quo. In less extreme situations, a small group of individuals may be able to extort payments in excess of their reservation prices if the rest of the legislature is very costly to influence or is equally divided on an issue permitting a small group to determine the outcome. For example, consider a legislature that uses majority rule, where 90% of the representatives have $\hat{p}$s close to .5, while 10% have safe seats. Suppose further that voters are knowledgeable and issue-oriented and that 45% of the representatives with $\hat{p} \sim .5$ have constituents who strongly support the bill under consideration whereas the other 45% have constituents who strongly oppose it. The constituents of the remaining 10% are divided. Since campaign contributions are of no use to incumbents, the decisive 10%, if it can organize, may now be able to extort high payments from those who favor the legislation. They can obtain these high bribes even if the bill would have passed without bribery and even if the opposition is completely unorganized.[30]

So long as the legislative agenda is not written in stone, some of the assembly's business must be transacted without resort to majority voting. Therefore, at some point in the political process, administrative procedures must be used to decide which issues are raised and to fix the wording of legislative proposals. Because majority support is not required for these decisions, they are an obvious focus for special interest group activity. Wealthy firms and individuals may be able to influence legislative outcomes by paying bribes or giving campaign contributions to those who control the agenda and define the issues.[31] In a legislative system like the United States Congress where standing committees develop legislative proposals and hold hearings, committee chairmen may be able to extort legal or illegal payments from the industries under their committees' jurisdiction.[32] For example, two Illinois legislators were recently charged with having introduced legislation unfavorable to the rental car industry and holding it in committee until paid $1500 by the Illinois Car and Truck Renting and Leasing Association (*Wall Street Journal,* December 5, 1974). This kind of implicit extortionary demand is probably behind Milbrath's finding (1963:284) that interest groups found it hard to refuse campaign solicitations even though they seldom volunteered funds on their own.[33]

---

[30] Similarly, if voters' preferences are unimportant and the legislature divides along ideological lines, a small group of pragmatic bribe maximizers may have considerable monopoly power because of the strong and divided beliefs of the rest of the group.

[31] In a legislature where committee chairmen fulfill this role, a friendly chairman in a safe seat can be a valuable long-term asset to an interest group (see examples in Allen, 1949; Deakin, 1966; and North, 1953). Although not obviously involving corruption, committee chairmen frequently have close relationships with the industries whose fortunes they affect (e.g., Albright, 1976; M. Levine, 1975; Nadel, 1971; *New York Times,* September 14, 1975, Section 4). In allocating campaign funds among United States congressmen and senators, interest groups do seem to favor members of committees that oversee legislation relevant to their concerns (Harris, 1971). Gelfand (1977), in a study of campaign contributions given by agricultural and banking interests to members of the House of Representatives in 1972, found that membership on the Agriculture or Banking and Currency committees, respectively, was an important determinant of interest group payments. His paper, however, does not completely resolve the problem of the causal linkage between committee membership and contributions. One cannot tell if congressmen who obtain large contributions are also the ones who seek membership on the relevant committees or whether committee membership spurs contributions.

[32] Thomas Dodd was apparently a skilled practitioner of this technique. See Boyd (1968).

[33] In this respect at least, the president of the United States has more power than any individual member of Congress, since he can single-handedly affect the profitability of a wide range of business enterprises. While covert extortion has apparently been practiced

Thus, while the dispersion of power among committees makes indus-try subject to extortionary demands, it also aids business groups by lowering the transaction costs of dealing with the legislature.[34] Interest groups may be able to choose at what stage in the political process to exert influence; and if defeated at one level, they can carry their fight to the next. Having a committee chairman "in one's pocket," however, is of little use if the bills reported out of committee are routinely defeated by the legislature. Therefore, special interests are more likely to be able to influence the content of legislation if the issues are of only minor concern to voters. For example, while citizens may care a good deal about having a modern air force, they are unlikely to care which company obtains the airplane building contract. Furthermore, if particu-larized legislation increases the profits of the successful firm, and if the public cannot measure these profits easily, political payments can be disguised as a cost of doing business. The power of committee chairmen or other influential legislators to favor one business firm over another is therefore a fertile area for special interest activity since the choices of these legislators are likely to be sustained by subsequent votes in the assembly.[35] Therefore, it is not clear a priori whether a strong committee

---

often in the past, the most clearcut recent examples come from the investigations of Richard Nixon's 1972 Committee to Reelect the President. Thus there is evidence that one multinational company provided campaign funds to President Nixon in return for a favorable antitrust ruling (see excerpts from the House Judiciary Committee's evidence in the *New York Times,* July 20, 1974). An administration increase in milk price supports was reported to have been conditional upon a dairy industry campaign contribution (*New York Times,* June 7 and July 18, 1974). A Senate Watergate Committee staff report concluded that President Nixon's reelection campaign "spanned the entire spectrum of corrupt campaign financing [reported in the *New York Times,* June 19, 1974]." Other allegations of extortionary behavior are reported in the *New York Times* on January 2, March 14, and March 20, 1974; February 26, June 10, and August 2, 1975.

[34] In an assembly where authority over particular issues has not been clearly apportioned, a firm or interest group runs the risk of paying legislators who claim to possess influence which they do not, in fact, have. Thus several Nigerian tailors paid town councilors to obtain a contract (Wraith and Simkins, 1963). One tailor paid £3 to a councillor to obtain a £16/7s. contract "in blissful ignorance of the fact that two of his colleagues on the Council had done the same in respect of other tailors. The resultant necessary division of this contract into three, to the value of £5/12s. for each part, was scarcely worth the layout of £3, as the tailors bitterly complained, "What we have here is not mere corruption, but corruption with cheating added [p. 24]."

[35] Thus, key Dutch legislators allegedly were offered bribes by aircraft companies in return for favoring particular fighter planes (*New York Times,* July 25 and July 27, 1975; Feb. 11, 1976), and the Northrup Corporation paid an agent for his assistance in obtaining the support of U.S. Representative, H. Mendel Rivers, Chairman of the House Armed

structure is on balance beneficial or harmful to special interest groups. The net benefits will depend upon the identities of the committee chairmen as well as the visibility and political importance of the issues affecting the interest groups.[36]

C. Conclusions

While the earlier discussion of an individualistic legislature identified the basic ties between voter preferences, corruption and other forms of influences, it did not explain one salient feature of real-world bribery. While efforts to corrupt large numbers of legislators are not unknown,[37] more commonly only a few key individuals receive payments. Thus, even in spectacular cases of corruption, like the Credit Mobilier scandal of the 1860s, many congressmen voted with the railroad without payment. However, "venal and greedy" they may have been, the organization costs were too high for them to exploit their willingness to be bought. A few congressmen, however, were in the position to exploit the monopolistic structure of the legislature by affecting the votes of colleagues and determining the details of the legislation and the speed

---

Services Committee, in the award of a contract (Albright, 1976). At the individual level, town councilors in Africa allocate market stalls, scholarship awards, and grants to study abroad. These benefits are often sold, sometimes at fixed prices (Scott, 1972; Wraith and Simkins, 1963.)

[36] Fenno (1973) has emphasized the difference between the behavior of six standing committees in the House of Representatives and their opposite numbers in the Senate. In some committees, Interior and Post Office in the House and Finance in the Senate, special interests and constituency groups are very active lobbyists. In others, Ways and Means and Appropriations, Fenno argues that the House committees have been organized to isolate members from lobbying groups. Fenno does not, however, look at campaign financing, and it may be that an examination of funding sources would force one to modify one's view of the "isolation" of "money committee" members. Furthermore, Ritt (1976) argues that committee position and seniority in Congress are not important determinants of the level of federal spending in one's district, and that simple incumbency appears to be the major fact determining the outcome of elections. Ritt's work, however, is similarly limited in not considering campaign contributions.

[37] Coulter (1933:187–192) reports that in 1795 all but one member of the Georgia legislature was bribed to pass a bill authorizing the sale of Georgia land to private interests at a low price. Lincoln Steffans reports a case where many members of the Missouri House of Delegates were bribed to obtain passage of a bill giving a St. Louis street railway company monopoly development rights (*Shame of the Cities,* 1904, reprinted in Gardiner and Olson 1974:197–204).

with which it passed through Congress. These were the people who obtained payments from the railroads.[38]

It is true, of course, that the existence of a few powerful political leaders may be as potent a source for honesty in government as for corruption. For if the powerful few are incorruptible, the costs of corrupting alternative majorities may be much higher than in the individualistic legislature. Nonetheless, the extortionary potential of a monopolistic legislature is high if leaders choose to make use of it and if voter preferences are not in themselves a strong deterrent.

4. INTEREST GROUP RESOURCES AND ORGANIZATION

Just as a legislator must trade off $\hat{p}$ and y in deciding whether to accept a bribe offer or how to allocate a campaign contribution, so must an interest group consider the benefits and costs of attempting to change a legislative outcome. Simple statements of the relationship between industrial categories and the likelihood of influence are, however, difficult to produce. On the one hand, the more competitive an industry, the more it "needs" government aid.[39] Economic profits tend to zero in the long run without government intervention. On the other hand, organizing a well-financed group may be difficult the more competitive the industry: Organizational costs may be high (Posner, 1974:346), finding a common position may be difficult, and the competitiveness of the industry implies that firms do not have many funds available to contribute to a trade association or lobbying group. Existing firms would benefit substantially from government imposed entry barriers, but they lack the resources to establish them, and banks may be unwilling to lend money for the risky task of obtaining favorable legislation. One excep-

---

[38] In the 1860s, in order to insure legislation favorable to the Union Pacific Railroad and its construction company, the Credit Mobilier, the promoters were accused of bribing the vice president, the secretary of the treasury, the speaker of the house, and 12 other members of Congress (Rhodes, 1906:7:1–18). The charges were made by the *New York Sun* during the election campaign of 1872. Representatives of the Central Pacific, building east from California, also paid for congressional favors. The company's Washington-based executive once wrote, "I believe with $200,000 we can pass our bill (Josephson, 1934:84)." Railroad leaders justified their corrupt payments on the ground that they represented the "public interest" better than the venal and greedy legislators (Cochran, 1953).

[39] See Posner (1974:345) and Stigler (1971). For a critique of their approach, see Goldberg (1974).

tion to this case is a competitive industry where entry takes time. Then an increase in demand or a decline in input prices could produce short-run profits for existing firms that are high enough to purchase legislative restrictions on entry.[40]

Once entry restrictions are on the books, however, they generate excess profits for firms in the industry. Some portion of these profits can now be "invested" by trade groups that seek to obtain even more economic benefits for member firms. The process may be inherently unstable, with the initial legislative benefit generating more and more political gains for the industry. If, however, annual profits are insufficient to obtain additional benefits, an industry group might accumulate funds for several years before making another effort to obtain favorable legislation. If this occurs, one might observe cycles in industrial regulation.

There is also a second means by which an initial piece of regulatory legislation can generate more. As a result of the first enactment, the industry may now have an agency within the executive willing to promote its interests before the legislature. Indeed, given an agency seeking both large budgets and expanded powers, a new kind of free rider problem arises. The agency may want the private firms to spend money on lobbying, campaign contributions, or bribery, while the firms would like the agency to exert influence. The agency is likely to be in a strong bargaining position in this case, however, since it can tie contracts or favorable regulatory treatment to the efforts of private firms.[41]

Conversely, while organization for political action may often be easier the fewer the firms in the industry and the less competitive they are, it may also be less necessary. For example, in a completely monopolized industry, no government program is required to set prices. The single producer can do it alone. If, however, an industry is oligopolistic and cartels are illegal, government price setting and entry barriers can provide a legal substitute for cartel activity. Trade associations, although they might have great difficulty in organizing a full-blown clandestine price fixing scheme, can fulfill the role of intermediary between produc-

---

[40] Entry barriers are not the only kinds of benefits industries seek. In addition, they may try to obtain government pricefixing, the legalization of private cartel activity, or outright government purchases of their product. In extreme cases, they may seek nationalization or government loans as alternatives to bankruptcy.

[41] A good example of this kind of close agency–industry relationship is found in Michael E. Levine's (1975) discussion of airline regulation. Similarly, the Department of Defense and NASA can rely on private contractors to undertake lobbying efforts. For example, see "Here Comes the Space Shuttle" (*New York Times*, September 5, 1976, Section 3).

ers and legislators.[42] Furthermore, where an industrywide organization cannot be achieved, individual firms may be large enough to attempt to influence votes, even though they know that others obtain a free ride from their actions.[43]

Beyond emphasizing the importance of market organization in studying the flow of special interest funds, the general analysis emphasizes the importance of moving beyond the traditional categories of monopoly and competition in discussions of the economics of political choice. To focus on only one dimension of the problem, consider the way in which the geographical distribution of an industry's plants will affect its legislative influence. Assume, for example, that the electorate is knowledgeable and issue oriented and that legislators represent different geographical districts. Then an industry seeking a benefit which would also aid employees or local residents may find that influence is relatively inexpensive if member firms have plants in a large number of districts.[44] Many legislators may find that favoring the industry is a $\hat{p}$ maximizing strategy, and in the absence of organized opposition, the industry will only need to influence enough legislators in districts without plants to create a majority. Alternatively, a geographically concentrated industry may find it easier to obtain legislation damaging to employees or nearby residents than one which is more dispersed. Here, concentration implies

---

[42] They can also intermediate with bureaucrats. For further discussion of these points see Chapter 4 and Posner (1974), Stigler (1974), and Wilson (1974). See the analogous work of Olson (1965) on the effect of group size on the provision of public goods.

[43] Thus in Chicago and New York in the 1930s the dominant taxi company lobbied for entry restrictions and may have used corruption to influence votes (Kitch, Isaacson, and Kasper, 1971).

[44] For example, congressional support for the controversial B-1 bomber was increased by the fact that contractors and subcontractors involved in the development of the bomber were located in 48 states (New York Times, July 3, 1977, Section 4).

A study of the Tariff of 1824 (Pincus, 1975) confirms in broad outline the model of the political process developed here. Because of the costs of communication in the early nineteenth century, Pincus hypothesizes that geographically concentrated industries will be more likely to organize, but that geographical dispersal will make a favorable hearing on tariff legislation easier to obtain since protective tariffs would be favored by both employee-voters and managers. His empirical results lend support to the first proposition, but data limitations make the second notion difficult to test.

Some evidence also suggests that when employee or consumer interests and company interests coincide, then legislation favorable to the industry is more likely, even in the absence of an industry educational campaign. Thus Pennsylvania railroads joined with local township officials to oppose increases in truck weight limits, and coal operators and miners combined in 1949 to prevent the Pennsylvania legislature from levying a tax on coal (Allen, 1949:100). The American Medical Association joined with consumer interests to support laws damaging to patent medicine manufacturers (Nadel, 1971:10–11).

that only a few legislators will be strongly opposed to the industry. Most others may have low reservation prices because their constituents will not be directly damaged. More generally, the relationship between structure and performance must be given the same prominence in studies of industry–government relations as it has already received in studies of the industry organization.[45]

5. CONCLUSIONS

This chapter has developed the interrelationships among voters, politicians, and interest groups by moving from the simple formulations of Chapter 2 to more complex and realistic situations. My first aim was to show how the *electorate's* motives and information affect both legislative and interest group behavior. My second object was to demonstrate how *legislative* organization affects the actions of interest groups, and my third was to consider how the characteristics of *interest groups* themselves help determine their political efficacy.

The analysis of the first, electoral theme began in Chapter 2, which showed that in an ideal system with knowledgeable and concerned voters, corruption was the *only* way special interest groups could influence political outcomes. My relatively simple model of the politicians' tradeoff between bribes and votes requires complication, however, as soon as different assumptions about the information available to the electorate are introduced. If voters are poorly informed about issues, and legislators know little about constituents' tastes, interest groups no longer need rely on bribery to gain legislative advantage. Instead, they can contribute to a politician's campaign fund in return for legislative support on issues of concern to the group. Thus, politicians may be less corrupt when the public has poor information, but special interests may be even more influential in the determination of policy. Furthermore, interest groups now have other options open to them besides campaign contributions to politicians. They can also try to "educate" either politicians or voters to obtain support for their positions.

In contrast, when voters are apathetic about political issues and only want personalized benefits from politicians, information will have little impact on electoral outcomes. Since politicians and voters are only concerned about the distribution of the money provided by interest groups, special interests are the only groups who care about policy.

[45] Two studies that try to take this approach are Caves (1976) and Pincus (1975).

Hence, politicians need not trade off electoral support against votes in favor of interest groups. The legislators' only problem is dividing their payoffs between personal enrichment and the "purchase" of votes.

The second major object of this chapter was to show how legislative structure can affect the incidence and volume of both corruption and campaign contributions. Moving beyond the individualistic legislature hypothesized in the previous chapter, I demonstrated that widely used political structures—political parties and the committee system—generate new varieties of influence. Similarly, in discussing the third theme, I pointed out that there is no reason to believe that interest groups will form with equal ease on all sides of an issue. Instead, I showed how market organization considerations as well as the geographical distribution of group members will help determine the wealth, organizing ability, and bargaining power of various groups.

Thus, these chapters provide a framework to enable a serious student of politics to go beyond one or another juicy political scandal to understand the basic factors that made the incident possible, even predictable. Legislative corruption need not imply the absence of popular control. Even when the electorate monitors its representatives closely, interest groups may successfully bribe legislators simply because reelection is not the politician's only aim in life.

This framework is not only useful, however, as a tool for positive analysis. It also provides the basis for normative conclusions which emphasize the difficult tradeoffs that must be made in any "reform" package that will seriously check corrupt incentives. Consider first a proposal that would require only modest changes in existing practice. Under this proposal, the government would commission independent research organizations to poll each congressional district frequently to determine constituent opinion on current issues on the legislative agenda. While many legislators now commission private polls, the public surveys would be part of the public record, and this visibility would make them a potent anticorruption weapon, permitting voters to infer the existence of corruption from persistent divergences between constituent preferences and legislative votes.

Even here, however, the anticorruption benefits of such a scheme can only be purchased at some cost. Putting aside the obvious problems of assuring the independence and competence of polling organizations, a public polling system that would deter corruption would also deter legislators from acting as something other than mechanical representatives of the majority of their districts' voters. Thus, every time congressmen took nationwide concerns into account, the public poll might lead others to think that the legislators' motives were private gain. In short, the same poor information that makes corruption possible makes it easier for principled legislators to blur the distinction between constituent interest and national interest. And it is not at all clear that we want to reduce the incentives for corruption at the cost of reducing the probability that politicians will take account of the extradistrict consequences of their decisions.

Much harder to justify are institutional structures that minimize the information required of voters at the cost of placing heavy restrictions on the operation of the political process. For example, a system where all legislative issues are specified at election time would make it easy for voters to detect broken promises, but prevent representatives from responding to new problems that arise during the legislative session. A rule that required legislation to be simple and easy to understand might inhibit the assembly from responding to complex, technical problems.

This analysis also sheds a new and different light on current efforts to reform congressional campaign financing by a system of public grants. It is easy to see that such a scheme may *increase* the amount of corruption if the proposal for public financing is coupled with a ceiling on the amount each candidate may spend. While some money that would have been legally contributed to campaigns will now be used for lobbying and educational campaigns, other funds may be given illegally to key legislators.

It seems then that the best checks on corruption are a well-informed and issue-oriented electorate and a political system that routinely produces challengers ready to take advantage of lapses by incumbents. If strong challengers are more easily generated in the context of a two-party system, however, this requirement must be traded off against the possibility that a legislature with a majority party may decide more issues on the basis of special interest contributions than an individualistic assembly.

To find a way out of these difficulties, then, we must imagine that legislators are motivated by more than a desire for income and reelection. Moral principles and a belief in majority rule can restrict the role of wealth as effectively as an informed and issue-oriented electorate. Similarly, representatives who follow their constituents' wishes not only because they maximize $\hat{p}$ but also because of personal commitment will probably be less subject to the influence of wealthy groups than representatives with no personal commitments to the stands they take. It follows then that a voter may well favor an ideological candidate over one who seems to have no deep personal convictions but whose platform positions are closer to the voter's own preferences. Nevertheless, while it may make sense for voters to favor ideological candidates, it does not follow that a legislature composed *partly* of ideologues will have a lower incidence of political payoffs than a body full of opportunists. If no group of ideologues has majority control, then the total cost of influencing the few opportunists who remain may be very low. It is not enough that "most" legislators be impossible to influence. If we are concerned not just with identifying "guilty" legislators but with developing a legislative system where few issues are decided on the basis of monetary payments, then almost all representatives must refuse payoffs in a democratic society where many legislative votes will be closely contested.

4

BUREAUCRATIC CORRUPTION
AND THE LEGISLATIVE PROCESS

---

1. INTRODUCTION

The political models in the preceding chapters contained three kinds of actors: voters, politicians, and private interest groups. Once a law was passed, however, its implementation was outside the range of concern. Given the possibilities for political influence in these three-actor models, I can now take a more realistic view by considering the way a functioning bureaucracy complicates the story. Introducing a bureaucracy requires an extension of the analysis of lawmaking in two different, if related, directions. First, corrupt bureaucratic implementation of laws will alter the way the legislature perceives the costs and benefits of its enactments, even if the bribery is itself kept secret. This, in turn, will lead the legislature to respond by cutting or increasing agency budgets as well as by changing the law itself. Thus, even if corrupt bureaucrats make no effort to provide personalized benefits to legislators, their administrative actions may nevertheless have an indirect but substantial impact. This effect of bureaucratic corruption is the subject of the first half of the chapter (Sections 2 and 3) where the main analytic task is an evaluation of the vague conventional wisdom which associates bureaucratic corruption with bloated agency budgets. Unlike the analysis of legislative behavior, this portion of the chapter only analyzes illegal payments to agents—*corruption,* as I have defined it. Thus, Section 2 shows that the corruption of low-level officials with no stake in the size of the overall budget may lower, rather than raise, the size of the budget an agency will obtain from the legislature. Section 3, in turn, explores the way top bureaucrats may consciously use the political power at the agency's disposal to skew budget requests and obtain output quotas and red tape in an effort to obtain kickbacks and bribes.

The second half of the chapter considers the impact of high level bureaucrats on a political process in which they can directly offer particular legislators increases in personal income and in the probability of reelection. Thus, Section 4 considers the extent to which high-level bureaucrats, like the special interest groups in Chapters 2 and 3, may influence legislators by trading some of the agency's scarce resources in exchange for extra political support. I contrast the bureaucrats' limited ability to make corrupt payments with the other ways in which agency heads may move legislative choices away from those that would have been chosen by a well-informed electorate. Finally, Section 5 explores the extreme case in which legislative and bureaucratic functions are merged in the same group of officials who can design an entire governmental system to maximize their returns.

2. LOW-LEVEL CORRUPTION

Let us begin, then, with a simple model of bureaucracy where corruption can occur only at "low levels" in the hierarchy. The defining characteristic of a low-level bureaucrat is that each one is such a small part of the total organization that he or she acts rationally in refusing to take into account the relationship between individual actions and the legislature's decision on the size of the agency's budget. Analogous to the price-taking entrepreneurs in a perfectly competitive economy, these bureaucrats are budget-takers, although in their dealings with the agency's clients they may have considerable monopoly power. Just as competitive firms have no individual impact on prices, low-level bureaucrats have no independent impact on their agencies' budgets. This first model concentrates on the overall budgetary consequences of low-level corruption. Hence, I assume that high-level bureaucrats—those who recognize that their actions will have an impact on legislative decisions—have a completely passive mentality. They take no steps to ferret out corruption amongst their underlings, and in their dealings with the legislature, they simply pass on their best estimates of the costs of providing the agency's services at different levels of output, without themselves engaging in any dishonest or strategic behavior.

Given this model, two types of low-level corruption are possible: bribery which increases the marginal budgetary cost of the public service and that which reduces these costs. Kickbacks paid in return for government purchases of inputs fall in the first category so long as these payments inflate the dollar value of the contract. The corruption of low-level bureaucrats by *suppliers* will raise cost estimates if honest bureaucrats would have picked low-cost suppliers or forced monopolistic suppliers to charge the government the true marginal costs of inputs.[1] While the opportunity for receiving corrupt payments may reduce the legal wages that the agency must pay bureaucrats, the illegality of corruption implies that this cost-reducing effect will generally be swamped by the "padded" contract terms which corruption makes possible.

In contrast, corruption in the distribution of government outputs—licenses, in-kind transfers, or other benefits—will not usually affect the budget directly, since the bribes paid to bureaucrats do not come out of the agency's budget but instead reduce the profits or incomes of clients. Indeed, corruption by *demanders* or clients may often *lower* the marginal costs perceived by the legislature. This occurs for two reasons. First, if the level of bribery receipts depends upon how fast low-level officials work, then corrupt bureaucrats may serve more people per day than their honest counterparts. Corruption, in this case, may actually increase the efficiency of the bureaucracy. Second, the promise of corrupt gains may lower the salaries which the government must pay to attract job applicants.[2] Even if the level of service provided is unaffected by corruption, budget costs will be lower.[3]

---

[1] This result will not follow if low-level bureaucrats have inadequate data about contractor costs. If the alternative to corruption is random selection, corruption might actually reduce budgetary costs. Instead of blindly choosing an inefficient producer, the bureaucrat may now obtain the output of an efficient producer at an inflated price (cf. Chapter 6).

[2] In New York City, construction inspectors were paid an average of $11,000 in legal wages by the city, but a corrupt official allegedly could expect to add $10,000 to $30,000 in illegal gratuities (*New York Times*, June 26, 1972). Historically, in many societies government office holders received no salaries and had to pay to obtain their jobs. Their reimbursement came in the form of fees collected in the performance of their duties. Tax collectors have often been paid in this way with the fees often paid to reduce tax liabilities (Swart, 1970).

Becker and Stigler (1974) point out that one way to deter corruption is to raise the salaries of officials above what they could earn outside of government. If dismissal is the main punishment for taking bribes, a salary differential increases the cost of this punishment.

[3] This effect would be most marked in a regulatory agency which makes few purchases and spends most of its budget on bureaucratic salaries.

Some bribes paid by "clients" may, however, increase marginal budgetary costs, so long as the impact of corruption on salaries is not too large. Many government activities are designed to impose costs on particular individuals or firms. The clients are not demanders but are unwillingly coerced into "consuming" the agency's services. Let us call them "avoiders." While the power of the police to arrest people is the most obvious example of this type of coercive program, other examples, such as the military draft, can easily be found. In these programs, bribes may be paid by clients to avoid the imposition of a cost.[4] Corrupt officials may then impose fewer sanctions than honest bureaucrats.[5] If output is measured by the number of arrests or the like, corrupt officials will appear to be less productive than honest ones, and the marginal costs of an arrest will increase. Of course, if potential criminals take into account the cost of bribes, the actual impact of bribery on the crime rate may be rather small.[6]

The simplest way to characterize the basic distinction is to say that bribes paid by *suppliers* and *avoiders* will generally raise marginal costs, and those paid by *demanders* who seek a particularized benefit will generally lower the marginal budgetary cost of a unit of *measured* output.[7] While I shall not treat them separately, combined cases are, of course, possible in which suppliers pay kickbacks while demanders pay for speedy service.

Given these distinctions—and the assumptions on which they are based—a fundamental concept in economic analysis provides a useful way of assessing the legislative response to corruption-induced increases or decreases in marginal costs. The key concept is the notion of

---

[4] If existing licensees bribe bureaucrats *not* to issue licenses to competitors, then this case must be analyzed along with the coercive programs discussed here. Similarly, in coercive programs, those who benefit from a high level of coercive activity might pay bribes to induce the agency to *increase* output. Thus farmers who use prison labor at less than the going wage might bribe the police to arrest more potential farmhands. If this type of corruption is pervasive, then these programs should be discussed along with others where bribery increases output.

[5] This result does not necessarily follow, however. Officials might simply substitute one individual or firm for another with no impact on the number of "units."

[6] Although corruption may reduce arrests, it might actually encourage greater effort from policemen eager to collect bribes. Stronger enforcement by the police will in turn deter crime. If foregone crimes were used as the measure of output instead of the number of arrests, corruption might lead to improved performance and lower perceived marginal cost.

[7] The text assumes that agency output can easily be measured in terms of the number of units of public service that is produced, the number of applications approved, or the number of individuals arrested. See Breton (1974) for a discussion of the difficulty of measuring the output of public programs.

elasticity of demand. Demand elasticity measures the percentage change in quantity demanded for a percentage change in price. If this ratio is less than 1 (in absolute value), total spending increases as price increases; if it is greater than 1, total spending increases as prices fall.[8] It is true, of course, that legislatures are unlikely to have neat easily estimated demand curves;[9] nonetheless, the concept of elasticity has heuristic value in this context, for it permits one to make clear the assumptions that must be made before the conventional correlation between bureaucratic corruption and bloated budgets can be established. Although deviant cases are possible,[10] I shall focus upon a legislature

---

[8] Thus, letting p and q stand for price and quantity, respectively, elasticity, η, is

$$\eta = -\frac{dq}{dp} \cdot \frac{p}{q}.$$

The change in spending, pq, for a change in p is

$$\frac{d(pq)}{dp} = q + \frac{dq}{dp} p = (1 - \eta)q.$$

Thus, if $\eta \lesseqgtr 1$, $d(pq)/dp \gtreqless 0$, respectively.

The price elasticity of demand for a good or service often depends upon prevailing prices. Demand may be elastic at high prices and inelastic at low prices.

[9] Two studies have attempted to estimate a tax price elasticity of demand for public goods. Bergstrom and Goodman (1973) use cross section data from a number of cities to estimate the demand for several local public goods. They assume that the cost of public goods is the same in all cities, but the tax price facing the voter with median income (who is assumed to be decisive) varies across the sample. They estimate that price elasticities for police services, parks, and general expenditures are all less than 1 in absolute value. Borcherding and Deacon (1972) also estimate price elasticities using a similar model. They find that police services, fire services, and parks all have elasticities less than one, but that hospitals, local education, and sewers have elasticities greater than one.

Other relevant empirical work has been performed by urban economists and students of charitable contributions. Bradford and Oates (1974) summarize work in local public finance indicating that households are sensitive to the tax–expenditure mix in alternative local jurisdictions. Feldstein (1975) has attempted to estimate tax price elasticities for individuals making charitable contributions to nonprofit institutions which provide public goods.

Although the empirical work does not deal with the problem, demands for various public programs may not be independent of one other. Thus one's tax–price elasticity of demand for schools may depend upon the individual burden of national defense spending and vice versa. Furthermore, the median voter models used in some empirical work are obviously poor descriptions of reality. The tie between citizens' preferences and political choices is tenuous, complicated by the poor information available to most voters (see the references in Chapter 3, note 1) and by the division of responsibility in the Congress between money committees and those which oversee substantive areas (Fenno, 1973).

[10] For example, if representatives from districts where suppliers are located hold powerful positions, then so long as the corruption is kept secret, high costs may look like benefits for their districts.

which responds to costs in the "standard" way—cutting back its demand if marginal costs rise and increasing its demand if marginal costs decline. Given this standard relationship, the impact of low-level corruption on budget size will be a function of two variables—first, whether corruption increases or decreases "marginal costs"; second, whether legislative demand is elastic or inelastic. If elasticity is less than one and "marginal costs" increase, for example, the budget will increase.[11] The four different ways of combining marginal costs and demand elasticities to yield budgetary impact are shown in Table 4.1.

Given this framework, first consider bribes paid by *suppliers,* which, as we have seen, are likely to cause an increase in marginal tax costs. The conventional association of corruption with high budgets will only prevail here if the legislature's demand elasticity is less than 1 (in absolute value) for all programs where suppliers pay kickbacks. Such a uniform association is clearly very improbable. The importance of a program in the total government budget and the existence of substitutes elsewhere in the government or private sectors will both be important in determining the elasticity of legislative demand. The smaller the budget share and the better the substitutes, the more likely it is that the elasticity exceeds 1 and the budget falls.[12] Furthermore, the legislature may simply be more sensitive to the costs of some programs than to

TABLE 4.1 The Impact of Low-Level Corruption on an Agency's Budget, *B*

Legislatures' elasticity of demand, η	Impact of corruption on marginal tax costs	
	MC higher	*MC* lower
$\eta > 1$	*B* down	*B* up
$\eta < 1$	*B* up	*B* down

[11] "Marginal costs" are *not* the true opportunity costs of providing the government service but only the marginal tax costs perceived by the legislature.

[12] This point may, however, be stretching the analogy between legislative and household behavior too far. The relationship between budget share and elasticity comes out of the Slutsky equations (Henderson and Quandt, 1971:32), but the intuition is simple. With a fixed income, demand elasticity cannot exceed 1 for all prices, or else the household would eventually spend more than 100% of its income on the good—an obvious impossibility. Legislators, of course, do not face the same kind of rigid budget constraint. A program could be a high proportion of the government budget and a small proportion of national income.

Furthermore, some feasible substitutes for existing programs may not be considered if, as Kaufman (1976) and Niskanen (1971) argue, government agencies are extremely hard to eliminate even if they are very inefficient.

those of others. Legislators, for example, might be very sensitive to changes in the costs of social welfare programs yet have a rigid demand for national defense that is relatively unrelated to costs.[13] If this is so, then if defense contractors pay kickbacks, the defense budget could increase, while if corruption inflated the costs of subsidized housing, the budget for subsidized housing could fall.[14]

The second group of propositions concern agencies where bribes are paid by "clients" and do not appear directly in the budget. Corruption of this type will tend to *increase* the marginal *tax* costs of coercive agencies as they cut back output in exchange for bribes by avoiders, while it will tend to *decrease* the marginal *tax* costs of licensing agencies as demanders pay for preferential service. Hence a corrupt situation can fall into any one of the four boxes in Table 4.1 depending on the elasticity of legislative demand. Is there, however, some reason to associate coercive agencies with elasticities less than 1 ($\eta < 1$) and licensing agencies with elasticities greater than 1 ($\eta > 1$)? For it is only if this is universally true that there is reason to support the conventional wisdom—at least for regulatory agencies—that associates corruption with bloated agency budgets.

It should be plain that such consistency is most unlikely. It is, however, possible to point to *tendencies* that give some support to the conventional wisdom. Thus, if the legislature wishes to condemn a particular type of activity, it may be reasonable to think that it will both be relatively insensitive to the costs of regulation ($\eta < 1$) and tend to choose a coercive program. In contrast, if the legislative commitment to the regulatory objective is lukewarm and lacking in moral fervor, it may be relatively sensitive to costs ($\eta > 1$), and may prefer a licensing program that limits but does not formally outlaw the regulated activity.[15] Yet these tendencies are precisely those required for corruption to lead to an increase in agency budgets in both cases.[16] The critical condition

---

[13] This is, of course, an empirical proposition, not an immutable fact of human psychology.

[14] Either strong militarists or strong pacifists could have a rigid demand for national defense. Although the first wants a large force and the second a small one, both could be insensitive to changes in marginal costs. Of course, even if the elasticity of demand for defense were less than the elasticity of demand for housing, it might be true that both are either less than or greater than 1.

[15] For example, public opposition to the use of heroin is generally much more rigid than public opposition to the use of alcohol. A coercive agency, therefore, typically regulates the former while licensing programs more typically oversee the latter. The distinction is similar to that made by Calabresi and Melamed (1972) between liability rules and property rules.

[16] Once again, however, both elasticities may be less than 1, or both greater than 1. To an economist the distinction between coercive and licensing programs looks like an unimportant one. If a coercive law is not perfectly enforced, its impact on an activity

here is my assertion of a possible association between cost sensitivity and the choice of regulatory technique. Although my hypotheses have at least a surface plausibility, there is as yet *no* convincing evidence on these points.

In concluding this section, we must consider the possibility, developed further in Chapters 6 and 8, that low-level corruption will change the composition of agency output rather than the number of units produced. One airplane design may be chosen over another on the basis of bribe payments; licenses may be given to poorly qualified applicants; a policeman may arrest a less important lawbreaker instead of a wealthy criminal who makes a payoff. The number of planes purchased, licenses issued, or arrests made may remain constant, while their composition changes. The important issue, then, is whether the legislature observes this distortion. If it does not, then corruption that simply shifts the identity of beneficiaries will not affect legislative choices since it has no impact on the measured output produced with a given budget appropriation. If the shift in quality mix is noted, however, then corruption will be perceived as inefficiency or incompetence, and the legislature may seek to reform or eliminate the program. Corruption can then affect the way the legislature defines issues and allocates programs to bureaus. Even if completely unobserved, it may induce the legislature to change the way a benefit is provided. For example, the legislature might decide to pay a housing subsidy directly to individuals if it found that subsidized dwellings built by private contractors and approved by a government housing authority were of poor quality.[17]

I have come, then, to a rather complicated conclusion. While there is some reason to associate corruption with increases in regulatory budgets, even this is far from a necessity. Moreover, corruption by suppliers will in many cases lead to a reduction in overall expenditure. My emphasis on budgets, however, limits the generality of the model. Looking at other types of low-level corruption and assuming that

---

can be similar to regulation which limits the number of entrants. Nevertheless, legislators and the general public obviously do not always think like economists. For a similar distinction between judicial decisions that ratify ordinary ways of thinking and a more scientific approach to the law, see Ackerman (1977).

[17] Although the analysis has concentrated upon output agencies that produce public goods, provide transfers, or regulate private activity, the basic framework can be applied to revenue raising. When corrupt tax collectors exempt individuals and firms from taxes in return for bribes, the result is a loss in the revenue raised from the particular tax. The legislature may react to this loss either by raising the rates for that tax or by relying on it less heavily through a shift to other forms of taxation or a reduction in overall government spending.

legislators can look beyond quantitative output measures to a program's "ultimate goals,"[18] opens up the analysis to a wider range of legislative actions. A model which took these additional possibilities into account would provide a richer view of the potential for legislative response. To accomplish this task, however, would take me too far from the focus of this book, and I turn instead to consider high-level agency corruption.

3. HIGH-LEVEL CORRUPTION

The preceding analysis assumed a model of bureaucracy in which high-level officials were essentially irrelevant. They had no independent policymaking role and could not detect low-level corruption on their own. Instead, they simply passed on cost information to the legislature, which made the ultimate decisions on outputs and budgets. However, high-level bureaucrats can usually assess the possible impact of corruption on budget appropriations and legislative demand for the agency's output. Abstracting from the wide variety of conflicting motives possessed by real officials, I assume that they seek only to maximize personal monetary gains. Thus they may want any of three types of legislative mandate: a padded budget, a quota on bureaucratic output, or a plethora of red tape to impose on "customers." To obtain any of these services bureaucrats must be able to persuade the legislature that they are providing accurate information about their agencies' operations. They must argue that padded budgets are actually lean and that quotas and red tape are in the public interest. Hence, my model will assume that bureaucratic credibility of this kind prevails. Furthermore, the bureaucrats' legislative dealings are limited to the provision of information to the assembly as a whole. I defer until Section 4 a discussion of bureaucratic attempts to provide personalized benefits to legislators.

To maximize their own corrupt receipts under any of these legislative strategies, top bureaucrats seek to ferret out low-level corruption as well as incompetence and laziness. They will only tolerate low-level corruption if it is necessary to their own survival, that is, if the corruption of subordinates prevents them from reporting payoffs received by their superiors. Therefore, this section assumes that low-level corruption does

---

[18] The difficulty of relating ultimate goals to direct outputs, with the resulting public policy distortions, has been studied in the context of current water pollution policy (Ackerman *et al.*, 1974) and in the administration of Veterans Administration hospitals (Lindsey, 1976).

not exist and that the agency head's peculation is kept secret from low-level civil servants so that they can neither demand a share for themselves nor engage in free lance low-level extortion confident that their superiors will be unable to punish them. Furthermore, agency heads can tell subordinate officials exactly how to behave. Thus top officials can predict the impact of their corruption on both their bureaus' output and on their agencies' appropriations.[19] Given these conditions, I develop the top bureaucrat's bribe maximizing strategy under different assumptions about the nature of the corrupt incentives. Thus, Part A hypothesizes an agency where the head can obtain kickbacks from suppliers, whereas in Part B, customers or clients have an incentive to pay bribes.

A. Milking Suppliers

Beginning with bribes paid by suppliers, assume that all corrupt payments received by agency heads are kickbacks concealed in their bureaus' budgets. Corrupt top bureaucrats know the true opportunity cost of producing any level of public services, and their bargaining power vis-à-vis contractors is high enough for them to appropriate any excess over costs in the form of bribes.[20] They will then seek to have the legislature approve budgets and output levels that maximize the difference between total budgets and contractors' costs.[21]

Even if the legislature has no independent information on the cost of producing public services,[22] an agency's requests are constrained by the

---

[19] In Chapter 9, I modify these assumptions and look at the whole organizational hierarchy. Actually the assumptions made in the text are too strong. All that is really required for the argument is the independence of high- and low-level corruption.

[20] Although I assume that the costs borne by top bureaucrats are independent of the level of their corrupt receipts, this is not likely to be strictly true. The larger the gains to agency heads, the more they may have to pass on to subordinates in order to buy their silence. Alternatively, low-level officials may engage in more petty graft the greater the difference between budgetary appropriations and contractors' costs. In addition, if the legislature has some rough notion of what the cost ought to be in an efficient agency, then the probability of detection may depend positively upon the level of the discretionary budget.

[21] In Niskanen's (1971) model of bureaucratic behavior, agency heads seek to maximize their total budgets. Migué and Bélanger (1974) criticize this aspect of his model and suggest instead that bureaucrats would maximize the excess of budget over costs. In responding to his critics, Niskanen (1975) admits this possibility as well.

[22] This is Niskanen's (1971) assumption. Breton and Wintrobe (1975) discuss the possibility that the legislature may itself expend resources to obtain information on costs.

assumption that the higher the costs of providing the public service, the less the legislature will want. If top bureaucrats know the legislature's maximum willingness to pay for various levels of output, they can make all-or-none offers to the legislature that leads it to accept kickback-maximizing output levels.[23] While in general the budgets approved under this scheme will be larger than those chosen when top administrators honestly report marginal costs,[24] this result is by no means necessary. In particular, if *private* goods are very *inferior,* in the economist's use of this term, the budget can be smaller in a corrupt system. An inferior good is one whose consumption falls as income increases. Thus, since corruption is an income transfer from the public to officials—if private

---

[23] Niskanen's (1971) budget maximizing bureaucrats also make all-or-none offers to the legislature. Thompson (1973) criticizes this approach and suggests that, at most, bureaucrats will be able to announce a marginal cost schedule.

[24] This can be shown analytically by adopting the political model used by Niskanen (1971) and many of his critics. Assume that the legislature always mirrors constituent preferences and that households have identical tasts, incomes, and tax shares. The task of the legislature is to fix the level of a single pure public good, Q. Letting $Y =$ an individual's after tax income, Figure 4.1 illustrates the indifference curves of a typical citizen with utility function, $U(Q,Y)$ and income $\hat{Y}$. Indifference curve U_1 passes through the point $(0, \hat{Y})$. The line $\hat{Y} = Y + (c/n)Q$ reflects the true opportunity costs of producing Q where c is the constant marginal cost of Q and n is the population. Thus c/n is the marginal tax cost of Q when everyone is taxed equally.

A corrupt agency head, capable of making all-or-none offers to the legislature, offers to

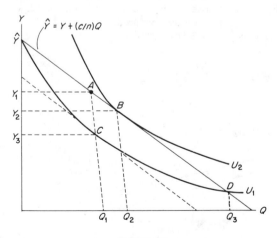

Figure 4.1

goods are inferior—this transfer induces an *increase* in the public's demand for private goods and a corresponding reduction in spending on the public good.[25]

B. Milking Customers and Clients

High-level corruption can also arise in the allocation of a bureau's services to clients or customers. The conclusions about budget size reached in Part A do not necessarily carry over to this kind of corruption. The relationship between budget size and corruption is more complex, because, unlike the simple case analyzed above, corrupt payments will not generally appear as kickbacks paid out of budgetary appropriations. Instead, the corrupt agency head's gain-maximizing budget request depends not only upon the costs of delivery and the

---

produce Q_1 at a cost of $n(\hat{Y} - Y_3)$, where $U_c/U_y = c/n$ (point C in the figure). In contrast, a bureaucrat whose power and prestige is linked to the size of his agency's budget (Niskanen, 1971) would offer point D, where the level of output is much too large but is produced at least cost.

In this simple case, one can compare the corrupt outcome with the "social optimum," where households attain the highest level of utility (i.e., the bureaucrat's utility is excluded from the calculation of the optimum). Utility is maximized at $B(Q_2, Y_2)$, where $U_q/U_y = c/n$. In general, $Q_1 \gtreqless Q_2$, depending upon the shape of the utility surface.

This characterization of the optimum differs from Niskanen's (1971) who uses the maximization of the *dollar* value of the surplus as his measure (point A, in Fig. 4.1). Although Niskanen's formulation seems clearly incorrect given this model, if his characterization were to be accepted, corruption would raise the government budget from $\hat{Y} - Y_1$ to $\hat{Y} - Y_3$ but would leave the level of output unchanged. This result stands in contrast with the conclusions of his budget-maximizing model, where bureaucratic actions raised output but assured least cost production.

[25] This observation can be illustrated by Figure 4.2, a graph similar to Figure 4.1. Clearly, $\hat{Y} - Y_3 < \hat{Y} - Y_2$.

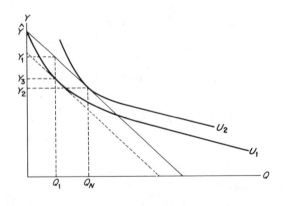

Figure 4.2

preferences of legislators and their constituents but also upon the preferences of clients or customers. In the analysis to follow, I consider how client preferences interact with the nature of the public program to generate preferred budget requests under two types of program structure. In the first, the agency's production and administrative costs per unit are predetermined for each output level, and the high level bureaucrat simply requests a level of output Q, where Q may represent any public service ranging from food packages for the poor to licenses to engage in a particular business. In the second, the agency head can request variations in the amount of "red tape" in order to create bribe-producing delays, thereby affecting the marginal tax costs of the agency's services.

Costs Predetermined

Beginning with the case where costs are fixed, the bureaucrat's choice of Q depends upon an ability to "bribe–price" discriminate. The bureaucrat is assumed to be charged with providing Q to the public at a fixed legal price, p_0, where $p_0 \geq 0$. For some levels of Q, the demand $Q = g(p_0)$ exceeds the supply. If the good provided by the bureaucrat can be traded among eligible households and firms, and if bribers have good information about the payoffs made by others, everyone who obtains the service will make an identical payoff. However, the illegality of the market is likely to foster price discrimination by keeping information about the amount of money that changes hands scarce. Furthermore, most actual programs encourage differential bribes by putting strict controls on the transferability of the public service. Controls can, of course, be circumvented, with the nature of the subsidized good determining the ease with which this can be done. Thus, circumvention will be practically impossible if the government is directly providing a service, such as aid to accident victims, where qualified beneficiaries are easy to identify. And it will be difficult when the government retains an interest in the beneficiary long after the assignment of Q occurs. For example, if the government retested physicians at periodic intervals, it would be likely to notice if licenses to practice had been reassigned. In these situations, corrupt officials may exploit the nontransferability feature of the public program to maximize their illicit income through price discrimination. If administrators know everyone's demand curve and can perfectly price discriminate among potential beneficiaries, top officials will seek legislative authorization to produce the maximum output demanded by beneficiaries. Thus if $Q_0 = g(p_0)$ is the amount demanded at p_0 and if the corrupt bureaucrat's price discrimination does not itself lower $g(p_0)$, the agency head seeks Q_0 from the legislature.

In contrast, if the good is easily transferable, no bribe–price discrimination may be possible. Assuming that all Q must be sold, corrupt administrators now maximize their bribery receipts by charging $p_0 + b$ with b set so that $Q = g(p_0 + b)$. If, however, administrators can affect the level of Q, they may be able to increase their corrupt receipts. They now act like monopolistic sellers and attempt to have Q set where the marginal bribery receipts from a marginal change in Q equal zero. This is the point where marginal revenue equals the legal price, p_0. Thus the inability to bribe–price discriminate implies that a corrupt administrator will ask the legislature to authorize a far lower quantity of output than in situations where bribe requests can be tailor made.[26]

RED TAPE AND CORRUPTION

A legislative majority will often refuse a bureaucrat's request to place an explicit numerical limit upon the number of people who can legally benefit from a program. The political benefits involved in enacting a program that is nominally open to all who qualify are often substantial since they do not require the legislature to make difficult tradeoffs among beneficiaries.[27] The legislature may, however, grant the agency permission to create costly procedures to serve as a low-visibility way of limiting access to the benefit. These procedures can then be used by corrupt officials as a device for generating bribes. When bureaucrats can

---

[26] An alternate way of looking at the issue of corruption in programs of this type is to take Q as fixed and ask how the volume of bribery and the distortionery effects of corruption can be reduced. Clearly, with a fixed Q, high total bribes are more likely when the government benefit cannot be traded. Therefore, it might appear that legislatures could reduce corruption by designing programs where bureaucrats sell vouchers to worthy householders permitting them to buy the good cheaply in the private market. If the private market is competitive, voucher holders cannot be forced to pay a higher price for the good than unsubsidized purchasers. The existence of a restriction on the supply of vouchers, however, will induce worthy households to bribe officials, just as in the case of direct government sale. However, if worthy households are permitted to sell vouchers to one other, officials will not be able to price discriminate. The dollar volume of bribery will be reduced, but its resource allocation effects will remain.

[27] This section concentrates on programs where all the bribes are paid to bureaucrats. As Section 4 demonstrates, however, legislators may prefer programs which are nominally open-ended but which, in fact, require them to intervene with the bureaucracy on behalf of applicants. This "legislative casework" can be a way of obtaining bribes, campaign contributions, or electoral support.

only create red tape, however, they will seek different output levels than those they would seek under explicit laws restricting output. Consider, for example, the problem of licensing liquor stores. How will the number of licenses change if a corrupt bureaucrat must impose red tape rather than request an explicit numerical quota from the legislature?

Of course, a corrupt bureaucrat will always prefer a numerical limit to the imposition of red tape. Red tape uses a bureau's resources and requires customers to spend time and money complying with the regulations. If all applicants must wait in a queue or carry out administrative tasks, their maximum willingness to pay is less than that found in a quota system.[28] Nonetheless, if red tape is the only way to prevent applicants from quickly obtaining access to the desired bureaucratic benefit, the official faces a tradeoff. On the one hand, long legal waits increase the amount an applicant is willing to offer to obtain priority service; On the other, the longer the delay and the higher the level of individual bribes demanded, the lower the total demand for the government service.

It follows that bureaucrats who are only able to impose red tape as a device for generating payoffs may want even lower levels of output than those who can collect bribes directly. This result is especially likely if individual waits are long and costly and if the marginal impact of corruption on waiting time is large.[29] Furthermore, the impact of increases in the legislated level of "delay" has ambiguous budgetary consequences. Delay can be produced either by firing personnel or by increasing rules and regulations. The first tactic reduces the budget; the second raises it.

C. Conclusions

Thus I have generated a range of strategies which top bureaucrats might follow in order to maximize their corrupt receipts. The novelty of the approach is not so much its concentration on corruption as the ability to relate the kind of tasks performed by the bureaucracy to the levels of budget, output, or red tape requested from the legislature. This distinguishes my analysis from that of Niskanen (1971; 1975) and his

---

[28] Since this chapter has not discussed the substance of the bureaucracy's activities, I have had nothing to say about efficiency in the preceding analysis. Nevertheless, if the costs of hiding bribery are not too high, a corrupt allocation system *might* be more efficient than a legally operating quota scheme. This section, however, permits a more definitive conclusion. Clearly, if red tape is established solely for the purpose of generating payoffs, then it is an inefficient use of resources.

[29] See the appendix for a demonstration of these points.

critics (Breton and Wintrobe, 1975; Migué and Bélanger, 1974; Thompson, 1973) who concentrate only on budget requests in a single type of stylized agency. While they have examined alternative bureaucratic maximands: budget size (Niskanen, 1971); excess of budget over costs (Migué and Bélanger, 1974); or some combination of the two (Niskanen, 1975), they have not distinguished between agencies which regulate behavior, dispense transfers, or purchase large quantities of inputs from the private sector. Yet the differences between agencies appear to be important. In my analysis, it is clear that only corrupt bureaucrats in a position to obtain kickbacks from suppliers will seek to maximize the excess of their budget over costs. Similarly, in the administration of transfer programs, only agency heads with enough monopoly power over clients to price–bribe discriminate will seek to provide as much output as would be legally demanded by applicants, in open-ended programs. Even these bureaucrats, however, will not try to maximize their budgets since large quantities of bureaucratic output provide no benefits unless they can be ''sold'' to applicants. Not all bureaucrats will be able to price discriminate. Those with less power over clients may accept smaller overall budgets in order to obtain explicit output quotas which increase their ability to collect bribes. Others may be relatively unconcerned with budget size per se and instead focus their energies on the bribe-creating potential of red tape.

4. TRADING FAVORS FOR VOTES

Even my attempt to enrich the analysis of bureaucracy by relating bureaucratic requests to agency business has taken an overly narrow view of the diverse forms of self-interested bureaucratic behavior. Instead of taking legislative preferences as given, corrupt bureaucrats may actively search for votes in support of new programs or high agency budgets. Top bureaucrats now resemble the leaders of private interest groups who sought to influence legislative outcomes in Chapters 2 and 3 through illegal payments as well as through legal campaign contributions and the provision of skewed information.[30]

[30] Bureaucrats may have any type of personal motivation for attempting to influence the legislature. Like the bureaucrats in the preceeding section, they may be seeking to maximize the corrupt gains of agency operation, or they may be budget maximizers or innovators trying to generate support for new activities. My principal concern here is the closeness of the analogy between interest groups and bureaucrats in their interactions with the legislature.

There is one major difference, however. Agency heads are generally unable to use surplus funds for direct payments to representatives. Instead, they must provide other kinds of benefits to substitute for monetary transfers. Most obviously, they may use their discretionary power to favor firms in which a legislator has an interest,[31] or devise more complex tripartite schemes in which the agency favors suppliers or applicants who in turn provide monetary or political support to the representative.[32] Of course, agencies will differ in their ability to disguise favors to legislators as legitimate bureaucratic choices, depending upon the ease with which their decisions can be monitored by journalists, watchdog agencies, and the public. As in the parallel treatment of legislative corruption in Chapters 2 and 3, however, I ignore the possibility of detection in order to concentrate on the structural incentives for private bureaucratic–legislative deals. My task is to show how the inability of bureaucrats to provide direct money payments leads them to a somewhat different course of action than that pursued by private interest groups.

Consider first legislators who will lose popular support if they vote in favor of high agency budgets and expanded agency activity. Since a favorable vote will lower their expected reelection percentages, $\hat{p}$, the legislators must receive a compensating increase in personal income, y, in order to vote in the agency's favor. While the formal choice can still be represented in terms of Figure 2.1, the indirect method of payment imposed on bureaucrats may sometimes make illegal transactions impossible. Thus in an individualistic legislature where an agency has little automatic support, the indivisibility of agency projects may create difficulties not faced by a special interest group using direct monetary

[31] These firms must, of course, be better off selling to the government instead of to private buyers, i.e., the competitive market assumptions can not all hold (see Chapter 6).

[32] Most recent examples of the corruption of members of the United States Congress involve payoffs in return for intervention with federal agencies. Thus Senator Edward Gurney of Florida was accused (and later acquitted) of extorting payoffs from real estate developers with pending business before the regional office of the Department of Housing and Urban Development (HUD). In this case, the senator's ability to influence bureaucrats legally was not in question, since employees of HUD were also accused of being part of the payoff scheme (New York Times, July 11, 1974; August 7, 1975; October 28, 1976). Representative Frank Brasco of New York was accused of accepting money in return for helping a trucking company obtain a mail delivery contract on which it was not the low bidder. In this case, an employee of the then Post Office Department was also named as a conspirator (New York Times, October 24, 1973). The Speaker of the Pennsylvania House of Representatives allegedly obtained money from parents in return for using his influence to have their children admitted to professional schools (New York Times, January 29, 1977).

payments. Even if legislators have very low reservation prices, the agency may be forced, by the nature of its activities, to favor only a few legislators. Agencies which make a large volume of private purchases are therefore in a better position to obtain majority support if they can spread their contracts broadly across firms; similarly, agencies which dispense transfer payments are advantaged if they have numerous clients. Legislators may, of course, overcome the disadvantages of indivisibility by coming to an agreement with a cartel of representatives under which the bureau promises to follow the cartel's recommenda-tions—which are then sold by the legislative cartel to the highest private bidder. These elaborate arrangements may not persist, however, since they not only are likely to be expensive to maintain but also are bizarre enough to come to the attention of even the most passive watchdog institutions.

It is a mistake, however, to think that bureaucracies can achieve their objectives only by increasing the personal income of crucial legislators. Like private firms, bureaucrats are often capable of affecting reelection probabilities. Although they are unable to make direct campaign contri-butions, three kinds of action are possible. First, if voters are knowl-edgeable, the agency can raise a legislator's probability of reelection directly by skewing its spending decisions to obtain the support of voters in key legislative districts.[33] Similarly, the power to dispense favors can be used to threaten legislators—bureaucrats delaying or denying re-quests for licenses or contracts initiated by firms in an unfriendly legislator's district. Second, if voters are issue oriented but not knowl-edgeable, bureaus can attempt to educate the public directly, trusting that legislators will follow the public's preferences. Education may well

---

[33] The Department of Defense creates support for its programs by using this strategy. The original Johnson administration proposal for the antiballistic missile system called for purchases from 28 private contractors with plants in 42 states, creating 1 million jobs, and directly affecting the constituents of 84 senators and 172 congressmen (Yarmolin-sky, 1971).

Similarly, Steiner (1971) reports that the Department of Agriculture rewarded con-gressmen for their support of the proposed food stamp program by locating experimental pilot programs in the appropriate congressional districts. The food stamp program was strongly supported by Democrats and opposed by Republicans, and the first 26 pilot programs were located in democratically controlled districts. By 1967, 19 of the 35 members of the House Agriculture Committee had food stamp projects in their districts.

The timing of spending may also be important. Tufte (1978) has noted that agencies making transfer payments, such as the Social Security Administration, often arrange for checks to be received by recipients several days prior to election day, favoring incumbent candidates.

be an especially effective strategy because of the imprimatur of a government agency may itself be a powerful persuasive tool.[34] Finally, when voters are neither knowledgeable nor issue oriented, an agency can favor a legislator's campaign contributors with contracts and regulatory benefits. The legislator's vote for the agency may then have little or no impact on $\hat{p}$, and the legislator can amass campaign funds on the grounds of superior influence with the agency.[35]

It is only in the second of these three cases, involving public educational campaigns, that an agency's inability to make direct cash payments is never a significant problem in obtaining support in an individualistic legislature. For even though an agency may only dispense a few indivisible projects, it may nevertheless easily divide up its educational campaign among legislative districts. In other cases, agencies whose outputs and contracts are both easily divisible and capable of national distribution will find themselves at an advantage since they can modify their behavior in response to changes in the number and geographical dispersion of potential opponents. In contrast, when political power is concentrated, an agency with indivisible contracts and outputs may be able to buy support, provided that it can shift its buying and spending habits to favor the districts of those currently in power. Two institutional factors will importantly influence this kind of flexibility. First, agencies with little control over their agendas obviously cannot choose to limit their concern to proposals which help their legislative cause. Thus agencies legally obligated to process all applications, like the Civil Aeronautics Board, are disadvantaged relative to those, like the Department of Housing and Urban Development, that can initiate projects. Second, even if the agency has formal control over its agenda, its political effectiveness will depend upon the speed with which it can adapt. While the Corps of Engineers cannot create rivers, it can move its dam-building activity around quite quickly, and hence would experience difficulty only if a key committee chairman came from a state

---

[34] The Department of Defense uses this technique to gain support: In 1969, it employed 2800 full time public relations workers. Among the educational programs they administered were the Joint Civilian Orientation Conference and Operation Understanding. In each of these programs, civic leaders from around the country were flown at government expense to receive briefings at military installations. In 1968, 618 persons, two-thirds of them from communities near proposed antiballistic missile sites, were taken to the White Sands Missile Range in New Mexico to view missile firings and to be briefed and entertained by high ranking military officers. Fulbright (1970) reports these and other Defense Department propaganda efforts.

[35] Boyd (1968) describes how Connecticut senator Thomas Dodd used these techniques.

with no rivers that can be dammed. (Of course, such a representative would have little interest in serving on this committee, let alone becoming its chairperson.)

In contrast, other agencies with indivisible projects may find it costly to respond quickly to changes in the identity of powerful representatives. For example, economies of scale in airplane construction imply that only a few plants will exist at any given time; and the geographical distribution of key committee members will help determine the location of those plants. Once these decisions are made, however, the capital intensity of the production process implies that the costs of changes in location are large. Hence the political power of the air force might be greatly reduced by the electoral defeat of a few critical congressmen. Agencies of this type can be expected to favor a rigid seniority system for assigning committee chairmanships: If they can predict who will be the future chairman, both they and their contractors can plan ahead. In fact, in a system where power is not concentrated in the chairman or where seniority does not determine leadership, these companies may give up some scale and transport economies in order to place their activities in a large number of legislative districts.[36]

Even if an agency has full flexibility, however, concentrated legislative power carries with it one serious risk. If powerful politicians recognize the extent of agency flexibility, they may attempt to divert a large proportion of agency budgets to activities that benefit them by increasing y or raising p. Just as private interest groups may try to appear poor in analogous circumstances, so many agencies attempt to reduce their flexibility by seeking public support and favoring public scrutiny and rigid rule-determined standards of behavior. If this combined strategy succeeds, the agency can prevent extortionary appeals while still obtaining legislative support.

To specify the pattern of bureaucratic influence, however, it is not enough to determine whether one is dealing with an individualistic legislature or one where power is concentrated in committees. For if the second case applies, one must also specify the principles under which legislators obtain especially powerful positions. The congressional practice, for example, of awarding committee chairmanships principally on the basis of seniority biases extortionary activities in a particular way.

---

[36] If logrolling is common in the legislature, then indivisibilities may be partially overcome. Agencies with a few large projects to dispense then have an incentive to form a cartel which allocates projects in a politically beneficial way. Legislators and bureaucrats could construct complex deals whereby political support for one agency's programs is given in return for concrete benefits from another agency.

Since seniority implies that most chairmen already have high ps, they may be particularly tempted to use their positions for private gain.

Speaking more generally, congressmen can be conceived as investing their time to establish seniority in a portfolio of committees overseeing one or more areas of government activity. Those who are not confident of reelection will seek to increase $\hat{p}$ by choosing committees that will permit them to deliver benefits to their own constituents. Hence, insecure junior congressmen will not choose committees with jurisdiction over agencies whose benefits are so indivisible that one can expect to obtain bureaucratic favors only after several elections. In contrast, secure legislators will not only have much greater freedom to make long-term investments in seniority but also will not need to choose committees in areas of particular concern to their constituents. If politicians lack personal commitments to particular policy areas and do not desire political power for its own sake, they will simply select powerful committees that will permit them, in the long run, to cash out their political power over agencies that provide indivisible benefits.

In short, while bureaucratic influence in the legislature has many similarities to the influence wielded by special interest groups, the constraints on agency actions imply important differences in the factors determining bureaucratic power. An agency head's inability to pay cash is especially important in dealing with politically insecure legislators concerned with $\hat{p}$. While all private interests may offer direct campaign contributions, only some bureaucracies will be able to favor one district over another or structure complicated arrangements that allow legislators to obtain cash from third parties. Even bureaucracies with contracts and favors to dispense may face a limited range of choices if they have only a few indivisible projects to allocate. A benefit bestowed on one legislative district may then imply that a cost has been imposed on another. For example, if two firms in two different districts are competing for a contract, the choice of either one imposes a cost on the other.

One should not, however, emphasize only the limitations of bureaucratic power. Especially when voters are knowledgeable and $\hat{p}$ is close to .5, the bureaucracy's capacity to bestow benefits on swing districts may be just as effective in generating voters as corrupt payments by private firms. Even when voters are ignorant and campaign funds are the major means of buying influence, agencies may not be at a disadvantage, given the leeway they often have in naming contractors and fixing terms. Instead of having to overcome free rider problems in order to obtain funds to use for legislative influence, bureaus have often been granted monopoly power by law. While they cannot accumulate profits, they can use their bargaining power to create political support.

5. POLITICAL SYSTEMS WITHOUT A SEPARATION OF POWERS

Thus far I have analyzed a political system containing two distinct groups of decision makers; the same person could not be both a legislator charged with lawmaking and a bureaucrat charged with implementing the law. While this separation of powers is a characteristic of some systems, notably the American national government, there are also many unitary governments which do not respect this principle. In the United States, for example, the legislators in many local governments are deeply involved in the process of hiring subordinate employees, letting contracts, allocating licenses, and granting administrative favors. These individual benefits can then be allocated in return for campaign contributions or kickbacks (Amick, 1976, gives examples). Of course, the centralized political machines common in American cities at the turn of the century are the archetypal examples of this kind of government, but the centralization characteristic of these local governments is by no means necessary.[37] Many modern local government politicians, although not organized under a strong boss, nevertheless allocate particularized benefits in return for political support, campaign funds, and increased personal incomes.[38]

Of course, just as in the preceding models, either apathetic or poorly informed voters are required before such a governmental system can persist. The main difference, however, between a unitary government and one where legislators are not administrators is the elimination of any

---

[37] Wolfinger (1972) has used the term "machine politics" to describe elective systems of this kind, where issues are unimportant and where the incentives to political participation are tangible and routine. The term is perhaps unfortunate, however, since it has traditionally been associated with centralized power. In his examination of New Haven, and in the other evidence he presents on New York and Indiana, however, a salient characteristic of modern "machine politics" is its decentralization. He argues that while the immigrant groups that formed the backbone of the old political machines may no longer need particularized benefits from politicians, the overall growth of government and of federal and state programs administered locally has created other groups, from wealthy businessmen to welfare clients, who want "help" from local officials and have little interest in the broader policy issues under the officials' jurisdiction.

[38] The Chicago city council made this division of authority explicit in the allocation of street railway contracts in the nineteenth century. In order to stabilize the system, they attempted to restrain the propensity of some aldermen to sell a franchise to several competitors at once, and gave each alderman the right to "auction" off street railway rights in his ward. The allocation of "market" shares was used to prevent bribe-reducing competition among aldermen. This case is reported in Lloyd Wendt and Herman Kogan, *Lords of the Levee* (New York: Bobbs-Merrill Co., 1943) excerpted in Gardiner and Olson (1974:50).

conflict of interest between lawmakers and bureaucrats. Since the same individuals perform both tasks, they can act to maximize personal gain subject only to the need for reelection. With apathetic or poorly informed citizens, the major risk is then the possibility that top officials will use their lawmaking power to pass legislation that gives them even greater extortionary power. For example, they might pass restrictive tax legislation in the hope of obtaining kickbacks from taxpayers (Riggs, 1963). Although this practice might lead the disadvantaged groups to support a new slate of electoral challengers, incumbents might respond with "bread and circuses" for the electorate as a way of neutralizing the vote-getting potential of challengers. In autocratic regimes, however, with no democratic checks on politicians' behavior, the promulgation of kickback-providing laws has sometimes reached an advanced stage of extortion.[39]

6. CONCLUSIONS: THE PUBLIC POLICY CONSEQUENCES OF CORRUPTION AND POLITICAL PAYOFFS

Up to the present point, I have assumed that the major variables to be determined by legislators were budget size, administrative procedures, and the identity of contractors and beneficiaries. I am now in a position, however, to complete the analysis and consider how the hope of personal and political gain will affect the basic structure of public policies.

The impact of corruption and political payoffs on program design will be similar regardless of whether only top bureaucrats are corrupt (as in Section 3) or whether legislators accept payoffs as well (Sections 4 and 5). Both groups will design programs in ways that permit them to appropriate the gains that would otherwise be received by nominal beneficiaries. Thus both corrupt bureaucrats and legislators in search of personal or political benefits will favor programs with complex, special purpose inputs that can not be bought off the shelf in competitive markets—this will make it difficult for outsiders to determine whether

---

[39] See V. T. LeVine (1975) and Johnson (1975). If a wealthy interest disapproves of an existing government's policies, it may use monetary payments not to coopt incumbents but to overthrow the government. See, for example, reports of International Telephone and Telegraph's attempt to pay the Central Intelligence Agency 1 million dollars to aid them in overthrowing Chile's president, Salvador Allende. They resorted to this expedient after their contributions to other presidential candidates failed to influence the Chilean election outcome (U.S., Congress, Senate, 1973:41–42; 520–627).

costs have been padded by kickbacks. Similarly, both groups of government officials will favor capital intensive inputs if they believe that suppliers of capital are more likely to have excess profits to use for payoffs than suppliers of labor (see Chapter 6). On the output side, neither bureaucrats nor legislators will want open-ended programs with simple, easy-to-observe qualifications for eligibility (see Chapter 7). In these situations, however, legislators face a tradeoff which is not part of a bureaucrat's decision-making calculus—since open-ended or labor-intensive programs may be very popular with constituents. Therefore, the establishment of programs that generate bureaucratic–legislative monopoly power may require both branches of government to "educate" the public about the value of closed-ended programs that require extensive purchases of special-purpose capital equipment.

Although corrupt bureaucrats and legislators who seek increases in y or p can be expected to cooperate on legislative provisions designed to increase the amount available for division between them, they will come in conflict over provisions that affect their relative bargaining power. Thus, particularly powerful legislators will want programs tied to their districts that cannot be shifted with a change in political favor. To accomplish this goal, they will favor immobile and capital-intensive projects for their districts and will be especially pleased if an investment requires a flow of federal dollars over time in order to keep the facility operating. Hospitals and army bases are attractive in this respect, dams and public monuments less so. In contrast, bureaus will seek to maintain their bargaining power by favoring programs that can be easily moved about the country.

In short, while conflicts between legislators and bureaucrats may surface, collaboration will often be in their mutual self-interest—often leading to programs that benefit both groups at the expense of more diffuse groups in the population (cf. Olson, 1965). Citizens may find that a new program improves their position without being aware that alternative ways of organizing the program exist that would have benefitted them even more at no additional expense.

When the analysis of bureaucratic–legislative interactions is combined with the preceding chapter's discussion of interest group activity, the picture of democratic government that emerges is far from a simple, elegant vision of a group of political leaders carrying out the popular will. Instead, the study of corruption and of political contributions generally leads one to stress the conflict between majority rule and the narrower concerns of interest groups, bureaucrats, and legislators who operate within the democratic framework. The resulting picture of government emphasizes the complex and shifting web of interpersonal and interorganizational relationships that lie behind democratic forms. Thus, an alliance between bureaucrats and interest groups to secure a large budget appropriation for an agency may be only a prelude to a struggle between interest groups and agency personnel over the division of the budget.[40] Similarly, legislators and bureaucrats may unite in wishing to strengthen an agency's statutory powers, despite the protests of contractors and clients. Legislators, however, will want the stronger agency to be dependent on Congress while bureaucrats, of course, will want the opposite distribution of power.

All of this, of course, amounts to a one-sided view of government. Observations of the actual behavior of legislators, bureaucrats and interest groups suggest that moral scruples, devotion to duty, ideological convictions, and respect for law play a major role in determining behavior. Nonetheless, the analysis serves to emphasize that the self-interested economic actors who inhabit models of perfect competition cannot be expected to operate a stable democratic state.

APPENDIX. THE RELATIONSHIP BETWEEN BUREAUCRATIC OUTPUT AND "RED TAPE"

This appendix demonstrates that bureaucrats who are only able to impose red tape as a device for generating payoffs may want lower mandated output levels than those who can collect bribes directly. To see this, consider a simple case where $p_0 = 0$ and x is the bribe paid per unit of service. Then the official seeks to maximize

$$G = xQ, \tag{1}$$

subject to:

$$h(Q) = x + wf(x, Q, z), \tag{2}$$

and

$$wf_x = -1, \tag{3}$$

---

[40] Alternatively, if the agency provides benefits to an industry, and if corrupt opportunities are created by the scarcity of benefits, then firms may lobby for large budgets while the agency seeks a cut in funds.

where

Q = units of output,

z = a red tape parameter,

w = the opportunity cost of a unit of time to an applicant (assumed constant for all people),

$h(Q)$ = the society's inverse demand function,

$f(x, Q, z)$ = the delay in units of time to obtain one unit of Q, $\ f_x < 0$, $\ f_Q > 0$, $\ f_z > 0$.

Equation (3) determines the bribe an individual will pay to obtain a marginal reduction in time spent waiting. The higher the price of Q, $x + wf$, the lower the total market demand, Q. Given this framework, one can examine how the bureaucrat's preferred Q depends upon whether or not he must use a queue in order to generate bribes. Let Q_1 be the level of output that maximizes profits when red tape must be used to produce bribes, and let Q_2 be the quota chosen by an official able to charge for the output directly.

First solve for x in terms of Q, and z in terms of Q so that the delay function can be written in terms of Q alone: $f(x, Q, z) = F(Q)$. This can be accomplished by solving (3) for x as a function of Q and z, i.e., $x = x(z, Q)$, substituting $x(z, Q)$ in (2), solving (2) for z as a function of Q, and substituting for z in $x(z, Q)$ and $f(x, Q, z)$. Therefore, $G = [h(Q) - wF(Q)]Q$. This function is maximized at $Q_1 = [h(Q_1) - wF(Q_1)]/[-h'(Q_1) + wF'(Q_1)]$. When no queues are needed to produce bribes, $F(Q) = 0$ and $-Q_2h'(Q_2) = h(Q_2)$. Therefore, $Q_1 < Q_2$, if and only if:

$$\frac{h(Q_1) - wF(Q_1)}{-[h'(Q_1) - wF'(Q_1)]} < \frac{h(Q_2)}{-h'(Q_2)}. \tag{4}$$

Since the market clearing price, $h(Q)$, is higher the smaller is Q, the inequality is more likely to hold if the delay, $F(Q_1)$, is large while the marginal change in $F(Q)$, $F'(Q)$, is either negative or small and positive. Even though $f_Q > 0$, it is possible for $F'(Q) < 0$ after substituting for x and z. However, if $h'(Q_1) - wF'(Q_1) > 0$, no corruption will occur at all.

Bureaucratic Corruption

5

LINING UP AND PAYING OFF

1. LOW-LEVEL CORRUPTION: AN OVERVIEW

The second part of the book leaves behind high-level policy choices and concentrates instead on the administration of public programs. I assume that the political process has established the basic legal framework and that the major issue is whether low-level officials will use their legal powers for corrupt gain. The shift in focus requires a fundamental change in the behavioral models. Thus far, the structure of the electoral process was the main check on corruption. Here, however, since I concentrate on low-level officials, bureaucrats are assumed to be insulated from political shifts. The officials either are protected by civil service regulations or are so far down the hierarchy that they can see no connection between their actions and electoral outcomes. The constraints on a low-level bureaucrat are, then, similar to the costs facing anyone contemplating a crime—the violation of moral principles,[1] and

[1] Beyond recognizing the potentially important role of moral costs in Chapter 6, I do not try to go behind these psychological factors to their determinants in education, culture, or the atmosphere of the workplace. See Williamson (1975) for a discussion of the importance of atmosphere and Gardiner, Balch, and Lyman (1977:15–18) for a summary of research on the sources of moral attitudes.

the fear of detection with the accompanying loss of a job and risk of legal sanctions. This portion of the book, therefore, focuses more singlemindedly on *corrupt* transactions. Although some favors given to bureaucrats are not illegal, I shall have less to say about these methods of influence than I did about campaign contributions and lobbying. Rather than the possibility of electoral defeat, criminal and administrative sanctions are the primary external restraints on behavior.

The substitution seems appropriate. Legislators seldom face criminal sanctions for their part in corrupt schemes; and in fact much of the special interest money they receive is not even illegal. Even more important, many legislators appear to believe that they have sufficient political power to deflect or quash prosecutorial attempts to uncover legislative misdeeds. In contrast, while the job security of civil servants is greater than that of politicians, their ability to suppress potentially hostile investigations is generally small.[2] Indeed, low-level bureaucrats not only may fear the intervention of criminal prosecutors, but they also may be threatened with oversight by superiors within their own organization. Thus, while it seems unrealistic to rely on the criminal law to check the activities of legislators, the fear of criminal prosecution and administrative sanctions can play an important part in deterring low-level corruption. This is not to say, however, that such sanctions do, in fact, serve as important deterrents in America today. Not only is criminal enforcement notoriously weak, but I shall argue that many existing statutes are fundamentally misconceived. Nonetheless, an analysis of criminal and administrative sanctions does seem worthwhile— both for purposes of serious reform and to gain an understanding of behavior under existing systems.

Given present realities, however, one cannot only work with idealized models which assume that criminal prosecutors and administrative superiors are waging an aggressive war on corruption. Instead, the present chapter begins with a more passive model of official oversight. Prosecutors and top bureaucrats (sanctioners) are not concerned with low-level corruption unless a victim of an extortion attempt complains to them. Moreover, the only penalty imposed on the official is the loss of a government job (Becker and Stigler, 1974). Under this passive sanctioning model, low-level bureaucrats can insulate themselves so long as they keep their honest customers satisfied. Moreover, those who pay bribes

---

[2] Accepting money from clients is formally prohibited in all the applications considered. While petitioners may be able to disguise bribes as job offers or gifts, officials are less likely than legislators or agency heads to have legal businesses on the side to serve as repositories for payoffs.

are similarly unconcerned with the possibility that their bribery will be uncovered. The next three chapters consider more complicated situations where outside law enforcement authorities or high-level officials make an active and systematic attempt to uncover corruption. Not only may the probability of detection depend upon the size of the bribe and the gains of the briber, but the level of the sanctions imposed may also depend upon these variables. Finally, Chapter 9 explicitly models the ways in which internal high-level review can modify low-level behavior.

While the change in the *structure of sanctions* is the most obvious break with our models of the political process, three other basic themes differentiate the analysis. First, I will emphasize the way two different types of *bureaucratic procedures* alter corrupt incentives. On the one hand, there is the impact of different *allocation rules*: Corrupt incentives differ depending upon whether an official is managing a first-come–first-served queue, using a sealed bidding process, choosing the "best qualified" applicant, and so forth. On the other hand, bureaucratic procedures specify the *class of officials* who are authorized to grant the governmental service in question. Most important here is whether procedures require that each beneficiary receive the service from only a single bureaucrat, or whether it gives applicants the right to approach several different officials in an attempt to obtain the government service. The former case is, of course, one where the official has considerable monopoly power. In the latter, however, competitive pressures may reduce the level of corrupt payments or even drive them to zero.

Second, the *tasks* the bureaucracy must perform will help determine corrupt incentives. Officials charged with contracting for inputs face incentives different from those of officials who must "coercively" enforce a law or who give subsidies and transfer payments to all qualified applicants.

Third, the *market structure* of potential bribers will often have an impact on the level and incidence of bribery. Firms that can cartelize may be able to obtain benefits through corruption that no individual firm would attempt on its own. Cartels may not need to pay bribes, however. The market power associated with cartelization may be sufficient for them to obtain high levels of profits without corruption. In contrast, more competitive firms may be required to pay high bribes as they vie for a government benefit.

To summarize, the bureaucrats in my model are constrained by the criminal law and the sanctions imposed by superiors, the structure of the bureaucracy in which they work, the kind of benefits and costs they are charged with dispensing, and the organization of beneficiaries. These factors cannot be considered independently, however. Bureaucratic procedures and legal and administrative sanctions are constrained by the nature of the benefits dispensed by the agency and by the market structure and organization of potential bribers. In the administration of some public programs, for example, the nature of the agency's business may prevent superiors from specifying correct behavior in a way that leaves little freedom of action for lower levels of the agency. It may be virtually impossible to avoid giving monopoly power to low-level administrators such as policemen or inspectors of housing, grain, meat, etc. And once these officials possess monopoly power, corrupt incentives are inevitably created.

But the analysis is not limited to corruption involving government officials. Turning from government bureaucracies to the private sector in Chapter 10, I show that much of the analysis of public institutions can be applied to private institutions as well. Many of the activities of private firms and nonprofit organizations produce corrupt incentives analogous to those which arise in the public sector. Market failure, rather than a governmental role per se, is responsible for the creation of many payoff opportunities, and large, complex firms face problems of controlling agents and employees similar to those found in government agencies.

The chapters which follow thus develop a theory of bureaucracy in which officials are self-interested and untrustworthy. They follow the rules only if they, on balance, gain. This stylized view of official motivation provides a way to argue both for structural reforms which limit corrupt incentives and for bureaucratic mores of trust and professional competence. To increase the precision of the analysis, some of the bureaucratic models use simple mathematics to illuminate underlying structures. Although readers with no formal economics training will miss some of the argument by skipping these more technical sections, they can absorb the main points from each chapter's introductory and concluding sections. The portions which can be omitted are noted in the text or footnotes to each chapter. (In the present chapter some readers may wish to omit Sections 3 and 4.)

2. THE EFFICIENCY OF BRIBERY

To begin this rather complicated analysis, I focus on a problem that will introduce the basic perspective of the next five chapters. Imagine that a single low-level bureaucrat is put in charge of an open-ended program that grants a benefit to all who apply.[3] Since the benefit is

[3] The problem of selecting qualified applicants is discussed in Chapter 8, Section 2.

desired by many individuals, a line forms, and the bureaucrat's time is spent processing applications. Thus the number of clients served each period depends upon the speed at which the official works. Moreover, in managing the queue, the official must announce an allocation rule that determines the order in which applicants obtain access. In short, if high-level policymakers hope to regulate the efficiency of their subordinates' conduct,[4] they must control both service speed and the allocation rule that prevails in the queuing process.

Each of these problems has a traditional solution. On the one hand, access is often regulated on a first-come–first-served basis. On the other hand, service speed is controlled by civil service sanctions that threaten low-level bureaucrats with discharge or other penalties if they fall below a certain minimal level of competence. And it is this context that social scientists seem to have in mind when they defend corruption as a more efficient way of conducting government business.

The case for bribery is easy to state. People waiting in line are using up valuable time whose worth is not transferred to the seller but is simply wasted.[5] Short of increasing the number of officials or lowering the quality of benefits, this inefficiency can be remedied in two ways. First, officials can be induced to process applications more speedily. Second, the applicants who join the line do not consider the delay costs they impose on those who come after them. If applicants value time differently, the total value of the time spent waiting can be reduced by "rearranging" the line. Corruption, it is thought, will remedy both deficiencies. Paying off officials will increase their service speeds, and applicants whose time is valuable will pay more for faster service than will those less inconvenienced by the wait.

---

[4] This chapter takes a partial equilibrium perspective and defines the efficient solution as one which maximizes the surplus generated by the public program. Conditions in the rest of the economy are unaffected by the particular queuing regime chosen. Readers interested in the general equilibrium question of the efficient allocation of resources to the service facility relative to the production of goods and services in the rest of the economy should consult Marchand (1971).

[5] See Barzel (1974), Leff (1964). The articles in the *New York Times* on the construction industry, June 26, 27, 1972, July 13, 1975, April 29, 1976 stress the costliness of bureaucratic delays. New York City's Building Commissioner is quoted in the 1975 article as saying, " 'What was being bought and sold, or so it's charged, was time, and the crucial permit often involves the certificate of occupancy,' which approves a building for occupancy. 'The c of o is the key permit for an owner to change his short-term, high-interest rate construction loan to long-term, lower-interest-rate permanent financing. On an $8 million or $10 million project that might mean about $1,000 a day for an owner and a big difference between whether he gets the permit on a Friday or the next Monday or two weeks later.' " Amick (1976:87–88) reports that entrepreneurs seeking a zoning change in Fort Lee, New Jersey, in 1974, calculated their willingness to bribe in terms of the interest they were paying on their money.

These simple arguments, however, are not equal to the complexity of the problem. This is not to deny that the traditional methods are inefficient, but only to argue that a simple cure may be worse than the disease. The case for corruption has three different defects. First, it oversimplifies the difficulty of designing even a *legal* price system that would produce efficient results. Second, it ignores the added inefficiencies generated by the illegality of corruption. Third, it assumes a particular model of bureaucracy that is not necessarily valid.

This last point requires no formal analysis and so will be developed first. The proponents of corruption assume that honest government officials are lazy and serve as few applicants as possible consistent with retaining their jobs. Only in this case will bribes necessarily speed up the rate of operation.[6] This cynical view of bureaucratic operations, however, will not always be empirically justifiable. To put the contrast starkly, consider the possibility that honest officials are perfectly conscientious, processing as many applications per period as they can during their limited working hours. The effort to extort payoffs could then only lead to a slower rate of service as officials threaten to slow down in order to make applicants pay for speed.[7] Thus, opposite assumptions

[6] This hypothesis is behind arguments that stress the favorable efficiency consequences of "speed" money particularly in underdeveloped countries (Leff, 1964; Nye, 1967). For example, a crackdown on corruption in Indonesian customs work produced widespread delays, and led the finance minister to appeal publicly for a speedup (*Wall Street Journal,* December 8, 1977). Harrison (1973) puts the point graphically: "No snail moves more slowly than administration in tropical countries. Kafkaesque offices are piled high with yellowed documents. If you want to get a permit while you're still around to enjoy it, you have to pay for preferential treatment [p. 289]." A *Washington Post* article described the Asian perspective. Some Asian businessmen contend "that their American partners often insist on paying a lot of money in bribes because they cannot be bothered to do things in the time-honored way of endless talk over tea. They therefore end up paying several times more in bribes than is necessary or even acceptable [quoted by Weiss, 1975:65]."

[7] Examples are provided by the *New York Times* reports on corruption in the New York City construction industry (June 26, 27, 1972), and in Gardiner's (1970) study of Wincanton (Reading, Pa.):

> At times . . . applying for a [building] permit became a cat-and-mouse game, with the official waiting to see how much he would be offered, and the applicant waiting to see if he could get his permit without paying for it. In one case uncovered by a reform district attorney, a desperate businessman paid $750 for a permit after his application had lain on an official's desk for three months. Other men, however, said that they received their permits simply by waiting or threatening to call the papers. Where time was important, however, many businessmen considered a $25 to $50 bribe the lesser of two evils [p. 83].

Gardiner and Olson (1974) also argue that "bureaucratic personnel may deliberately slow down service after the initial payoff and create more red tape in order to establish additional inducements for others to make payments or to raise the ante [p. 196]."

lead to opposite results: Under one, corrupt payments speed up service; under the other, they slow it down. Moreover, it seems likely that the real world will usually be somewhere between the two poles—in which case the net effect of corruption on performance will be difficult to predict a priori.

Even under the extreme, lazy official model, however, high-level policymakers should not generally tolerate low-level corruption. For legal incentive systems that will increase speed without the need for bribery generally exist. The superior official may, for example, pay bureaucrats a bonus for every application they process. Bureaucrats will then work as fast as possible so long as the cost to them of speeding up is less than the bonus paid per customer.[8] Thus, corruption is at most a second-best response to the inefficiencies of the traditional solution.

Increasing the speed at which bureaucrats work, however, is only one of the policy objectives of an efficient queuing process. If applicants value the program benefit differently, or if they have different opportunity costs of time, then it may be possible for a corrupt official to exploit these facts by charging beneficiaries different bribe–prices for different service priorities (cf. Nichols, Smolensky, and Tideman, 1971). In modeling the corrupt marketplace, I shall assume that officials cannot price discriminate and require some people to pay more for a given priority than others. Thus, bureaucrats cannot strike individual bargains with applicants who threaten blackmail. While this degree of rigidity is consistent with plausible assumptions about the corrupt environment,[9] a more complete analysis could incorporate game-theoretic elements into the problem. Nevertheless, the main points can be made without including additional analytic complexities.

Section 3 shows that when price discrimination is impossible, even a *legal* pricing system can fulfill only very limited efficiency goals if the official is restricted to the use of a single queue. An efficient solution will, instead, generally require a more complex priority-queuing system. Under this more complicated approach, officials make several different

---

[8] Previous work on agency has analyzed the way superiors can set fines or rewards that induce agents to perform efficiently. See especially Ross (1973, 1974) and Wilson (1968). Bonin (1975), Bonin and Marcus (1976), and Weitzman (1976) discuss a related problem—how to set fees so that agents pass along correct information.

[9] Either of two alternative assumptions will make price discrimination impossible. On the one hand, officials may know the overall distribution of beneficiaries by willingness to pay but be unable to identify the relevant characteristics of any particular demander. On the other hand, the public benefit may be transferable with information available to beneficiaries about the bribes paid by others. This is not to say, however, that bargaining does not occur. Many of the payoffs made by developers and contractors seeking speedy action from government officials are essentially the result of bilateral bargains.

queues available to applicants. They serve those in the highest priority queue first and when it is empty move to the second priority and so forth. While the added costs of managing such a complex system may sometimes be greater than the gains, even for an *honest* policymaker, a *corrupt* bureaucrat is less likely to establish such a system since its very complexity will make it difficult to keep illegal activities hidden. This, however, is only one way in which the illegality of corruption will encourage inefficiency. Even if sanctioners are not themselves aggressively searching for corruption,[10] low-level bureaucrats may nevertheless fear a hostile response if their clients complain to superior authorities. I shall introduce this factor in two different stages. Section 3 moves from a model in which a monopoly bureaucrat does not fear detection to another in which the corrupt official can operate safely so long as the lowest priority of service is free. If a corrupt bureaucrat closes this option, outside law enforcement authorities are immediately alerted to the existence of a corrupt system and proceed at once with successful prosecutions. In either of these simple cases, it is not generally possible for corrupt officials to capture all the surplus generated by the program. It follows that it will be in their interest to design systems of queues and bribe prices that a policymaker seeking efficient solutions might reject as unacceptable. Finally, Section 4 considers the possibility that even clients willing to pay bribes may bring evidence of corruption to the attention of the prosecutor. If the probability of turning state's evidence is a positive function of the size of the bribe requested, then this fact will lower the overall level of bribes charged by the official and may be sufficient to prevent corruption entirely. Inefficiency will be introduced by the official's need to consider variations across applicants in the probability of reporting the corrupt solicitation.

---

[10] The relative indifference of U.S. legislators to payments of speed money versus bribes paid to obtain a sale is indicated in the law signed by the President on December 20, 1977. The new law makes it a criminal offense for an American corporation or its executives to make payments to foreign government officials or political organizations for the purpose of influencing governmental decisions. The payment of "speed" money is, however, not prohibited under current laws and regulations (See N. Jacoby, P. Nehemkis, R. Eells, "Foreign Payoffs Law: A Costly Error," *New York Times,* January 22, 1978, Section 3.) Many writers on corporate payoffs have attempted to distinguish between small expediting payments and either large political payments or bribes paid in return for illegal benefits. For example, Louis Wells, as quoted by Weiss (1975), states:

> It seems to me the important question is: Are you paying small sums to just speed up action on something that is perfectly legal, or are you paying for something illegal—something not in the best interest of the home country [p. 68].

3. SINGLE LINES AND PRIORITY QUEUES

Our model of administrative behavior assumes a stochastic queuing process[11] where the actual number of people waiting changes over time. A queue forms because servicing applicants takes time and applicants may arrive more rapidly than the server can accommodate them. Since I have assumed that corrupt officials cannot price discriminate, they may wish to follow the alternative strategy of differentiating their product to take advantage of differences in willingness to pay.[12] Since product differentiation takes the form of making rapid service more expensive than slower service, demanders pay different combinations of time and money to obtain the program benefit. With a single queue, priority service can be provided by permitting applicants to purchase any place in line. Since a future demander may enter the queue ahead of the applicant, demanders are essentially purchasing lottery tickets where the probability of service in any future time period depends upon one's choice of a place in line and the probability that future demanders will purchase more favorable places.

Individual demanders can be classified into groups, $i = 1, \ldots, m$, which may have different average service times, $1/\mu_i$, waiting costs per period, c_i, evaluations of benefits, R_i, and average arrival rates, λ_i. (An arrival rate is the number of type is expected to arrive in any period.) To simplify the exposition, assume that people who wait in line can obtain only one unit of service apiece when it is their turn to be served. If they want additional units, they must reenter the queue. If the cost of providing service depends only on the time involved and not upon other characteristics of i, then the total surplus generated by a program will be larger if those with long service times, low waiting costs, and low R are given relatively low service priority. People with high waiting costs should either be given high priority or eliminated from the system. Designing pricing systems that efficiently account for these differences may prove complicated, particularly because individual applicants are

---

[11] The pool of potential beneficiaries each period is assumed to be independent of the number served in previous periods, i.e., the affected group is never exhausted, either because those already served may join the queue as many times as they desire or because enough new applicants appear every period to maintain the pool of qualified beneficiaries.

[12] The officials' behavior is analogous to the behavior of oligopolists who differentiate their product as an alternative to price discrimination when demanders have different tastes and incomes.

not concerned with the externality imposed on those behind them in line.

To begin the analysis, assume that demand is stochastic,[13] with $\Sigma \, \lambda_i/\mu_i < 1$ and independent of the queuing procedure chosen. This last assumption is a restrictive one,[14] but it permits one to concentrate on the externalities which applicants impose on each other. If a single queue is to be maintained, then charging legal prices for different places in line cannot produce an efficient solution. To see this, suppose that applicants have identical R_i and service times, $1/\mu_i$, but differ in their waiting costs—individuals are classified so that $c_1 > c_2 > \cdots > c_m$ where c_i is waiting cost per unit of time. Given this situation, the efficient policy is clearly to place an individual of type i ahead of those of type $i + 1$ to m who are already in the queue and behind those of type 1 to $i - 1$. Unfortunately, however, the official who wishes to generate this result through a set of constant prices $p_1, \ldots, p_n$, for different *places* in line, will fail because the composition of the line is constantly changing.[15] The cost that applicants impose on those behind them in line cannot accurately be reflected in the prices because this cost varies over time for each position in line. The closest that the official can come to efficiency is to set fees that minimize *expected* waiting costs, given that a single queue must be maintained.

It is possible, of course, to improve on this result by permitting the

---

[13] In particular, it is common in queuing models to assume that both arrival and service rates follow a Poisson process. Arrivals, λ, follow a Poisson process if $p_n(t) = [(\lambda t)^n e^{-\lambda t}]/n!$, where $p_n(t)$ is the probability that n applicants arrive during a time interval of length t. This expression will hold if (1) $p_n(t)$ depends on t alone and not upon the initial instant, i.e., the process is homogeneous in time; (2) two events cannot occur at precisely the same time; and (3) the probability that one applicant will arrive in interval dt is proportional to dt and is written λdt (Kaufmann, 1963:79–85; 343–347). In most queuing models, service times are also assumed to be distributed exponentially.

[14] The assumption implies that demand is perfectly inelastic. This assumption will be changed when discussing corruption, since if demand is truly inelastic corrupt officials can charge everyone infinite prices whatever queuing procedures they use.

[15] People who purchase jth place in line are purchasing an expected wait which depends upon the expected number and types of people who will purchase places in line ahead of them. Service is provided without preemption, i.e., if an applicant is being served, no one can bribe the official to stop serving the applicant currently being serviced.

In situations when the line contains r people of types $i = 1, \ldots, v$, efficiency requires that a person of type v pay p_{r+1} to enter the line behind the rth person. In other cases, when the line contains s people of types $i = 1, \ldots, v$, where $s \neq r$, that same person should pay p_{s+1} to enter the line behind the sth person. No price system which is stable over time can generate this result. Applicants notice only the set of prices for each place in line. They are indifferent to the identity of those already in the queue. Hence if an individual paid p_{r+1} in the first case, he would also choose to pay p_{r+1} in the second.

official to price discriminate—changing prices as the composition of the line changes. If, however, the official can price discriminate this perfectly, it is not clear why a price system is needed to achieve efficiency. Instead, a set of administrative orders can assign applicants to places in line in an efficient way.[16] Even a *legal* price system, then, cannot realistically be used to produce efficiency if all applicants are obliged to line up in a single queue. And if this is true for a legal system, it is obvious that a corrupt pricing system will suffer from at least equal difficulties.

One institutional reform, however, promises greater efficiency gains if combined with a sophisticated pricing system. Under a priority queuing system, applicants may be placed in one of several lines to wait for service. The official then processes those in queue one first and if it is empty moves to queue two and so forth. Applicants may be assigned to lines on the basis of waiting costs, c_i, and *expected* queue lengths, or they may choose which line to join, given a set of entry fees x_j and a set of *expected* waits in line, t_j. Expected waits, of course, depend upon the expected arrival rates and servicing times of the other applicants.[17] An individual i who enters line j expects to wait for $t_j + 1/\mu_i$ before receiving the benefit.[18] If μ and R are constant for all types of people and if $c_{j-1} > c_j$, then the prices, x_j, which generate efficient results in *expected value terms* are[19]

$$R - x_j - c_j t_j > R - x_k - c_j t_k \quad \text{for all} \quad j \quad \text{and} \quad k \neq j. \tag{1}$$

The inequality implies that given the set of prices, $\{x_j\}$, individuals of type j prefer priority j to all the other priorities. Information about the c_i and λ_i for all i are required in order to choose an efficient set of prices, but the price system itself is quite simple. The price of the lowest

[16] This point is made in different contexts by Rose-Ackerman (1973) and Weitzman (1974).

[17] Arrival rates, λ_i, follow a Poisson process and service times, $1/\mu_i$, are distributed exponentially.

[18] Service time, $1/\mu_i$, is independent of which line is chosen. Furthermore, while a program designer can establish a priority queuing system in several ways, I concentrate upon nonpreemptive systems where the official will not stop servicing an applicant even if someone of higher priority arrives.

[19] A similar result is reported in Levhari and Sheshinski (1974). The result in (1), however, differs from their (7.46) since their upper bound for $x_{j-1} - x_j$ depends upon expected waiting times under a permutation of j and $j - 1$. This appears to be an error, since for any given set, $\{x_j\}$, applicants choose priorities on the basis of actual expected waits, and stable results can be generated only if type $j - 1$ chooses queue $j - 1$ when all previous js and $j - 1$s chose queues j and $j - 1$. Hence type $j - 1$ will choose queue $j - 1$ if: $c_{j-1}t_{j-1} + x_{j-1} < c_{j-1}t_j + x_j$.

priority queue can be set arbitrarily at some level, zero for example. Then x_{n-1} can be set to satisfy $x_{n-1} < c_{n-1}(t_n - t_{n-1})$ since $c_{n-1} < c_j, j \neq n - 1, n$. Given x_{n-1} and (1), x_{n-2} can be chosen and so on up to x_1.[20] These prices will lead individuals with high opportunity costs of time to choose service priorities at least as high as individuals with lower costs. This condition of a legal pricing system must also be met by an illegal one.

Corrupt officials may not, however, find it possible to establish a priority queuing system. It is one thing to take under the table payments; quite another to attempt a major institutional reform without gaining the attention of even extremely passive superiors.[21] Even if corrupt officials *could* set up n priority queues, however, they might not want to do this. Since they are not concerned with efficiency per se but only with maximizing their returns, they might well make different choices. To simplify, first suppose that officials can set prices without any fear of arrest. They realize, however, that applicants will refuse to join the queuing system if net returns are negative. While they wish to capture as much of the surplus generated by the program as possible, they are constrained by the fact that uniform bribe–prices must be set for each

[20] If applicants have different expected serving times, $1/\mu_i$, then expected costs are minimized when applicants are assigned to priorities on the basis of $c_j\mu_j$—the higher the value of this fraction the higher the priority. In this case, a complex pricing scheme may be required. When type i occupies queue i for all i, suppose that $\mu_{j-1}c_{j-1} > \mu_j c_j$ at the same time that $c_{j-1} \leq c_j$ for at least one pair of applicant types. Thus group $j - 1$ ought to be placed ahead of group j in spite of the fact that $j - 1$'s waiting cost is low. In that case, an efficient set of $\{x_j\}$ satisfying (1) for all j priority queues will not be possible. Since applicants make their choices of queue without taking their own servicing costs into account, whenever $c_j \geq c_{j-1}$, type j must choose a priority queue at least as high as type $j - 1$ so long as the prices depend upon the queue chosen and not upon the c_i of the customer. Hence, to generate efficient prices in this more complex situation, the price of joining a particular priority queue must depend upon type is expected servicing time. Levhari and Sheshinski (1974) do not make this complexity clear in presenting their equation (7.46). In fact, their results seem to imply that even when the μ_i are unequal, a single price for each priority queue can be established. However, in the discussion which follows (7.46) they present an example in which prices do depend upon expected service times. The appeal of a price system is substantially lowered in this case since prices must often be essentially tailor made, with applicants facing a set of prices which depends upon their own expected servicing time. In fact, if applicants can be assigned to queues only through prices which are not calibrated by applicant type, a simple first-come–first-served regime might dominate a priority queuing system.

[21] It is not, however, impossible, although all of my examples are of corrupt schemes that were discovered. Thus, officials at a federally financed housing complex in West Haven, Connecticut apparently operated queues with two priorities. The low priority queue, for which no bribe was required, involved a wait of around six months. Payment of a bribe shortened the wait to several weeks (*New Haven Register*, April 1, 1976).

priority queue. Prices cannot be set separately for each applicant. This single constraint may be enough to force the monopolistic official in an inefficient direction. Assume, for example, that $\mu_j = \mu$ for all j and that the monopolist begins by considering a queuing system where the number of queues is set equal to the number of applicant types, i.e., $R - c_j(t_j + 1/\mu) - x_j \geq 0$ for all j. Since prices attach to queues and not to applicants, the monopolist cannot capture all of the applicants' surplus by setting $x_j = R - c_j(t_j + 1/\mu)$ for all j. To see this, assume that the official does choose $x_j = R - c_j(t_j + 1/\mu)$, and substitute in the inequality in (1) for $k = j - 1$, which yields,

$$0 > (c_{j-1} - c_j) \left(t_{j-1} + \frac{1}{\mu}\right).$$

This is a contradiction since $c_{j-1} > c_j$. Since applicants are free to join any queue they wish, everyone wants to join the highest priority queue.

As soon as one recognizes that monopolists may not obtain the total surplus, it is easy to see that they may design queuing systems which do not maximize this surplus[22] unless the relationship between monopoly profits and total surplus is a simple one that is independent of the number of applicant types who do not join the system. To demonstrate that no simple relationship need exist, consider a priority queuing system with n types of applicants. If returns are negative in all priorities for class i, that entire class of applicants will refuse to join any queue. With uniform service rates, μ, and $1 = \Sigma\lambda_i < \mu$, consider the way the monopolist chooses between two different priority queuing systems. Under the first, prices, $\{x_j\}$, are set so that no applicant balks, i.e., refuses to line up, and each applicant type chooses a different line. In contrast, consider an alternative queuing system, which prices type one's out of the market and establishes only $n - 1$ lines with prices z_j. In the first case, the monopolist sets prices equal to their upper bounds in

---

[22] Other work has considered the relationship between monopoly pricing behavior and that of the surplus maximizer in simpler models without priority queuing. Thus Naor (1969) and Levhari and Sheshinski (1974) show that a monopolist will not internalize all of the externalities of a queuing system under certain assumptions about a monopolist's ability to levy tolls. Edelson and Hildebrand (1975) show that with a two-part tariff the equivalence of monopoly and surplus maximization can be reestablished. If applicants differ in their cost of waiting or their valuation of the service, they show that the single monopolist's toll is not equal to the single toll of the surplus maximizer. It can, in fact, be either greater than or less than the surplus-maximizing toll. Edelson and Hildebrand also examine a case where an uncongested alternative exists. Clearly, both monopolist and surplus maximizer make the same choice in this case, although calling the seller a monopolist is surely a misuse of words.

(1). (For convenience in exposition assume that if applicants are indifferent between two queues, they always choose the one of highest priority. This assumption permits the official to set x_j equal to its upper bound instead of just short of it.) Thus:

$$x_{n-1} = c_{n-1}(t_n - t_{n-1}) + x_n,$$

$$x_k = \sum_{i=k}^{n-1} c_i(t_{i+1} - t_i) + x_n \quad \text{for} \quad k \neq n. \tag{2}$$

However, to prevent balking, the x_j must also satisfy $R - x_j - c_j(t_j + 1/\mu) \geq 0$ for all j. These two conditions imply that[23] $x_1 = R - c_1(t_1 + 1/\mu)$ and $x_k = R - c_1/\mu - c_k t_k - \Sigma_{i=2}^{k} t_i(c_{i-1} - c_i)$ for $k \neq 1$. Maximum expected profits, W_1, are $W_1 = \Sigma_{k=1}^{n} \lambda_k x_k$. Substituting for x_k from the above expressions, it is easy to show that $S_1 - W_1 \geq 0$, where S_1 is total surplus.[24]

The monopolist compares W_1 with his profits, W_2, when type ones are priced out of the market, and $n - 1$ priorities are established.[25] The

---

[23] To see this, note that for $j = 1$, $x_1 \leq R - c_1(t_1 + 1/\mu)$ or from (2):

$$x_n \leq R - c_1\left(t_1 + \frac{1}{\mu}\right) - \sum_{i=1}^{n-1} c_i(t_{i+1} - t_i). \tag{i}$$

It is easy to show that if (i) is satisfied, then no one balks, i.e., $R - x_j - c_j(t_j + 1/\mu) \geq 0$ for all j. Furthermore, $x_n = R - c_1(t_1 + 1/\mu) - \Sigma_{i=1}^{n-1} c_i(t_{i+1} - t_i)$ is the largest value of x_n which satisfies these n inequalities.

[24]

$$W_1 = \sum_{k=1}^{n} \lambda_k x_k = R - \frac{c_1}{\mu} - \sum_{k=1}^{n} \lambda_k c_k t_k - \sum_{k=2}^{n} \lambda_k \sum_{i=2}^{k} t_i(c_{i-1} - c_i).$$

The first three terms equal total surplus, S_1. Since $c_{i-1} > c_i$,

$$S_1 - W_1 = \sum_{k=2}^{n} \lambda_k \sum_{i=2}^{k} t_i(c_{i-1} - c_i) \geq 0.$$

[25] When type ones are priced out of the queuing system applicants of type j occupy priority $j - 1$ and

$$z_{k-1} = \sum_{i=k-1}^{n-2} c_{i+1}(T_{i+1} - T_i) + z_{n-1},$$

where T_i is the expected wait in the ith priority queue with type ones excluded. In order to exclude type 1's and include 2's we must have $R - c_2(T_1 + 1/\mu) \geq z_1 > R - c_1(T_1 + 1/\mu)$. The monopolist can set z_1 equal to its upper bound, $R - c_2(T_1 + 1/\mu)$, which implies:

$$R - c_2(T_1 + \frac{1}{\mu}) - \sum_{i=1}^{n-2} c_{i+1}(T_{i+1} - T_i) = z_{n-1}.$$

difference between the monopolist's profits and total surplus is greater with n lines than with $n - 1$ lines.[26] Therefore, if a surplus maximizer would choose to exclude type ones, then so would a monopolist (if $S_2 - S_1 > 0$, then $W_2 - W_1 > 0$). However, if the surplus maximizer would design a queuing system that included all types of applicants, the monopolist might well seek to exclude type ones ($W_1 < W_2$).

Thus far, I have been considering the analytically simplest case—where the monopolistic official can set prices without any fear of sanctions. It should be plain, however, that an official who must take steps to avoid sanctions also need not choose the efficient queuing system. Assume, for example, that corrupt officials must make the lowest priority queue free if they wish to escape criminal prosecution. They then maximize their receipts subject to this free-entry constraint and will sometimes design a queuing system that diverges from that selected by either surplus maximizers or monopolists. Since the fee for the last queue is zero, this requirement lowers the bribes that can be charged for higher priority queues as well. As the appendix to this chapter demonstrates, this restriction implies that corrupt officials may well price fewer applicants out of the market than would surplus maximizers.

Three points, then, cut against a presumption in favor of corrupt expediting payments. First, when a uniform fee must be charged for

---

Once again this value of z_{n-1} is the largest one satisfying $R - z_k - c_{k+1}(T_k + 1/\mu) \geq 0$ for all $i > 1$, i.e., no one balks except type ones. Thus

$$z_{k-1} = R - \frac{c_2}{\mu} - c_k T_{k-1} - \sum_{i=3}^{k} T_{i-1}(c_{i-1} - c_i),$$

for $k \neq 2$ and profits, W_2, are:

$$W_2 = \sum_{k=2}^{n} \lambda_k z_{k-1} = (1 - \lambda_1)\left[R - \frac{c_2}{\mu}_3 - \sum_{k=2}^{n} \lambda_k c_k T_{k-1} - \sum_{k=3}^{n} \lambda_k \sum_{i=3}^{k} T_{i-1}(c_{i-1} - c_i)\right],$$

where $(1 - \lambda_1)[R - c_2/\mu] - \sum_{k=2}^{n} \lambda_k c_k T_{k-1}$ is total surplus, S_2, and thus $S_2 - W_2 \geq 0$.

[26] To see this, substitute for $S_1 - W_1$ and $S_2 - W_2$ in

$$S_1 - W_1 \lessgtr S_2 - W_2.$$

$$\sum_{k=2}^{n} \lambda_k \sum_{i=2}^{k} t_i(c_{i-1} - c_i) \lessgtr \sum_{k=3}^{n} \lambda_k \sum_{i=3}^{k} T_{i-1}(c_{i-1} - c_i).$$

$$\sum_{k=3}^{n} \lambda_k \sum_{i=3}^{k} (t_i - T_{i-1})(c_{i-1} - c_i) + \sum_{k=2}^{n} \lambda_k t_2(c_1 - c_2) \lessgtr 0.$$

Since $c_{i-1} > c_i$ and $t_i > T_{i-1}$, the left-hand side of the inequality is positive, and $S_1 - W_1 > S_2 - W_2$ or $S_1 - S_2 > W_1 - W_2$.

each type of service, efficiency may require institutional change as well as the introduction of a pricing system. Second, even if anticorruption laws are not enforced, the queuing system chosen by a monopoly official will often diverge from efficiency. Third, when fear of detection leads the official to make the lowest priority queue free, a correspondence between efficiency and the official's choices will also be unlikely. The official who fears detection, however, might provide more or less service than the monopoly official able to charge for the lowest priority queue.

4. CORRUPTION AND THE RISK OF DETECTION

The sanctions imposed by the criminal law and by bureaucratic superiors are generally not so easy to avoid as assumed in Section 3. Instead of knowing for sure that particular actions will prevent detection, bureaucrats will generally face a finite risk of detection which depends upon the size of the bribes they accept. This section begins to add realistic complexities to the corrupt bureaucrat's decision making calculus, and shows that when the risk of detection is taken into account, the official's bribe–price decisions will continue to diverge from those legal prices that would produce efficiency. Inefficiency arises because applicants must be classified not only in terms of service times, waiting costs, and benefit levels, but also in terms of their willingness to report corruption.

The analysis of the risk of detection in this section continues with the basic model developed earlier. In particular, the official is a monopolist and is assumed to initiate all bribe requests. Outside law enforcement authorities and bureaucratic superiors are relatively passive. They do not ferret out corruption but instead wait until an applicant reports a bribery solicitation. The sanctioning process is characterized in simple terms. Once an applicant reports a corrupt solicitation, the official cannot appeal and immediately loses his job. His expected salary in the private sector multiplied by the probability of detection is, therefore, the benchmark which he compares to his earnings as a corrupt government official.[27]

To develop the model, I need to specify both the official's preferences for high bribery receipts, versus a low risk of being apprehended, and

---

[27] This view of the expected penalty for taking bribes follows Becker and Stigler (1974). Their analysis is simpler, however, because both the probability of detection and the opportunity wage are fixed independently of the size of the bribe. Becker and Stigler also make the strong assumption that the opportunity wage is independent of the official's reason for leaving government service. Officials' opportunity wages might,

demanders' behavior given their returns in corrupt and honest situations. I first analyze the behavior of demanders and then represent the official's strategy and the resulting bribe–price equilibrium. Assume that applicants will report bribe solicitations when they expect that the benefits of doing so exceed the costs. Applicants know the benefits of participating in the corrupt regime, $\Pi_i{}^* = \max[0, \max \Pi(i, j)]$, where $\Pi(i, j)$ is the net gain to i of entering the jth queue. The benefits of a change to an honest regime with no pricing system are, however, uncertain. First, demanders must guess the length of the wait when no bribery exists. Second, they must estimate the cost of changing from a corrupt distribution to an honest one. Hence, the delay occasioned by the law enforcement process itself may be enough to deter demanders from reporting the crime. This delay will weigh less heavily in beneficiaries' calculations, however, if they expect to return repeatedly to the queue. They may then be willing to bear the cost of delay in the present in return for a series of higher gains in the future. If an applicant has already paid a bribe, another cost of reporting corruption is, of course, the penalties levied on bribers who reveal their peculation.[28] While

---

however, depend both upon the fact that they were fired for corrupt dealings and upon the size of the payoffs they accept. Thus, individuals are more likely to resist corrupt incentives altogether if they belong to a profession that puts a high premium on honest behavior. For example, in a study of corruption in the implementation of a Kentucky strip-mining law Broadus (1976) found that the more highly trained inspectors were less likely to be corrupt than those without training, presumably because of the impact of a bribery conviction on future professional opportunities. The relationship between one's opportunity wage and the seriousness of one's crime is especially evident in instances of high-level corruption. See Rosenblum (1962) for a discussion of the difficulties faced by a corrupt member of the Federal Communications Commission. Some of those businessmen involved in the bribery of foreign nations have, however, been protected from financial reverses by their employers (*New York Times*, August 25, 1975). Furthermore, those convicted of corruption may sometimes reenter government service, albeit at a lower salary. Thus, an official convicted of 32 counts of corruption while working for the Philadelphia Department of Licenses and Inspections was rehired by another city agency several years later at $7000 to $8000 less pay (*Philadelphia Inquirer*, May 8, 1974).

[28] The corrupt official may try to lower the benefits of disclosure by neutralizing law enforcement authorities and by threatening extralegal sanctions against "squealers." For example, in Newark, New Jersey and Wincanton, Pennsylvania government officials apparently had ties to organized crime that gave them an added bargaining advantage and, in addition, had appointed "friendly" police chiefs. See Gardiner (1970); George Amick (1976); Ron Polumbo, *No Cause for Indictment: An Autopsy of Newark* (New York: Holt, Rinehart and Winston, 1971), excerpted in Gardiner and Olson (1974:85–96); and Michael Dorman, *Payoff: The Role of Organized Crime in American Politics* (David McKay, 1972) excerpted in Gardiner and Olson (1974:140–144). Dorman, cites the testimony of Paul Rigo, an engineering contractor doing business with the city of Newark: "Asked if he wanted to pay [the kickback] Rigo said, 'No, but if we didn't we'd have lost God knows how much money and, in addition, there was always the fear.' "

informers may be treated leniently, they may nevertheless be expected to face substantial costs in employing legal counsel, testifying at trials, and obtaining unsavory reputations.[29] To simplify the exposition, assume that the demander ignores the possibility that someone *else* may report the corruption after the applicant has joined the queue. In realistic situations this may be an important deterrent to bribery and will be taken up in subsequent chapters.

Given the uncertain gains from reporting corruption, it seems appropriate to adopt a probabilistic approach. That is, if the expected net return to applicant i of paying a bribe is below a threshold level, $\bar{\Pi}_i$, the probability of i turning state's evidence, v^i, is an increasing function of the x_j. If expected returns exceed $\bar{\Pi}_i$, the applicant will never report the corrupt official. The threshold, $\bar{\Pi}_i$, could be infinite, but it will be finite if there are substantial costs to the applicant from reporting corruption. Thus: $0 \le v^i(X) \le 1$ for all i, where $X = (x_1, x_2, \ldots, x_n)$ is the bribe–price vector which determines Π_i^*.[30]

For any set of bribe–prices, some types of individual are likely to gain more from reporting corruption than others. Thus individuals with low opportunity costs of time may be more likely to report corruption than those with high opportunity costs because, with corruption, they are located in low-priority queues and may expect a shorter wait if bribery is eliminated.[31] In an effort to prevent reporting by applicants who do not value time highly, the official may therefore establish fewer priority queues than would be required for efficiency. Similarly, if efficiency requires that a group of applicants with very high service times or

---

[29] For example, a firm granted immunity in return for testifying that it had paid kickbacks to officials in Philadelphia and New Jersey was removed from a $200-million regional sewerage project in Camden County. The New Jersey attorney general ruled in 1973 that firms—even though immunized—that had admitted to "bad acts" could not bid on future state contracts (*Philadelphia Inquirer,* April 9, 1974).

In New York, a lawyer, who taped a conversation with a construction inspector demanding a bribe, went to the authorities and had the inspector discharged and arrested. Since then, through four years of waiting, she has been unable to get a certificate of occupancy for a supermarket in which she had an interest (*New York Times,* June 27, 1972).

[30] I assume that $\partial v^i/\partial x_j \ge 0$, and v^i approaches 1 as the x_j increases and equals zero for X such that $\Pi_i^* \ge \bar{\Pi}_i$.

[31] This is not necessarily true, of course. While those with high opportunity costs of time expect a longer wait without corruption, this may be compensated for by the fact that no prices are charged. Furthermore, in some corrupt systems, those with very high opportunity costs of time may be eliminated. Alternatively, waiting may be costly only because the benefit is deferred, not because applicants must actually waste time in a queue. Individuals may simply submit an application and go about their business until an answer arrives. In that case, those with low discount rates or who place a low value on the benefit will be most likely to report corruption.

waiting costs be excluded, this group may be included in a corrupt system in order to prevent them from reporting the existence of payoffs. Finally, the behavior of those who occupy the lowest priority queue and pay no bribes (or who do not queue at all when bribery exists) is especially important. This group has very high incentives to report corruption, since no legal or psychological penalties can be levied against them. Thus the stability of a corrupt equilibrium may depend upon preventing those who would choose not to pay bribes from discovering the existence of bribery. They must believe that they are participating in an honest but slow-moving queue.

Given the set of functions, $v^i(\mathbf{X})$, determined by the factors discussed above, the official must choose a bribe vector, $\mathbf{X}$, that takes account of the probability that someone may report the official's corruption to law enforcement authorities. I continue to assume that the official cannot price discriminate and arrange special deals with individual applicants. Thus the official can lower the v^i both by setting the x_j close to their lowest feasible levels, given a fixed number of queues, and by changing the number of queues.

Since officials are establishing bribe–price vectors that will persist over time,[32] they are not interested in the expected returns in any particular period, but rather in the discounted present value of expected returns earned over time. If the official is risk neutral, the discounted present value of expected returns, $L(\mathbf{X})$, can be calculated for various feasible price vectors, $\mathbf{X}$, and the highest expected return chosen.[33] As

---

[32] This assumption implies the existence of a stable ongoing corrupt allocative system. The assumption is dropped in subsequent chapters which discuss the establishment of bribe–prices at a given point in time.

[33] To derive the expression for expected return, $L(\mathbf{X})$, assume first that T is the last period. Then expected return in period T, given a price vector $\mathbf{X}$ is

$$E(T, \mathbf{X}) = \sum_{i=1}^{n} f(i)x^i[1 - v^i(\mathbf{X})],$$

where $f(i)$ is number of people of type i expected to arrive each period, x^i is the price paid by people of type i, and $1 - v^i(\mathbf{X})$ is the probability that type is will not report the corruption in that period. Thus:

$$E(T - 1, \mathbf{X}) = \sum_{i=1}^{n} [f(i)(1 - v^i(\mathbf{X}))]\left[x^i + \frac{E(T, \mathbf{X})}{1 + r}\right].$$

$$= \sum_{i=1}^{n} f(i)\, x^i[1 - v^i(\mathbf{X})] + \sum_{i=1}^{n} \frac{f(i)(1 - v^i(\mathbf{X}))}{1 + r} \sum_{i=1}^{n} f(i)x^i[1 - v^i(\mathbf{X})].$$

$$E(T - 2, \mathbf{X}) = \sum_{i=1}^{n} f(i)[1 - v^i(\mathbf{X})]\left[x^i + \frac{E(T - 1, \mathbf{X})}{1 + r}\right].$$

$$= \sum_{i=1}^{n} f(i)x^i[1 - v^i(\mathbf{X})]\left[1 + \sum_{i=1}^{n} \frac{f(i)[1 - v^i(\mathbf{X})]}{1 + r}\right] + \sum_{i=1}^{n} \frac{\{f(i)[1 - v^i(\mathbf{X})]\}^2}{(1 + r)^2}\right).$$

the footnote demonstrates, the maximum value of $L(\mathbf{X})$ depends upon the discount rate, r; expected return per period, $F(\mathbf{X})$; and the probability that the official's corruption will not be reported, $s(\mathbf{X})$. It is not necessary, however, to solve the problem explicitly to obtain an intuitive sense of the official's behavior by considering his willingness to trade off $s(\mathbf{X})$ against $F(\mathbf{X})$. Any given level of expected per period returns, $F(\mathbf{X})$, may correspond with several different price vectors, each associated with a different probability of escaping detection, $s(\mathbf{X})$. The official's preferences depend only upon the sums $F(\mathbf{X})$ and not upon the particular values of the x_i. Thus in Figure 5.1 the lines labeled L_k are isoutility lines for the official in terms of $F(\mathbf{X})$ and $s(\mathbf{X})$. Under the assumption of risk neutrality each L_k represents a different level of $L(\mathbf{X})$. The higher the L_k and the lower the discount rate, the steeper the slope of L_k (see note 33).

Figure 5.1 also contains a representative opportunity locus, Z, confronting the corrupt official. While the smooth shape of Z is not required by the model's assumptions, certain of Z's features represent general characteristics of the official's set of opportunities. Thus, $F(\mathbf{X})$ must

---

Let

$$\sum_{i=1}^{n} f(i)x^i[1 - v^i(\mathbf{X})] = F(\mathbf{X}) = \text{expected return earned per period,}$$

and let:

$$\sum_{i=1}^{n} f(i)[1 - v^i(\mathbf{X})] = s(\mathbf{X}) = \begin{array}{l} \text{probability corruption will not be} \\ \text{reported to law enforcement} \\ \text{authorities in each time period.} \end{array}$$

Thus:

$$E(T - 2, \mathbf{X}) = F(\mathbf{X}) \sum_{i=0}^{2} \left[\frac{s(\mathbf{X})}{1 + r}\right]^i.$$

By induction it can be shown that:

$$E(k, \mathbf{X}) = F(\mathbf{X}) \sum_{i=0}^{T-k} \left[\frac{s(\mathbf{X})}{1 + r}\right]^i.$$

At the present, i.e., $k = 0$, the limit of $E(k, \mathbf{X})$ as T goes to infinity is

$$L(\mathbf{X}) = \lim_{T \to \infty} E(0, \mathbf{X}) = F(\mathbf{X}) \sum_{i=0}^{\infty} \left[\frac{s(\mathbf{X})}{1 + r}\right]^i.$$
$$= F(\mathbf{X}) \left[\frac{1 + r}{1 + r - s(\mathbf{X})}\right].$$

The final step is to find the vector of prices for priority queues that maximizes $L(\mathbf{X})$ subject to the condition that the prices meet the feasibility rules defined in the previous sections. This vector is calculated by estimating the fee paid by each type i, x^i, given any vector $\mathbf{X} = (x_1, \ldots, x_n)$.

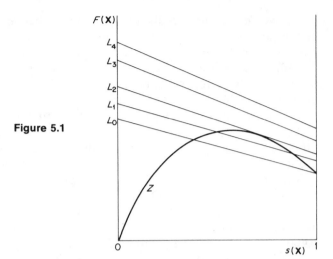

Figure 5.1

equal zero when $s(\mathbf{X}) = 0$ since the crime is certain to be reported. Similarly, at $s(\mathbf{X}) = 1$, $F(\mathbf{X})$ will be positive if each type of individual, i, has a threshold level of net benefit, $\bar{\Pi}_i$, above which $v^i(\mathbf{X}) = 0$. At this point, the official can set bribes so that $\Pi_i^* > \bar{\Pi}_i$ for all i, and a corrupt regime can be maintained with no risk that bribers will report their crime. For intermediate levels of $s(\mathbf{X})$, the maximum $F(\mathbf{X})$ will be positive, but $F(\mathbf{X})$ need not be a convex differentiable function of $s(\mathbf{X})$. Clearly L_k must be maximized somewhere along this function.[34] In the example, the lower the discount rate, the higher is the equilibrium level of $s(\mathbf{X})$ and the lower is $\mathbf{X}$. The more present oriented are officials, the higher the bribe–prices they will seek from applicants.[35]

---

[34] The possibilities can be narrowed further by noting that at the maximum feasible L_k, either $s(\mathbf{X}) = 1$ or $F(\mathbf{X})$ must be constant or falling when $s(\mathbf{X})$ increases. If $F(\mathbf{X})$ were rising, the official could unambiguously improve his position by moving to the feasible points providing higher levels of both $F(\mathbf{X})$ and $s(\mathbf{X})$. When $F(\mathbf{X})$ falls as $s(\mathbf{X})$ increases, this implies that $\Sigma_{i=1}^n f(i)x^i$ must be falling. A fall in this sum, which measures the return when no one reports the corruption, occurs either through changing the length of the line or setting prices closer to the lower feasible bounds given some length of line. Since Z need not be either convex or continuous, local maxima may exist, and Z may not have a derivative at the actual maximum, but, in principle, there is one preferred choice of $F(\mathbf{X})$ and $s(\mathbf{X})$ corresponding with some particular price vector, $\mathbf{X}$. Ceteris paribus, a corner solution at $s(\mathbf{X}) = 1$ is more likely the higher is r, i.e., the steeper are the L_k.

[35] Another way to view the variation in corruption propensities across officials would be to consider variations in risk aversion or in the costs of being discovered. Risk preferers will charge higher bribe–prices than risk averters, and those with little to lose from being discovered (e.g., officials earning salaries below their opportunity income) will also risk setting higher prices.

Clearly, once one admits the possibility that applicants themselves may report the crime, the efficiency of bribery is further compromised. Not only are the resources spent on law enforcement a clear waste, but the official's decision will depend, in part, on the applicant's willingness to "rat," a characteristic of demanders that is irrelevant to the establishment of an efficient set of prices and priority queues. There might, however, be a distributional gain over the model of corruption presented in Section 3. Because of the heightened risk of exposure, a corrupt official may charge lower prices for all priorities. Instead of maximizing profits, subject to the free entry constraint as in Section 3, the official is constrained by the possibility that *any* applicant may report the official. Hence applicants may obtain a higher proportion of the program's benefits than they would under a simpler sanctioning system and will also generally obtain more benefits than they would when an official can behave like a legal monopolist. Of course, officials' legal salaries might adjust in response to changes in corrupt receipts (Barzel, 1974). This would not change the conclusions about the benefits obtained by applicants but would imply that as bribe payments fell, budgetary costs would rise (see Chapter 4).

5. CONCLUSIONS

While the use of prices as an adjunct to a queuing system can undermine a program's distributional goals, the efficiency of prices is often assumed to be beyond dispute. In choosing to reject a pricing system, one is assumed to be demonstrating a willingness to favor equity over efficiency. This argument has been expanded to include bribes which are assumed to promote efficiency in spite of their illegality. My analysis, however, permits a critical assessment of such simple appeals to the market paradigm. First, as we shall see again in subsequent chapters, the illegality of bribery distorts the allocation system. Officials take actions to reduce the risk of arrest which have no justification in efficiency terms.[36] Second, payoffs designed to make officials work faster may either increase or decrease the overall efficiency of officials. Third, legalizing bribery or failing to enforce the corruption statute may not have favorable efficiency consequences. If officials cannot price discriminate perfectly between applicants but must instead sell various

[36] For a related discussion of the inefficiency of illegal transactions see Bhagwati (1974) on smuggling and Kreuger (1974).

priorities of service at fixed prices to all comers, then they may make inefficient choices. Perfect price discrimination, however, implies that officials obtain all of the program's benefits for themselves. It is thus an unappealing strategy on distributional grounds, so long as one has any concern at all for the nominal beneficiaries.

Finally, the role of even legal prices in producing efficient outcomes depends upon the institutional setting. It is a mistake to imagine that the policy options available are *either* prices *or* administrative orders. Instead, prices may only be useful if they can be *combined* with an institutional change such as a shift from a single queue to a system of priority queues. Thus, bribes paid to obtain a favored place in a single line may fail the efficiency test on all four counts. While they might still be better than an honest single queue, they should not be confused with the efficient prices of economic theory. Bribery in a system of priority queues may be more efficient, but even if legal and administrative sanctions do not distort a bureaucrat's decision, a monopoly official may not make efficient choices. Furthermore, when expected sanctions do influence behavior, a complex priority queuing system may produce only limited efficiency gains.

APPENDIX

This appendix demonstrates that a corrupt official may provide a higher level of service than a "surplus maximizer." The analysis builds on the case in the text where the decision maker can choose between a system with no "balking" and one where type ones refuse to queue. The corrupt official cannot set $x = 0$ and set the other prices equal to those chosen by a legal monopolist. For if this were done, customers of type $n - 1$ would choose queue n. Instead, all prices must be lowered so that type k chooses queue k for all k when the lowest priority is free. In fact, all prices must be reduced by a constant amount equal to, x_n, the price chosen for queue n by the legal monopolist.

If no balking occurs, the corrupt official can obtain, $G_1 < W_1 < S_1$, where:

$$G_1 = W_1 - \sum_{i=1}^{n} \lambda_i x_n$$

$$G_1 = W_1 - R + c_1\left(t_1 + \frac{1}{\mu}\right) + \sum_{i=1}^{n-1} (t_{i+1} - t_i).$$

Similarly, if prices are set to exclude type ones, profits are G_2, where:

$$G_2 = W_2 - (1 - \lambda_1)\left[R - c_2\left(T_1 + \frac{1}{\mu} \right) - \sum_{i=1}^{n-2} c_{i+1}(T_{i+1} - T_i) \right].$$

To compare the behavior of the surplus maximizer and the corrupt official, examine:

$$S_1 - G_1 \underset{<}{\overset{>}{=}} S_2 - G_2.$$

Substituting for S_i and G_i and collecting terms, yields:

$$\lambda_1 R + (1 - \lambda_1)\frac{c_2}{\mu} + \sum_{k=3}^{n-1} \lambda_k \sum_{i=3}^{k} (t_i - T_{i-1})(c_{i-1} - c_i)$$

$$- (1 - \lambda_n) \sum_{i=3}^{n} (t_i - T_{i-1})(c_{i-1} - c_i) - \frac{c_1}{\mu} \tag{i}$$

$$- \lambda_1(c_1 - c_2)t_2 - \lambda_1 c_2 T_1 - c_n(t_n - T_{n-1}) \underset{<}{\overset{>}{=}} 0.$$

The first three terms of (i) are positive, and the remaining terms are negative. The sign of the inequality cannot be determined without specific information about λ_i, c_i, R, and μ. The basic ambiguity can be easily seen in a simple case with only two types of applicants, a Poisson queuing process, and $1 = \lambda_1 + \lambda_2 < \mu$. In this situation, officials will never set the bribe for the first priority line high enough to exclude type ones since then they would be unable to collect any bribes. Hence the surplus maximizer would make a choice different from the corrupt official when total benefits are maximized by excluding type ones, i.e. when

$$\lambda_2 R - \frac{c_2}{\mu - \lambda_2} > (\lambda_1 + \lambda_2) R - c_2\lambda_2 t_2 - \lambda_1 c_1 t_1,$$

where $1/(\mu - \lambda_2)$ is the average time in the system for type twos when ones are excluded and t_j is the expected time in the system if applicants of type j join line j for all j.

6

MONOPOLISTIC BUREAUCRACY

1. INTRODUCTION

But there is more to government administration than simply waiting in line. While an analysis of this common bureaucratic phenomenon has made it clear that bribery cannot be mechanically equated with efficiency, it can serve only as an introduction to the corrupt incentives that may confront government officials.

First, in focusing upon the problem of managing a first-come–first-served queue, Chapter 5 assumed away the problem of selecting those applicants who best fulfill governmental objectives. This question, however, raises an important new area for corrupt dealings. Superiors may issue vague directives about government objectives that give a good deal of discretion to low-level officials. Bureaucrats who seek corrupt gains can then sell their discretionary power in the illegal market.

Second, while I have already modeled some of the ways in which sanctioning policy can affect corrupt behavior, a more comprehensive analysis is required. Thus far, I have assumed that a bureaucrat confronts a "passive" sanctioning system which acts only if a dissatisfied customer complains; moreover, the only sanction imposed on corrupt officials was discharge from their lucrative positions. A more active enforcement policy, however, is not only possible but often desirable as well. Hence, there is a need for a more general analysis of sanctioning that will permit discussion of a wide variety of penalty strategies.

Third, I have thus far ignored the importance of private market structure in affecting the incidence of corruption. While this was acceptable when the only issue was managing a queue, market structure will be of critical importance in determining whether low-level officials can sell their discretionary power without a high risk of detection.

This chapter, in short, presents a more wide-ranging analysis of the interaction between governmental objectives, criminal sanctions, and market structure in generating corrupt incentives. To accomplish this goal, however, I will assume away the problems of queuing theory raised in the last chapter. Rather than servicing a flow of applicants, a bureaucrat's task is, instead, to select a single applicant who "best" fulfills the government's needs. This assumption, of course, often fits the facts quite well. Thus, a contracting official may have the task of signing a contract with the supplier who provides the best product at the most advantageous price, or a bureaucrat may have the job of allocating a franchise to provide some public service—water, electricity, or cable television. For simplicity, however, I shall speak of the official as a purchasing agent contracting for inputs. Although the analysis has broader applications than this, there are also many cases where it inadequately describes the activities of the bureaucracy. While later chapters begin the task of broadening and enriching our view of administrative processes, much more work is required before the task can be completed.

Having sketched the basic differences between the two chapters, I should emphasize a critical feature they have in common. Just as in Chapter 5, I assume that each low-level official has monopoly power. While firms and individuals may have other options in the private sector, they cannot turn to another official if the first turns them down or demands a high bribe. In some situations the grant of an official monopoly follows almost inevitably from the nature of the bureaucratic task. Thus, it seems reasonable to assume that each low-level contracting official in a public agency will be given sole responsibility for a particular group of purchases. If, for example, the government gave two low-level officials the right to accept offers to fill its annual paper-clip contract, it would run the risk of getting twice the number of paper clips needed.[1] Similarly, development rights to a particular parcel of land or

---

[1] A striking example of what can happen when contracting authority is not effectively centralized occurred in Nigeria. Several officials sought contracts for cement from companies throughout the world, apparently accepting large bribes in return for signing

permission to operate a cable television system or a water supply company in a defined geographical area cannot be given to more than one applicant.[2]

In many other cases, however, the efficiency case for giving officials monopoly power is much more problematic and is supported by little more than conventional bureaucratic wisdom. Chapters 7 and 8 will examine this common bias in favor of monopoly. I will argue that a competitive bureaucratic structure—where clients are free to deal with any number of officials—may be a powerful deterrent to corrupt practices. It makes sense, though, first to analyze the role of sanctions in traditional monopolistic bureaucracies before considering the potential of structural reform.

2. A SUMMARY OF THE RESULTS

The basic results can be stated quite simply and are presented without technical detail in this section. Readers without an interest in mathematical models may omit the technical discussion in Section 3 and concentrate instead on the summary argument below.[3]

A. Competition and No Vagueness

In one very simple case, legal sanctions are irrelevant. Suppose that the government knows exactly what product it wants and finds a large

---

contracts. The result was that the Nigerian government ordered five times more cement than it needed (*New York Times,* December 4, 1975). The newspaper article includes a photograph of Lagos harbor jammed with cement-carrying boats waiting to be unloaded.

[2] Corruption in the granting of government contracts and in the issuance of franchises and development rights is well documented. For a recitation of state and local government cases see Amick (1976), Gardiner and Lyman (1978), and Pinto-Duschinsky (1976). Recent cases of the bribery of foreign government officials in return for contracts are summarized in Jacoby, Nehemkis, and Eells (1977). Of course, some of these decisions are made, not by individual bureaucrats, but by collective decision-making bodies like city councils or zoning boards. Since these political bodies are often quite small and lack any complex organizational structure, the individualistic model presented in Chapters 2 and 3 is likely to describe the situation facing a developer or potential contractor. Since it is unnecessary to repeat our earlier discussion of legislative corruption here, the text concentrates on the case where a single official has authority to approve a contract or award a monopoly franchise.

[3] These results were first published in Rose-Ackerman (1975) and are reprinted with the permission of the North-Holland Publishing Company.

number of sellers willing to supply it. If a private market for the good exists, and if there are no cost advantages in selling large quantities to a single purchaser like the government, the state will simply purchase the good at the private market price.[4] Corruption can be avoided since a sale made at a price above the competitive level can be easily detected. Furthermore, under a regime of perfect competition, sellers[5] have no incentive to bribe the government simply to obtain the contract since each firm can sell all it wishes privately. If no private market exists, bribes can be eliminated by using sealed bids to choose the contractor with the bids made public after the low bidder has been determined.[6]

In only slightly more complex and realistic competitive situations, however, constraints other than those imposed by the market will help determine the outcome. For example, the government might confront an imperfectly competitive market structure where many sellers compete to fill the government's demands but where each offers a somewhat different product.

To begin the analysis, it is necessary to specify the rules under which low-level government officials operate. Imagine, then, that a high level policymaker defines the state's preference function over the available alternatives. Assume that the policymaker discharges this task perfectly and specifies the relative prices that must prevail if the government is to

[4] Gardiner and Olson (1974:279) also make this point. If selling in large lots to the government is cheaper than selling the product privately, bribery might still occur as sellers compete for the limited but more profitable government business. This case is similar to the product differentiation case discussed later.

[5] This chapter assumes that there is no distinction between the seller's gains and losses and the gains and losses of the firm's representative. A fuller treatment would, however, include the agency relationship between the firm and its representatives. Clearly the seller is free to organize itself in ways that makes bribery more or less attractive to its agents (see Chapter 10).

[6] Corrupt officials, however, have sometimes been able to extract bribes in spite of formal bidding requirements. If only a few contractors are willing to pay bribes, purchasing officials may refuse to permit other firms to pass prequalification standards, may throw out the low bid of an honest contractor on a technicality, or may simply falsify records to indicate that a contract was awarded competitively when, in fact, it was not. Amick (1976) provides examples of all these practices, drawing mostly on New Jersey cases.

Even if a sealed bidding procedure does eliminate bribery, it leaves the way open for collusion if the number of suppliers is relatively small. Since sellers have no private market to fall back on if they lose the government contract, since price is the only means of choosing between products, and since each contract may represent a large share of the firm's business, sellers will have a high incentive to collude both to fix prices and to divide the market. See Herling (1962) and Smith (1963) for case studies of price fixing in the sale of electrical equipment to large purchasers.

be indifferent between the competing products. Once this task has been discharged, the job of negotiating a contract is delegated to a lower level bureaucrat whose purchasing decision will later be reviewed by the policymaker. If firms have perfect knowledge of the state's preference function, one would expect suppliers to offer a spectrum of price and quality packages which all appear equally desirable to the government. If one producer clearly dominated the others at the initial offering prices, the other sellers could be expected to lower prices or raise quality to bring themselves into line with the dominant seller if this can be done without causing losses.

Once the sellers have made their price–quality offerings equivalent to one another, the contracting official can satisfy the policymaker by making a deal with any of the competitors. Thus, firms may attempt to win the contract through bribery. The contracting official, in turn, is assumed to organize the bribery market by truthfully informing each corrupt firm of the size of the bribe offers received.

Given this framework, it is possible to develop a model determining the conditions under which bribes will occur and the manner in which their level will be set. The official's net gain from accepting a bribe is the value of the bribe minus the official's expected penalty and the moral costs of engaging in an illegal action. The level of moral costs and the way in which they depend upon the size of the bribe will be a function both of the individual's preferences and of the public agency's attitude toward corruption. Since a bribe will not necessarily be discovered, the expected penalty can be determined by multiplying the average penalty levied upon conviction by the joint probability of arrest and conviction.[7] The penalty may be a fine, a jail term, or simply the loss of a high-paying job with its associated fringe benefits.[8] If fixed costs are not high enough to deter all corruption, then the way in which moral costs[9] and expected penalties depend upon the level of the official's bribery receipts will determine the maximum bribe acceptable.

On the other side of the corrupt transaction, the gain to a successfully corrupt firm is simply the net increase in profits that bribery makes

---

[7] In emphasizing expected penalties I assume that both bribers and bribees are risk neutral.

[8] Compare Chapter 5, Section 3, where I followed Becker and Stigler (1974) and assumed that the possibility of losing one's job is the only major deterrent to corruption.

[9] Officials with high scruples may be offered especially high bribes on the theory that one's scruples do not increase in proportion to the money one is offered. Thus in 1974, when the mayor of Fort Lee, New Jersey turned down $200,000 to support a zoning change, he was offered first $400,000 and then $500,000. He turned down each offer (Amick, 1976:89).

possible minus expected penalties and moral costs.[10] For a firm, the main penalty may be lost business both inside and outside the government. The legal penalties levied on firms are often low, however, because of the common prosecutorial practice of granting immunity for incriminating testimony. Since there are very rarely any witnesses to a bribe, prosecutors are almost invariably forced to grant someone immunity, and the official is usually considered the more prestigious conviction.[11]

When the official is corrupt, the successful firm will be determined by the maximum bribe each firm will pay[12] and the maximum bribe the official will accept. On the one hand, the officials' expected penalties might increase rapidly as the level of bribes increased. They would then refuse to accept bribes that exceeded a threshold amount.[13] If several firms were willing to pay the maximum bribe, corruption can not solve

---

[10] The expected gains must be discounted by the possibility that officials will not perform their side of the illegal contract. Therefore, corruption is more likely if an official provides an immediate and tangible benefit to the bribe payer. When the expected penalties for corruption are high, bribers will only accept a delayed response if ties of mutual trust are strong, if they are willing to use extralegal threats of violence, or if they can threaten to destroy the reputation of the corrupt official.

[11] For example, 31 federal meat inspectors were charged with accepting bribes from meatpackers and processors in the New York area, but no company officials were charged (*New York Times,* June 3, 1977). Similarly, New York City prosecuted corrupt construction inspectors while ignoring the firms paying the bribes (*New York Times,* June 27, 1972). An exception is reported in the *Philadelphia Inquirer* (January 18, 1974). Two accountants were charged with bribing an Internal Revenue Service official for a favorable tax ruling. No charges were filed against the official, who had recently retired.

[12] In a recent Indonesia example, an executive of a company which turned down a bribe demand of $40 million indicated that the company's reason was not a principled opposition to all payoffs but simply a belief that the bribe was too high. The executive asserted that if the bribe request had been reduced to the "usual" agent's fee of $3 million to $4 million, then the company might have gone along (*New York Times,* January 25, 1977).

[13] For example, Gardiner (1970) reports the testimony of Police Chief Phillips of Wincanton (Reading, Pa.). Phillips testified that "'I told Irv [Stern, the underworld boss of Wincanton] that Walasek [the mayor] wanted $12 on each [parking] meter instead of the $6 we got on the other meter deal. He became furious. He said, 'Walasek is going to fool around and wind up in jail. You wait and see. I'll tell Walasek what he's going to buy' [p. 26].''

Caro's (1974, 719) biography of Robert Moses reports a similar aversion to high payoffs on the part of Carmine DeSapio, head of Tammany Hall in the 1950's. Moses offered DeSapio a large insurance commission in return for his influence with New York City. DeSapio refused the offer on the ground that he was not prepared to exert the required influence. Instead only a part of Moses' insurance business was given to a company associated with DeSapio.

an official's decision-making problem. The official would still have to determine which of the competing firms should receive the contract.

On the other hand, the penalty function might have high fixed costs for the official, but costs might be little affected by the dollar value of the bribe. Thus, small bribes would be unacceptable, but once the threshold was reached, the official would seek out the firm with the highest willingness to pay. If the expected penalty does not vary between firms, all firms willing to pay bribes must be earning excess profits. The successful firm will then be the one with the largest gap between revenue and the sum of production and moral costs at its maximum willingness to pay. If production costs and moral costs are treated in a parallel fashion, the size of the maximum bribe a firm is willing to pay can fall, either because production costs rise or because a management reshuffle elevates more scrupulous executives.

B. Competition and Vagueness

The first model assumed that agency heads had specified their willingness to tradeoff various price–quality combinations so clearly that corruption could be used only to determine a low-level official's choice over fungible alternatives. Consequently, corruption had no efficiency consequences. It was simply a transfer from a firm with excess profits to a contracting official. Corruption of this kind, however, implies that even honest contracting procedures are likely to be inefficient. Since high-level officials have no independent information about the cost functions of contractors, they will unwittingly approve purchases which permit sellers to earn excess profits. I must, however, also examine the corrupt incentives created by another type of high-level failure. In addition to having little independent cost data, agency heads may also be very unclear about what they want their agents to purchase.[14] The second model takes this into account by assuming that a low-level official who accepts a bribe in return for a high purchase price or a reduction in quality does not face certain detection but simply increases the probability that both briber and bribee will be punished. Firms may then be willing to bribe, even if they earn zero excess profits in the

---

[14] In fact, in many cases of local government corruption there are no high-level officials who set purchasing requirements. While states may try to impose general standards of contracting activity on local governments, states cannot tell local officials what they need to buy. Therefore, if local government officials know which contractors are willing to make payoffs, they may be able to rig the contract specification to favor a particular firm. See Amick (1976:35).

absence of corruption, so long as the higher profits they receive by paying a bribe overcome the additional moral and arrest costs.[15]

Corruption in this model is controlled not only by the probability of detection but also by the penalties imposed upon those found guilty of bribery. The best way to deter corruption through expected sanctions (i.e., the probability of conviction times the penalty) is to tie them to the size of the gain obtained by each of the participants in the illegal deal. Thus firms' expected penalties should be tied to their *profits*[16] and the officials', to their bribery receipts. Furthermore, *marginal* expected penalties should be set so that a dollar of corrupt gains is associated with more than a dollar of expected costs. Unfortunately, however, these basic principles are not followed systematically in existing American law. So far as corrupt government officials are concerned, statutes permit, but do not require, the judge to impose a fine which is a function of the size of the bribe.[17] Since there are no reliable data on actual fining practices, however, one cannot know how often judges actually follow

---

[15] Although I refer to firms in the text, the analysis also applies to individuals seeking state employment in governments without a strong civil service system. Individuals may be willing to kickback part of their salaries if their best private sector alternatives pay less than the state. So long as job descriptions are vague and monitoring lax, the poorer one's private sector alternatives, the more one will be willing to pay to obtain a government job. Andreski (1968) reports that in Africa competition for jobs "sometimes takes the form of a kind of auction in which the prize goes to the highest bidder while the rest forfeit their bids [p. 355]." In Brooklyn, a former law clerk charged that he and others obtained court positions through payoffs to the Democratic party (*New York Times*, March 26, 1974). In Indiana, according to McNeill (1966), state employees routinely kickback 2% of their salaries to the party in control.

[16] Clark (1977) makes a similar point in discussing corporate illegal behavior in general.

[17] 18 U.S.C. 201, 1962, provides that the penalty for accepting a bribe shall be a fine of "not more than $20,000 or three times the monetary equivalent of the thing of value, whichever is greater, or imprisonment for not more than fifteen years, or both." Furthermore, 18 U.S.C. 3612, 1949, provides that if the bribe itself can be recovered, it shall be deposited in the registry of the court. Therefore, the bribee could be penalized an amount equal to four times the bribe. The judge, however, is not required to tie the fine to the size of the bribe, and the second part of the penalty, the jail term, is not tied by statute to the size of the bribe. Furthermore, there is another statute, 18 U.S.C. 203, 1962, that provides that a bribee "shall be fined not more than $10,000 or imprisoned for not more than two years or both." This statute contains no provision for tying the fine to the size of the bribe, although it does not, of course, explicitly prevent it. In addition, many bribery cases are actually tried as tax evasion cases, and different penalties may apply for tax violations. For example, Amick (1976:80) documents the case of a Chicago alderman indicted for evading taxes on $50,000 he received from two developers. Similarly, officials of the meatcutters union and supermarket executives were charged with tax evasion for failing to report bribes and kickbacks on their income tax forms (*New York Times*, March 26, 1974).

this practice. While it seems plausible to hypothesize that penalties actually imposed increase with the size of the bribe, *expected* penalties might fall if the probability of detection and conviction falls as the amount paid increases. Furthermore, it would be surprising if *marginal* penalties acted as a potent deterrent over the entire penalty function.

So far as the corrupt firm is concerned, penalty policy seems even less satisfactory. While the statutes permit the government to deprive the firm of any of the excess profits it earns from the corrupt transaction, this provision cannot itself deter bribery since the corrupt firm can never do worse than break even.[18] Even if the firm is also subject to a penalty that is a function of the size of the *bribe* it pays,[19] this strategy will not be as effective as a penalty tied to the *profits* the firm has gained through its corrupt dealings.

Indeed, given prevailing penalty functions, it is easy to construct cases where the criminal law will not impose any significant constraint on corruption. Suppose, for example, that the expected penalty facing the firm increases with the size of the bribe paid but is always outweighed by the more favorable price–quality combinations which higher bribes make possible. Assume, in addition, that the official's expected penalty increases by less than a dollar for every dollar of extra bribe accepted. This combination of penalty functions, then, imposes no constraint on corruption. This is not to say, of course, that bribes will actually be unbounded, but merely that legal penalties and bureaucratic controls will not be a sufficient deterrent. Instead, the inability of the firm to raise capital or the legislature's refusal to appropriate money may be the ultimate constraints on the size of kickbacks.

Of course, the effectiveness of the criminal law depends not only upon the penalty levied upon conviction but also on the probability of detection and conviction. Nevertheless, unless the sanctions actually imposed are administered with deterrence in mind, there is little assurance that even a substantial enforcement effort will make much difference.[20]

---

[18] 18 U.S.C. 218, 1962. Of course, if jail terms are imposed or extralegal costs are important, the deterrent effects would be greater. Some state laws provide for penalties which depend upon the size of the briber's gain, however. In a New York meat sales scandal, for example, the district attorney unsuccessfully sought to impose the maximum sentence of "twice the illegal gain" on a convicted briber (*New York Times*, October 8, 1974). Expected losses from resulting civil suits might also affect the structure of the penalty function.

[19] The penalties in 18 U.S.C. 201 and 203, 1962 also apply to the giver of a bribe.

[20] Thus a properly designed fine schedule could prevent corruption so long as the probability of arrest and conviction does not fall as the severity of punishment increases. However, while there is little direct evidence on the subject, an inverse relationship

Whenever expected penalties do not completely deter bribery, the firm which offers the official the highest net gain, but not necessarily the highest bribe, wins the contract.[21] The conditions which favor success are high efficiency, few moral scruples, and political influence that makes heavy punishment less likely. Furthermore, some firms may be "punished" by future customers more severely than others if their corruption is uncovered. If the firm is solely engaged in selling goods or services to the government, a conviction may lead to blacklisting by government agencies.[22] In contrast, a firm with a mixed public and private business can turn its energies to the private sector. In a perfectly competitive private market, all products are homogeneous and sold at a constant price; hence the identity of the seller is irrelevant. If, however, products are sold by brand name or if private sales depend upon a reputation for honesty, a conviction could seriously hurt nongovernment business as well. Finally, the quality of the firm's products has an ambiguous impact on the level of the bribe paid. On the one hand, the higher the quality, the lower the risk of detection at a given contract price. This factor implies that high-quality firms will pay higher bribes than low-quality firms. On the other hand, if private-sector buyers can evaluate quality better than high-level bureaucrats, then low-quality

---

between legal penalties and the probability of conviction does not seem implausible. If conviction implies a high penalty, then mistakes are costly and greater certainty may be required to produce a conviction. Therefore, increases in legal penalties might be counterproductive. They could lower the probability of conviction so much that *expected* penalties might actually fall.

[21] The model of competitive bribery discussed here may be particularly applicable to the international arms market. American arms makers often compete with French and British manufacturers "who have no compunction to agreeing to excessive fees," according to a Pentagon document (*New Haven Register,* May 16, 1975). The Indonesian example cited above also apparently fits this case. In 1973, General Telephone and Electronics and Hughes Aircraft were competing to sell Indonesia equipment to construct a satellite communications system. General Telephone and Electronics refused to meet a $40-million bribe demand for one sale, and the contract was awarded to Hughes. Hughes has denied that it made payoffs, but other sources directly involved in the negotiations claim that payoffs totaled at least 20% of the purchase price on all contracts obtained by Hughes (*New York Times,* January 25, 1977).

In the local government examples in Amick (1976), however, the "cost" of corruption appeared to be remarkably standardized—10% of the value of the contract was the usual kickback, and there is seldom evidence of explicit competition through bribery. Honest firms occasionally challenged the grant of a contract to a corrupt firm, but corrupt firms seldom competed openly. Instead, informal market sharing arrangements such as that used in awarding engineering contracts in Maryland (Amick, 1976:43) are apparently not uncommon.

[22] Kriesberg (1976:1108).

producers may be especially attracted to government business and may be willing to pay more than their high-quality competitors.[23] Thus, when purchasing orders are "vague," corruption will increase governmental costs and will not necessarily favor efficient, high-quality producers.

C. Bilateral Monopoly

When a government agent faces a single monopolist, bribery will be unnecessary if the firm can simply make a single take-it-or-leave-it offer. The government obtains the good or service at a price far above marginal cost, without any illegal influence being exercised.[24] In fact, however, the government will often also have considerable bargaining power in a bilateral monopoly situation. It may, for example, be able to wait until the monopolist, eager to keep his capital stock occupied, makes a better offer. Once the potential for bargaining is introduced, corrupt incentives enter, since the agent charged with negotiating the government's terms has no responsibility for raising the money to pay the contractor. Thus, I analyze bilateral monopoly in terms of a bargaining model where firm and official move closer together as time passes.[25] While this is only one of several possible ways to view the bargaining process, it does concentrate upon the critical role of time. The analysis suggests that bribes are likely to be attractive to the firm when it finds waiting costly while the government official does not,

[23] I am grateful to Gregory Neugebauer for stressing this point in private correspondence. Officials may be induced to buy very shoddy products if the bribes are high enough. "One country bought used aircraft that were plagued with maintenance problems so bad that only two or three of them were able to fly at any time. Another desert country dealing with the same agent, bought European-style vehicles that overheated and stalled in the hot summer months [*New Haven Register,* May 10, 1975]." From a different era, a congressional investigation in the late nineteenth century revealed that Cornelius Vanderbilt sold rotten ships to the government during the Civil War (Deakin, 1966:66).

[24] See, for example, the discussion in the *New York Times* (October 11, 1973) of kickbacks paid by engineering firms in return for contracts from the state of Maryland. The article reports that "a few companies developed in time a size, expertise, and stature that insulated them to some extent from this system [of corruption]. One or two developed an expertise, for example, in large bridge design, that other local companies could not match. One or two grew so large and had been awarded so many contracts that the state could not do without their services unless out-of-state consultants were employed. In these ways, a few companies in effect graduated in time from the system to a position of less vulnerability, and they could afford to resist, and perhaps in some instances refuse to participate."

[25] Cf. Schmidt (1969), who emphasizes the importance of bilateral negotiations in a wide range of corrupt situations.

either because the project is not of urgent importance or because the government has some legal tool that, if used, can effectively hold down costs. For example, when the government announces that a particular area will be subject to urban renewal at a specified future time, honest government officials will never buy sites offered for sale at prices higher than the discounted present value of the prices expected to emerge from condemnation proceedings. Their concession rates are low while landowners will have high concession rates since their properties are likely to have little use as income-earning investments. Thus, there is a strong incentive for landowners to pay bribes to induce government officials to agree quickly to prices favorable to owners. Incentives for corruption are increased by the difficulty with which third parties can assess the price a court would have awarded the landowner in a condemnation proceeding.

In the formal analysis, I work through a model where firms offer bribes to passive officials as a way of inducing them to speed up the rate at which they concede to the firms' wishes. In order to compare corrupt with honest outcomes, however, I must also examine the possibility that the corrupt official takes a more active role and adopts a rigid uncompromising position in the expectation that this will induce the firm to offer payoffs.[26] If the official refuses to bargain unless paid off, the firm may eventually agree to terms close to those which would result from an honest negotiation. In that case, the corrupt official essentially gives the firm a worse initial bargaining position than an honest bureaucrat. When corrupt officials take a less active role and do not let the hope of payoffs determine their initial positions, bribery undercuts the government's bargaining power, and contracts may be made at terms less favorable to the government. Thus, if it is difficult to motivate honest government officials to be hard bargainers, extortionists may be less destructive of government interests than officials who passively take bribes. In both cases, however, contracts will include considerable slack, although extortionists will generally obtain a higher proportion of the excess profits than will less active officials.[27]

---

[26] Descriptions of local government corruption in bilateral monopoly situations frequently see the official as the initiator of the corrupt deal (e.g., Amick, 1976).

[27] Local officials in New Jersey have created bilateral monopoly situations by waiting to demand payoffs until after a contract is awarded (Amick, 1976:32–34; 60). An official then demands payment as a condition for releasing a check due to the contractor. The contractor can sue to obtain payment, but since going to court will introduce an additional delay, the contractor may decide to pay off instead. The bribe payment often cannot be added onto the value of the contract, and thus it simply reduces the contractor's profits.

3. FORMAL MODELS

A. Competition and No Vagueness

In the first formal model the government has specified its needs clearly, and therefore the firms competing for a government contract cannot influence the quantity sold or the selling price of their product through bribery. Corrupt payments come entirely out of a firm's profits and can only be used to determine which firm obtains the contract, not the terms of the sale. Only the firm that obtains the contract makes a payoff. Expressing all of the relevant variables in dollar terms:[28]

$$G(X^i) = X^i - J(X^i) - R(X^i), \tag{1}$$

where

G = gain to the official if seller i obtains the contract;

X^i = total bribe paid by seller i;

$J(X^i)$ = expected penalty to official; $J_x \geq 0$

$R(X^i)$ = moral cost in dollar terms to official, $R_x \geq 0$.

The statements, $J_x \geq 0$ and $R_x \geq 0$, mean that both penalty and moral costs are either constant or increasing as X^i increases.

The net gain to any successfully corrupt firm is simply its afterbribe profits. These profits are the firm's revenues minus its production costs minus the bribe paid minus the moral and penalty costs of bribery. I assume that the firm's opportunities elsewhere in the economy are such that it is willing to pay bribes up to the point where profits equal zero. Production costs are defined in economic terms to include a return to entrepreneurship. Hence when economic profits equal zero, the firm is

---

No systematic evidence exists on the question of how kickback costs are divided between the government treasury and the contractor's profits. Amick (1976) cites cases in which the payoff is simply added onto the bill submitted to the government. In other cases, contractors complain about the loss in profits that a kickback entails. See the *Wall Street Journal* (July 19, 1972) where a contractor complained that kickbacks reduced his return on investment from 10 to 2%.

[28] The formal model is similar in general form to Becker's (1968) analysis of crime. If penalties include jail terms, then both moral costs and penalties ought to be expressed as losses of utility, not dollars. The formal condition permitting the use of dollars in the equations is a constant marginal utility of money for the individual involved, so that the rate at which utility is translated into dollars is not affected by wealth. If officials and sellers are not risk neutral, the expected values could be translated into certainty equivalents.

earning a competitive rate of return and continues to operate. Assuming that the quantity demanded by the government is fixed, with only the price subject to corrupt influence:

$$\pi_i(X^i) = P^i q - T^i - X^i - D^i(X^i) - N^i(X^i), \qquad (2)$$

where

π_i = profit of seller i,

P^i = price per unit of seller i's product,

q = quantity demanded by government (assumed given),

T^i = total cost of producing q units for seller i,

$D^i(X^i)$ = expected penalty to seller, $D_x \geq 0$,

$N^i(X^i)$ = moral cost in dollar terms to seller i, $N_x \geq 0$.

The set of bribes acceptable to the official includes all those where the level of the bribe, X, is at least as great as the expected costs, i.e., such that $X \geq J(X) + R(X)$. Four cases are considered here: (1) No bribes are acceptable; (2) All bribes are acceptable; [29] (3) All bribes less than some maximum will be acceptable, but anything larger will fail because marginal moral costs or marginal expected penalties or both increase as X increases; (4) Bribes greater than or equal to some minimum bribe will be acceptable because, for example, expected costs do not rise as fast as bribery receipts. [30]

Consider, first, Case (4), where any bribe greater than some X_{min} is acceptable. If several firms are willing to bribe and each firm's selling price, P^i, and product characteristics are fixed, each supplier has a feasible set of bribes that it will pay rather than lose the contract. This set includes all X^i where net returns are greater than or equal to zero, i.e.:

$$X^i \leq P^i q - T^i - D^i(X^i) - N^i(X^i). \qquad (3)$$

Thus, in order for any bribe to be feasible, it is necessary for $P^i q - T^i > 0$. This means that unless every firm in the market is corrupt the potentially corrupt firm must be earning excess profits either because it is more efficient than the marginal firm[31] or because barriers to entry

---

[29] For example, because $J_x + R_x < 1$, $J(0) + R(0) = 0$, where $J(0)$ and $R(0)$ are the fixed costs of accepting a bribe.

[30] That is, $J_{xx} + R_{xx} \leq 0$ and $J(0) + R(0) \geq 0$.

[31] This is the case mentioned by Leff (1964) in discussing, not contracting, but the allocation of investment licenses.

generate monopoly profits for all firms. For every seller, i, we can now find the maximum feasible bribe: X_0^i, where equality holds in (3). If $\max_i[X_0^i] = X_0^m \geqq X_{\min}$, then firm m will get the contract. Firm m may not, however, actually have to pay X_0^m. Instead, a bidding process can be expected to occur, with the actual bribe paid falling between X_0^m and X_0^{m-1}.

Since Cases (1) and (2) are trivial, consider, finally, the operation of the bribery market when Case (3) holds. The case might prevail, for instance, if larger bribes are easier to detect than smaller bribes or if the penalty levied upon conviction is an increasing function of X. The payoff, $\bar{X}$, that maximizes the official's gain, occurs where the marginal gain from accepting a slightly higher bribe just equals the marginal penalty cost plus the marginal moral cost, i.e., $1 = J_x + R_x$. If several suppliers are willing to offer bribes at least as great as $\bar{X}$, then corruption will not solve the official's decision-making problem. He still must determine which of the competing corrupt firms should receive the contract.

B. Competition and Vagueness

THE BASIC MODEL

Since Section 3, Part A assumed the existence of a well-defined government preference function, a contracting official induced by a bribe to accept a price–quality combination ranked lower than that offered by another seller was certain to be punished.[32] I now assume that government preferences are "vague" so that increases in P^i or reductions in quality only increase the probability that corruption will be discovered. While firms produce goods with varying quality levels, Y^i, the model does not permit them to change Y^i. This simplification does not limit the analysis substantially—allowing price to vary for a given quality is essentially identical to allowing quality to vary at a given price.[33] Thus expected penalties to both seller and official depend on

---

[32] Even with well-defined preferences, officials might escape punishment if their superior concludes that they are incompetent rather than corrupt and reprimands them or gives them further training.

[33] Dealing with quality changes is more complicated than dealing with price changes because of the difficulty of specifying the units of measurement and the fact that the production function for quality, $T^i(Y^i)$, can vary between firms. Nevertheless, since the basic conclusions reached in this section appear to carry over to the case where both P^i and Y^i are permitted to vary, this more complex case will not be treated separately.

price and quality as well as the size of the bribe. In symbols:

$$J = J(P^i, Y^i, X^i), J_p \geqq 0, J_y \leqq 0, J_x \geqq 0, J(0, Y^i, X^i) = 0, \quad (4)$$

$$D^i = D^i(P^i, Y^i, X^i), D_p \geqq 0, D_y \leqq 0, D_x \geqq 0, D^i(0, Y^i, X^i) = 0. \quad (5)$$

Assuming that each firm, i, has a different fixed quality level, Y^i, and that each can vary its price P^i, then for any firm, i, the feasible set of bribes includes those for which total profits are greater than or equal to zero,

$$0 \leqq P^i q - T^i - X^i - D^i(P^i, Y^i, X^i) - N^i(X^i). \quad (6)$$

Letting the function, $X_0{}^i(P^i)$, represent the price–bribe combinations that yield zero profits for each firm, the shaded area and the function $X_0{}^i(P^i)$ in Figure 6.1 represent one possible form for a firm's feasible set of bribes and selling prices. For all bribe and price combinations in the shaded area or on the line $X_0{}^i(P^i)$, the firm earns a nonnegative return.

Up to the present point, I have simply specified the bribes that a given firm is willing to pay in return for particular levels of P. I must now consider how corrupt officials will behave if they wish to maximize their net gain, G. In this model:

$$G^i = X^i - J(P^i, Y^i, X^i) - R(X^i). \quad (7)$$

If firm i were the only firm in the market, then an official's gain would be maximized at G_{max}^i, where the difference between $X_0{}^i(P^i)$ and costs, $J + R$, is at a maximum. If many firms, each operating independently, are competing for the government business, then the official can try to choose the firm where G_{max}^i is the greatest, G_{max}.

If there is no time limit on reaching a final bargain, firm i does not need to know G_{max}^i in order to bribe an official. It can instead

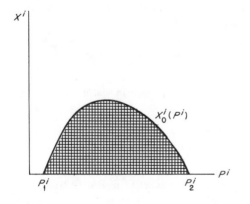

Figure 6.1

experiment with various price–bribe combinations provided it receives information on the preferred price–bribe–quality offers made by other firms. Eventually, this trial and error process can be expected to produce the gain-maximizing offer. If, alternatively, firms are operating within a time constraint, their ignorance of the official's preferences could prevent the attainment of G_{max}.

Since the special concern of this chapter is the relationship between legal penalties and deterrence, I begin the analysis by specifying two plausible penalty functions for the firm and two for the official. I then demonstrate that, under these partial equilibrium assumptions, it is sometimes possible for a firm to be willing to tender an infinite bribe and for an official to prefer this outcome to all others. Having isolated the cases in which a finite bribe will be offered and accepted, I then consider the characteristics of firms that will make them likely to be the successful briber.

Two Penalty Functions for the Firm

In this section, I shall show that when the firm's penalty depends on the size of the bribe (Case 1), the sanctions may be ineffective in reducing or preventing bribery, even when the probability of arrest is close to 1. Alternatively, if the firm's penalty upon conviction depends upon the revenue it earns (Case 2), a determinate finite solution always exists which may, of course, occur at $X^i = 0$. More formally stated, I will consider firm behavior, if, on the one hand, the expected penalty is concave and increasing in P^i, i.e., $D_p \geqq 0$, $D_{pp} < 0$ (Case 1) or, on the other hand, the firm's penalty is convex and increasing in P^i (Case 2). Case 1 is consistent with a sanctioning strategy under which the penalty upon conviction is solely a function of the size of the bribe paid and the probability of conviction levels off gradually as the firm's revenues increase. Case 2 describes a situation in which the penalty imposed is an increasing function of the revenues earned by the firm, with the penalty increasing faster than the revenues, and where the probability of arrest and conviction is independent of the firm's revenue.

Case 1: To assess the impact of the first penalty function, it is necessary to specify the way in which the firm's maximum bribe changes as P^i changes. Assuming that moral costs are constant at $\bar{N}$, and differentiating X_0^i with respect to P^i, omitting the superscript i and the subscript 0, yields:

$$\frac{dX}{dP} = \frac{q - D_p}{1 + D_x}. \tag{8}$$

Equation (8) reaches an extremum at $q = D_p$. However, when $q = D_p$, the second derivative of (8) is positive if $D_{pp} < o$.[34] This implies that in Case 1 the maximum feasible bribe as a function of P reaches a minimum when $q = D_p$ and rises thereafter. In addition, the maximum X acceptable to the firm might go to infinity as P goes to infinity if d^2X/dP^2 is positive for all P greater than some P.[35] If the official will also accept infinite bribes, there will be no finite solution to the problem of finding the X^i that maximizes G^i. From a general equilibrium perspective, of course, this solution cannot occur since society's resources are finite. Instead, this case can be understood as one in which the legal sanctions themselves do not determine the solution.

Case 2: When the firm's marginal expected penalty rises as P^i (or revenue) rises, $D_{pp} > 0$, then the function X_0^i reaches a finite maximum. Assuming that $D(X^i, P^i) = 0$ when $P^i = 0$ and that X_0^i is positive for some P^* and negative for some $P^{**} > P^*$, then the maximum bribe at $q = D_p$ is positive and the function $X_0^i(P^i)$ is a single-peaked function like the one illustrated in Figure 6.1.

Two Penalty Functions for the Official and the Equilibrium Bribe

In framing penalty functions for the official I shall attempt to isolate those situations under which the level of bribes is unbounded and compare them with others in which the official's gain is maximized for a finite bribe. The important cases are, first, those where the marginal penalty with respect to X is less than 1 ($J_x < 1$) even for very high prices (Case A) and second, those where $J_x \geqq 1$ for all P greater than some $\hat{P}$ (Case B). In both cases, assume $J = 0$ for $P = 0$, $J_p \geqq 0$, and $J_{pp} \leqq 0$. Case A can occur when legal penalties for convicted officials are independent of the size of the bribe paid while the probability of arrest depends only upon the price at which the contract is negotiated. Case B is consistent with a legal regime that levies penalties upon conviction that are at least equal to the bribes received. Since it seems most

---

[34] The second derivative of (8) is

$$\frac{d^2X}{dP^2} = \frac{-D_{pp}(1 + D_x) - (q - D_p)D_{xp}}{(1 + D_x)^2}.$$

Since $q = D_p$ at the extremum, $d^2X/dP^2 > 0$ if $D_{pp} < 0$.

[35] To see this, notice that beyond the minimum, $dX/dP > 0$, and in addition, $d^2X/dP^2 \geqq 0$ as $-D_{pp}(1 + D_x) \leqq (q - D_p)D_{xp}$. Since we would expect D_{xp} to be positive, both sides of the inequality are positive, and d^2X/dP^2 can be $\geqq 0$.

realistic, I assume in both cases that the penalty upon conviction is independent of P—which implies that $J_p \to 0$ as $P \to \infty$ and the probability of conviction approaches 1.

Assuming constant moral costs, $\bar{R}$, and differentiating (7) with respect to P, yields:

$$\frac{dG}{dP} = \frac{dX}{dP}(1 - J_x) - J_p. \tag{9}$$

When Case 2 holds, $X_0{}^i$ reaches a finite maximum for firm i, and G must also be maximized for some finite P and X since the firm will never wish to offer infinite bribes in return for infinite prices. The form of J_x is irrelevant, and G^i is maximized where the slope of $X_0{}^i$ equals the slope of $J + R$ (See Figure 6.2). However, when Case 1 holds, the form of J_x become crucial. If Case A holds, gross marginal return from agreeing to a higher price dX/dP will be greater than the marginal cost of accepting the bribe $[J_x(dX/dP) + J_p]$ beyond some P, if $J_p \to 0$ as $P \to \infty$ (Figure 6.3a).[36] Hence infinite prices will be preferred by both firm and official, and if $d^2X/dP^2 > 0$, infinite bribes will be desired as well. When case B holds, as P increases, $dG/dP < 0$ beyond some P since $J_p \to 0$ and $J_x \gtreqqless 1$ as $P \to \infty$. Neither infinite prices nor infinite bribes will ever be acceptable to the official, whatever the sign of d^2X/dP^2 (Figure 6.3b).

If expected penalties are not so high as to deter bribery completely, the firm that wins the contract is the one for which $G^i_{\max}$ is the greatest.

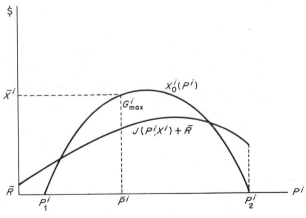

Figure 6.2

[36] If the penalty upon conviction did depend upon P so that J_p is greater than $(1 - J_x)(dX/dP)$, G will reach a finite maximum in this case as well.

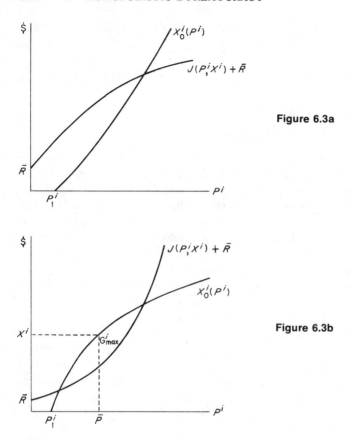

Figure 6.3a

Figure 6.3b

Of course, if "infinite" bribes were acceptable to both sides, the identity of the successful firm would depend upon other constraints—its ability to borrow, for example. Furthermore, even if legal and bureaucratic sanctions provided no check on corruption even the most passive legislature would ultimately impose budgetary constraints on an agency whose contracting behavior revealed a total lack of concern for costs.

The preceding analysis assumed a stable bribery market in which firms that lose a contract either do not learn of the bribe or fail to report the winning firm to law enforcement officials. While an honest firm obviously has an incentive to both search out and report corrupt transactions,[37] the problem is more complex for a firm that offers a bribe

---

[37] Firms who refuse payoff requests, however, often fail to report bribe solicitations to law enforcement authorities. See Amick (1976) for evidence of this in the New Jersey context.

that is refused. Despite the loss of an individual contract, it may be profitable to refrain from discovering and reporting the corrupt transaction, if the firm hopes to win future contracts by means of bribery. The incentive to remain silent is increased, moreover, by the fact that the criminal law imposes sanctions upon those who attempt to bribe officials, regardless of their success.

If, however, a losing contractor does credibly threaten to expose corrupt practices, it is in the winner's interest to propose a cartel in which contractors share in the bribes and the benefits. Taken to its extreme, the competitive case analyzed in this section could thus be reduced to the bilateral monopoly problem to which we now turn.[38]

C. Bilateral Monopoly

When only a single buyer and seller bargain without recourse to bribery, the range of indeterminacy in the price and quantity sold depends upon the ground rules under which the contract is negotiated. Under certain conditions, the quantity sold will not be in doubt but only the division of the surplus, that is, the price per unit. In particular, agreement on quantity can be expected when the participants see both price and quantity as negotiable.[39] In this context, the price per unit can vary between the minimum price the seller can receive and still cover costs and the maximum the government will pay rather than do without the good entirely. The efficacy of bribery depends upon the relative bargaining strength of the participants in the absence of payoffs. If sellers believe that they can appropriate most of the surplus "fairly" they are unlikely to engage in corruption. To analyze this point rigorously, however, it is necessary to develop a workable definition of bargaining strength for use in a formal model.

Cross (1969) provides a paradigm of the bargaining process which will serve as my point of departure. Cross's most important contribution is his explicit consideration of the passage of time in measuring "bargain-

---

[38] Evidence of collusion was uncovered among contractors bidding on the South Side Sewer in Newark. An engineering consultant "told selected listeners that his engineering company would have full control of the sewer job. [He] said he was assembling a group of contractors to work as a team, which would cut down the competition and make it possible to set a contract price high enough to include a $1 million payoff [Amick, 1976:63–64]."

[39] See, for example, Machlup and Taber (1960). The alternative case, in which buyer and seller both believe that only price is under their control, is discussed by Mansfield (1970:270–272).

ing strength.''[40] Suppose that the total surplus to be divided is M dollars and that the initial demands of the two participants are Z_1 and Z_2 dollars respectively.[41] If $Z_1 + Z_2 > M$, then one or both of the participants must modify their demands to achieve an allocation of M between them. Since each participant is free to choose any level of initial demand, the problem each faces is to set Z_i so as to maximize the present value of the return actually received. Letting player 1 represent the firm, I shall examine the firm's behavior under normal profit-maximizing assumptions. Assume that a delay of 1 period in reaching agreement costs the firm C_1 dollars and, of course, delays the receipt of any gains by 1 period. Player 1 expects to benefit from a delay because if this player waits an additional period, player 2, the government official, reduces his demands by r_2. The concession rate, r_2, is thus a measure of the government contracting official's bargaining strength: The lower is r_2, the stronger is the official's position. Given the official's initial demand Z_2, the time required until a demand of Z_1 can be satisfied is $w = (Z_1 + Z_2 - M)/r_2$. Assuming continuous discounting at rate a, the total present value of player 1's insistence on Z_1 is

$$U_1{}^* = Z_1 e^{-aw} - \int_0^w C_1 e^{-at}\, dt. \tag{10}$$

Equation (10) reaches a maximum with respect to Z_1, where[42]

$$\left[Z_1 + \frac{C_1}{a} \right] \frac{a}{r_2} = 1. \tag{11}$$

Equation (11) means that player 1's return is maximized when the extra waiting costs plus the cost of delaying the receipt of Z_1 by $1/r_2$ equals the benefit of 1 more dollar of return. If the second player does not concede at the expected rate, then player 1's demands will be modified over time. In Cross's work, players react to changes in each other's rates of concession but do not try to influence these concession rates directly. The possibility of corrupting one's opponent is not discussed,[43] but Cross's model can be extended to include this case by assuming that corruption can be used to raise the official's concession

[40] The discussion that follows is based on Cross (1969:42–64).
[41] Cross's initial analysis is in terms of utility, not dollars. See note 28 for a statement of the assumptions behind the use of dollar values.
[42] At this point $(U_1{}^*)'' = (-a/r_2)e^{-aw} < 0$.
[43] Cross (1969:120–180) does discuss other bargaining strategies such as the use of force, threats, promises, dirty tricks, and bluffs.

rate, r_2.[44] The government official is assumed here to be a passive recipient of the bribe. The concession rate is affected by the size of the bribe offered, but the official does not try either to hold out for a higher bribe than the seller offers, or to bribe the entrepreneur to raise his concession rate.

Assuming that the total cost to player 1 (the entrepreneur) associated with making a bribe of X is $g(X)$, the present value of the total return is[45]

$$V_1^*(X) = U_1^*(X) - g^*(X),$$ (12)

where the bribe is offered in the present but actually paid at the time of agreement so that $g^*(X) = g(X)e^{-aw}$. The firm is, of course, only interested in the net gain that bribery can bring over the maximum return when $X = 0$, or $\max[U_1^*(0), V_1^*(\bar{X})]$, where $\bar{X}$ is the bribe that maximizes (12).

The optimal level of X to the firm can be found by first determining the optimal level of Z_1 given any particular bribe, second, choosing the bribe, $\bar{X}$, that maximizes gain, V_1^*, and third, determining whether or not $V_1^*(\bar{X}) - U_1^*(0) > 0$. The first part of this decision problem is solved by maximizing V with respect to Z_1, given any fixed X. The maximum occurs at:

$$\frac{r_2(X)}{a} = Z_1(X) - g(X) + \frac{C_1}{a}.$$ (13)

Since (13) must hold for each X, the second part of the decision problem can be solved by substituting (13) into $V^*(X)$ and maximizing $V^*(X)$ with respect to X. This operation yields

$$g'(X) = w(X)r_2'(X),$$ (14)

which determines the gain maximizing bribe so long as the second derivative is negative.

Figure 6.4 illustrates a possible situation where a bribe of $\bar{X}$ dollars satisfies (14). I have assumed that $g'(X)$ falls as X increases, approaching B as a limit where $B \geq 1$. Assuming $g(X) = X + D(Z_1, X, Y) + N(X)$ (using the notation of Sections A and B), such a shape is consistent with the assumption that $D_x + N_x > 0$ and $D_{xx} + N_{xx} < 0$. In Figure 6.4,

---

[44] One might also think of bribery as being used to lower the initial demand, Z_2, made by the government. Since the end result would be the same, i.e., a higher return, Z_1, and a shorter bargaining time, w, this case will not be analyzed separately.

[45] $V_1^*(X)$ can be written as:

$$V_1^*(X) = [Z_1(X) - g(X)]e^{-aw(X)} + (C_1/a)e^{-aw(X)} - C_1/a.$$

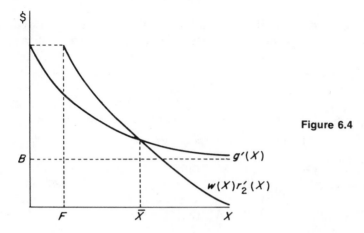

Figure 6.4

$w(X)r_2{}'(X)$ is zero for $X \leqq F$, where F equals the fixed costs of bribery to the government official.[46] Beyond F, $r_2(X)$ is assumed to rise, but at a steadily declining rate.[47] Since $w(X)$ also falls as the size of the bribe increases, the whole expression $w(X)r_2{}'(X)$ falls. Given these conditions, if $g'(F) < w(F)r_2{}'(F)$, (14) will hold for some positive $\bar{X}$.

Once $\bar{X}$ has been determined, the final task for the private contractor is to compare returns at $\bar{X}$ with returns at $X = 0$. While many of the factors that make bribery likely here are also those that determine the size of the successful bribe in the case of many sellers, one distinctive aspect of the problem must be considered separately. Since I have assumed that the total surplus to be divided is fixed at M, the level of return when $X = 0$ has an important relationship to the incremental benefit of bribery. If the contractor's bargaining costs and rate of time preference are high relative to the corresponding variables for the government official, bribes will, ceteris paribus, yield higher incremental gains that if C_1/C_2 and a_1/a_2 are low.

4. POLICY IMPLICATIONS

While corruption can be kept at a low level if purchasing agents contract for standardized products in competitive markets, less rigorous

---

[46] In the notation of Sections A and B, either moral costs are constant, $\bar{R}$, or J is independent of P^i.

[47] The less knowledge the government has about the return that it can expect in the absence of corruption, the less likely is an official's compensation or arrest to be tied closely to the size of the government's return, $M - Z_1$, and hence the more likely is an official to lower r_2 rapidly as X increases.

competitive pressures provide little check on corruption. So long as a government contract or "franchise" is more profitable than a firm's other private market alternatives, and so long as agency heads have no independent information about firms' production costs, firms can compete by offering bribes to the low-level official.

When this occurs, the analytical framework developed in this chapter permits a critical evaluation of the efficiency of corruption. In a simple case, where the selling price of each firm's output is fixed, corruption will not necessarily lead to the choice of the most efficient producer because moral and penalty costs are symmetric to production costs. A firm with high costs and low scruples may outbribe a more efficient and more scrupulous competitor. The basic difficulty is a fundamental lack of competition in the market for the government benefit, combined with poor cost data available to high-level policymakers. The extortion of bribes is simply a means by which low-level officials can take advantage of the monopoly profits they perceive.

In the more complex case, when preferences are vague and price is negotiable, corruption might raise the budgetary cost of a good purchased by a corrupt agent or increase the price which customers of a franchisee must pay. This is not necessarily so, however, if production costs vary widely among bribers while moral and penalty cost do not, and if honest officials are unable to identify low-cost producers. Nevertheless, it is a likely result of the added negotiating power of agents in this model. Furthermore, with negotiated prices, the tie between efficient production and high bribes is likely to be even more tenuous than in the simpler case.

There is an obvious parallel between this movement from clarity to vagueness and the discussion of legislative corruption in Chapters 2 and 3. With perfectly informed voters and active challengers, legislators were certain to be defeated if they changed their votes in return for payoffs. When voters know what they want and can monitor legislative votes, challengers can take advantage of actions by the incumbent that do not reflect majority preferences. Similarly, when top-level bureaucrats know what they want and the market system provides perfect information about marginal costs, corruption will once again be checked. Introducing uncertainty of various kinds implies that taking bribes will only increase the probability of defeat or the risk of being disciplined by superiors or the law. Thus, if voters have clear preferences for legislative outcomes, while both legislators and voters have poor information about the tastes of the entire electorate, then corruption can occur. The situation is similar to a case where agency heads have well-defined preferences over various price–quality combinations but no independent information on contractors' costs. Finally, when voters have poorly defined preferences and bureaucratic superiors issue vague guidelines, money payments, be they bribes or campaign contributions, can easily influence the choices of legislators or low-level officials. Political and bureaucratic decisions can be determined by payoffs because of the lack of any clear standards specifying correct behavior.

With bilateral monopoly, the efficiency of corruption depends upon the relative bargaining power of firm and government agent in an honest negotiation. The final result could be either an increase or a decrease in the costs borne by the public, depending upon whether bureaucrat or firm initiates the corruption. Once again there is a parallel here between the bureaucratic model and legislatures with strong political parties which face a single, well-organized interest group. In both cases, bilateral bargaining models can illuminate the corrupt situation. In the legislative case, the need to be reelected checks the greed of those politicians who are willing to accept payoffs; while in the bureaucratic context, bargaining is constrained by legal and administrative sanctions. In both cases, however, the final outcome depends upon the relationship between the initial offers of corrupt officials and the positions of similarly situated honest politicians and bureaucrats. Extortion demands initiated by government agents may be less costly for the general public than payoff offers initiated by special interests or monopoly firms. I have not, however, attempted a general treatment of bilateral monopoly. Instead, I concentrate on both the bureaucrat's and the firm's mutual interest in speed. In the formal analysis, bribery was initiated by the firm and produced rapid agreement at terms favorable to the private producer.

Since corruption in contracting and in the granting of one-of-a-kind benefits has little normative appeal, and since high standards of personal honesty may not prevail, bureaucratic sanctions and legal penalties will often be needed to increase the likelihood of honest activity. I have argued, however, that existing legal remedies are inadequate. Not only is the probability of being prosecuted low, but the penalties levied are often not tied to the gains of officials and firms. To act as an effective deterrent, a firm's expected penalties must be tied to its profits, while for officials, penalties must be a function of the size of the bribe received. Furthermore, marginal expected penalties must rise at least as fast as marginal expected gains or else only small bribes will be deterred.

The analysis also suggests the wisdom of considering basic changes in the relationship between government and the private sector. First, I have shown that when the government purchases a good also sold on the private market, the incentives for bribery are substantially less than those obtaining when government is the sole purchaser. Thus, when policymakers recognize that there can be hidden corruption costs involved in ordering goods especially for state use, the purchase of standard items sold on private markets will often be justified despite some quality loss. Since corruption costs can seldom be accurately assessed, however, the extent to which government purchasing policy should favor goods generally available in the private market must be left to good judgment informed by the factors previously discussed. Second, when goods must be ordered especially for government use, policies should be designed to reduce vagueness in purchasing instructions given to officials, thereby reducing the costs of effective surveillance and increasing the probability of detection of serious peculation. Unfortunately, neither of these strategies will prove feasible in every case—the private demand for spaceships is currently nonexistent, and research contracts are necessarily vague as to outputs. This leads to a third policy option: Instead of purchasing the ill-defined good from private enterprise, direct government production may be considered.[48] Under this strategy, the state firm will enter the market only to purchase standardized inputs, thereby minimizing the incentives for private businessmen to pay bribes out of their excess profits. Of course, corruption is not limited to transactions involving private individuals. If the managers of state-owned firms are compensated on the basis of the profitability of their enterprises, the incentives for bribery will be the same as those in private corporations. Just as bribes can be paid out of a private firm's excess profits, so may bribes be paid out of a public firm's budget allocation.[49] Even if the funds allocated to a publicly held firm cannot be translated into private profits unless officials are willing to embezzle as well as bribe, maintaining a high level of firm activity could well mean improved working conditions, increased power in shaping government policy, and promotions for the officials involved.[50]

[48] The argument for expanded government production of goods and services parallels the discussion of vertical integration in Williamson (1971).

[49] If bureaucrats' salaries, opportunities for promotion, and the like are related to their ability to fulfill legislated output goals, they may use agency budgets to bribe the agents of suppliers of specialized inputs to assure that supplies are received. This type of corruption is apparently common in the Soviet Union's state enterprises where the major problem for managers is obtaining raw materials and other inputs. A second related problem for Soviet managers is obtaining a production plan from the state that is easy to achieve. To accomplish both of these aims, enterprises may hire special agents adept at exerting influence on both suppliers and members of the state planning apparatus (Berliner, 1959; Smith, 1976).

[50] Downs (1967, Chapters 2, 8, and 9). Niskanen (1971; 1975).

7

COMPETITIVE BUREAUCRACY: CORRUPTION IN REGULATORY AND SOCIAL PROGRAMS

1. INTRODUCTION

The models of bureaucracy presented in the previous chapters have been limited by one powerful simplifying assumption. In all of the cases discussed so far, officials had monopoly power. Applicants were required to seek the government benefit from a single official and could not reapply to another bureaucrat if the first turned them down. While applicants might compete with one another to obtain a government benefit, officials did not compete among themselves. The agency might be very decentralized and fragmented, with numerous low-level officials, but each individual official was granted exclusive authority over a particular group of customers. This careful division of responsibility, while characteristic of a wide range of administrative procedures, is not a necessary feature of many bureaucratic allocation procedures. Especially when an agency is charged with dispensing a large number of licenses, subsidies, or in-kind transfers, there is no fundamental reason why bureaucrats cannot have overlapping jurisdictions. While permitting applicants to reapply may increase the budgetary costs of administering a program, these costs may be balanced by the reduction in corrupt incentives which competition makes possible. Interofficial competition thus opens a new line of inquiry that had no relevance in the cases already discussed. While in the preceding chapters it was only criminal penalties and moral compunctions that could prevent crime, here overlapping jurisdictions can generate a dynamic in which corruption is eliminated or reduced. Thus, if applicants have a chance of obtaining a bribe-free benefit from an honest official, they may be unwilling to pay corruptible officials enough to compensate them for the risks of illegal behavior. I can, then, isolate situations in which a reversed Gresham's Law applies—where the honesty of some officials breeds legality in others. Given my general concern with the way structures other than the criminal law affect the incidence of illegality, a model of decentralized competitive bureaucratic behavior seems particularly important.

I begin the analysis of interofficial competition in this chapter with a stylized bureaucratic procedure where applicants can approach any one of a large number of officials in an attempt to obtain a governmental benefit.[1] Assume that all the applicants are, in fact, legally qualified to receive the benefit and that the level of individual benefits is fixed exogenously. Bribes only determine access and do not affect the quality or quantity of service.

If the total supply of the bureaucratic good is outstripped by the demand at the legal price, bureaucratic discretion is necessary, with corruption being one of the ways officials may resolve their problem in nonmarket allocation.[2] I shall show, however, that even if many officials will accept bribes, corruption is hardly foreordained—while competition among applicants will create incentives for bribe offers, the refusal of a few officials to accept bribes may lead to the elimination of bribery throughout the entire decentralized system. The bribe-reducing potential

---

[1] The analysis in this chapter may be difficult for readers with no technical training. The main conclusions, however, are summarized in Section 5.

[2] Although seldom allocated by competitive officials, the programs which most closely approximate the model's other assumptions are closed-ended social welfare programs like public housing, where only a fixed number of units are available in any period. Even nominally open-ended programs fit this model reasonably well if the approval of an application takes time. In that case, however, officials might be able to increase their daily output of q by working faster (see Chapter 5).

Two good examples of corruption in the allocation of a fixed supply are the "sale" of import licenses in Ghana (LeVine, 1975:25) and of market stall permits in Africa (Andreski, 1970:348; McMullan, 1970:326; Wraith and Simkins, 1963:20). McMullan writes that "the allocation of market stalls by Local Government Councils in West Africa is a regular cause of scandals. The trouble is that these exceedingly valuable properties are usually let at rents greatly below what they are worth. The difference inevitably transforms itself into bribes. The simple device of charging as much rent as the traders would be prepared to pay does not, perhaps understandably, commend itself to the Councillors and officials [326]."

of competition between bureaucrats does not, however, carry over in a simple way to other more common types of regulatory and social programs. Thus, Chapter 8 looks at models of other public programs in an attempt to see how the nature of the bureaucracy's tasks determines the ease or difficulty of controlling corruption.

2. THE BASIC MODEL

Assume then that each official behaves very much like a private profit maximizer who is willing to accept a bribe if the expected costs, both criminal and moral, are lower than the bribe offered. During each time period, each bureaucrat is given a fixed supply of the good to distribute within a system analogous to a competitive market. "Buyers" (applicants) are also identical to private consumers in that they are numerous, unorganized, and free to seek or refuse the bureau's services. There are no externalities in consumption between beneficiaries. An individual "customer" is indifferent to the consumption of others except insofar as it raises the bribe–price of service.[3] The service is homogeneous, perfect information is available about both service quality and bribe–prices, and the risk of detection is independent of which applicant deals with which official. The number of bureaucrats and their legal earnings are fixed by legislative fiat.[4]

Like the purchasing agent in the preceding chapter, the jth bureaucrat is assumed to be risk-neutral and to maximize expected income, G^j. Both the probability of detection and the punishment if caught may depend upon the number of corrupt transactions, n_j, and the total volume of bribes collected, x_j. Thus the official maximizes:[5]

$$G^j = x_j + J^j(n_j, x_j), \qquad j = 1, \ldots, N, \tag{1}$$

where

$$J^j(n_j, x_j) = \text{expected penalty to } j\text{th official},$$
$$N = \text{number of officials}.$$

[3] Just as in a competitive market the number of customers is so numerous that no one individual has any discernible impact on the bribe–price.

[4] While this restriction on entry would be a major simplifying assumption in an analysis of the free market, it seems realistic here. The number of officials does not automatically expand as a result of an increase in the number of job applicants, and civil-service salaries are often set on a governmentwide basis using the legal characteristics of jobs to determine pay scales.

[5] To simplify the discussion, I have omitted the moral cost term used in Chapter 6.

The function J is completely general and may or may not include the loss of a job or a requirement to pay back x_j.

The model of applicant behavior is also very simple. I shall assume that no one ever demands more than one unit of the good or service provided by the agency. Thus for applicant i:

$$q_i = 1 \quad \text{if} \quad p \le p_i,$$
$$q_i = 0 \quad \text{if} \quad p > p_i, \quad i = 1, \ldots,$$

(2)

where q_i is the quantity demanded by i, p_i is i's reservation price, and p is the agency's price.

Having described the objectives of both bureaucrats and consumers, I can specify the conditions under which corruption may affect the process of distribution. Low-level bureaucrats are each assigned $\bar{q}_j$, where $Q_s = \Sigma_{j=1}^{N} \bar{q}_j$, to distribute and are told to charge p_s per unit. If the quantity demanded at p_s exceeds the supply, Q_s, the market clearing price exceeds p_s, and the possibility for corrupt deals arises. An individual applicant with reservation price p_i may not, however, be willing to pay $p_i - p_s$ in bribes, because of moral scruples or the possibility of arrest and punishment. Thus, the expected cost to i of a bribe of x^i dollars is $x_i + D^i(x^i)$, where D^i is the expected penalty expressed in dollars, $dD/dx \ge 0$. Applicants are assumed to be risk-neutral and capable of estimating D.[6] In short, under a corrupt allocation system:

$$q_i = 1 \quad \text{if} \quad p_s + x^i + D^i(x^i) \le p_i,$$
$$q_i = 0 \quad \text{if} \quad p_s + x^i + D^i(x^i) > p_i.$$

(3)

The ranking of applicants in terms of x^i may differ from their ranking in terms of p_i. Individuals with high reservation prices may only be willing to pay small bribes if they have a high expectation of being caught or if the costs associated with arrest and conviction are high. Thus, the illegality of the pricing systems can have important distributional consequences. The level of individual gains generated by the program is not the sole determinant of willingness to bribe. Instead a corrupt system also favors those with low scruples and low expected costs and risks of arrest.

3. SUPPLY AND DEMAND FUNCTIONS

Before analyzing the corrupt marketplace, the way in which the decisions of individual bureaucrats and applicants can be aggregated to

---

[6] Once again I omit any explicit consideration of moral costs.

determine the supply of and demand for illegal activity at each bribe–price must be considered. Of primary importance is the link between the penalty functions, J^j and D^i, and the number of bureaucrats and applicants willing to engage in corrupt deals. To simplify the discussion, assume that each bureaucrat has only a single unit of q to dispense, that $p_s = 0$, and that even if the J and D functions deter some buyers and sellers from paying or accepting bribes, enough corrupt agents remain to prevent them from cartelizing to set bribe–prices. Thus $x^j = x^i = x$ for all i and j, i.e., a single bribe–price prevails in equilibrium.

$$G^j = x + J^j(x), \qquad j = 1, \ldots, N, \tag{4a}$$

and

$$q_i = 1 \quad \text{if} \quad x + D^i(x) \le p_i,$$
$$q_i = 0 \quad \text{if} \quad x + D^i(x) > p_i, \qquad i = 1, \ldots. \tag{4b}$$

Depending upon the form of the J^j, some bureaucrats may choose not to accept bribes for some x. When this is so, two cases must be considered. In the first case, bureaucrats with $x + J^j(x) < 0$, simply throw away their units of q. While this, of course, may seem unrealistic when the bureaucrats are distributing a tangible good, it is more plausible where officials are charged with the task of granting exemptions or issuing licenses to engage in a regulated activity. Here, once bureaucrats have decided that bribery is too costly, they may well find it easiest to do nothing.[7] In the second model, I shall ignore the problem posed by lazy bureaucrats and assume that officials who do not accept bribes assign their unit of q to an individual i on the basis of some nonmarket criterion. Thus some customers who have $x + D^i(x) < p_i$ may not actually need to pay x in return for the service, and others with $x + D^i(x) > p_i$ may obtain it free.

To examine the relationship between a corrupt marketplace and one where the sale of q at the market clearing price is legal, I must specify the penalty functions for bureaucrats and individuals, J^j and D^i. The demand side is simple to model. If there are no moral or legal penalties, i.e., if $D^i = 0$ for all i, the quantity demanded for each level of x, Q, is identical to the quantity demanded at that level of p, Q_D. As x falls, Q increases. If the penalty function, D^i, has both a fixed and a variable component (not necessarily equal for all i) then fewer units of Q are demanded at each x, $Q < Q_D$. The demand curve (R_1) shifts down and changes shape although, of course, the slope will always remain negative (i.e., as x falls, Q increases).

[7] This model is analogous to the lazy official case discussed in Chapter 5.

The supply side is more difficult to characterize. The shape of the officials' penalty functions, $J^j(x)$, will determine whether or not total corrupt supply increases as the bribe–price, x, increases. Moreover, under some conditions, the supply function may take a rather complicated form. For instance, the penalty for accepting a bribe may rise so rapidly with x that the corrupt supply is "backbending"—it increases to some maximum and then falls as x increases. One should, then, build the model carefully—first considering the decision-making calculus of the individual official before moving to the entire bureaucracy's supply of corrupt services.

Two simple cases can be quickly disposed of. An official whose moral costs are zero will accept any bribe offer if the expected penalty is zero, i.e., $J^j(x) = 0$, for all j, x; or if fixed costs, $J^j(0)$, are zero, and penalty costs rise less rapidly than bribes, $dJ^j/dx < 1$. In contrast, under other conditions even an entirely unscrupulous official will never accept a bribe. In particular, if penalty costs rise at least as rapidly as bribes, $dJ^j/dx \geq 1$, for all j and x, then no bribes will ever be taken.

The more complicated cases, of course, are those in which the officials are willing to accept bribes only if x falls within certain ranges. Under some conditions, they may refuse small bribes while accepting large ones. A penalty function which produces this last result is one where fixed costs are positive, $J^j(0) = \bar{z}$ for all j, but where costs rise less rapidly than bribes, $dJ^j/dx < 1$. Bribes less than some breakeven $\bar{x}$ where $J(\bar{x}) = \bar{x}$, $\bar{x}$ will not be taken, and any bribe greater than $\bar{x}$ will be acceptable (see Figure 7.1a which illustrates the more general case discussed in note 8).[8] For example, suppose that the officials' expectations of being caught are one-third whatever size bribes they take and that the penalty is dismissal plus a fine equal to the bribe collected. If the financial loss from dismissal is \$6000, then officials will accept no bribes less than \$3000, where $\bar{x} = \frac{1}{3} (6000 + \bar{x})$.

In contrast, there does exist a penalty strategy which will deter large bribes without preventing all smaller ones. If the second derivative is positive, $d^2J^j/dx^2 > 0$, the marginal increase in the expected penalty increases with x, and there may be some range $\hat{x}_j < x < \hat{\hat{x}}_j$ where $x > J(x)$ (see Figure 7.1b). All bribes in this range will be acceptable, while larger or smaller bribes will be turned down.[9] When this is the case, a bribers' expected returns are maximized for some $\bar{x}$ where $dJ/dx = 1$.

---

[8] Whenever the penalty function increases at a decreasing rate (i.e., if the second derivative is negative), only small bribes will be deterred. Even if the penalty more than keeps up with x for small x, $dJ^j/dx > 1$, the rate of increase eventually falls so that $dJ^j/dx < 1$ for large x.

[9] If $x = J$, the official refuses the bribe.

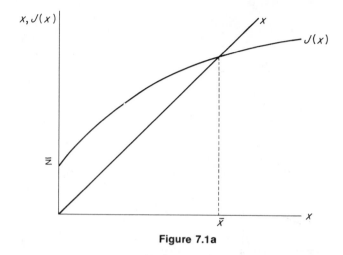

Figure 7.1a

To complicate the problem further, bureaucrats will typically differ in their evaluation of the expected costs of accepting a bribe. One may take this fact into account without undue technical complexity by assuming that while bureaucrats differ in their evaluation of the costs of accepting a bribe of a given size, the general shape of all $J^j(x)$ functions is represented by one of the illustrations in Figure 7.1. This assumption is realistic so long as the general shape of the penalty function is not determined by subjective fears entirely unrelated to the objective behavior of sanctioning authorities. If this is so and if the number of officials is large, there are no switching points where a completely

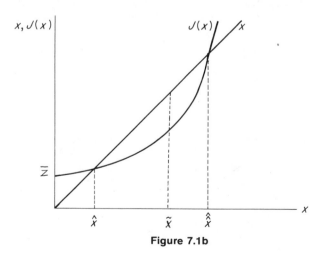

Figure 7.1b

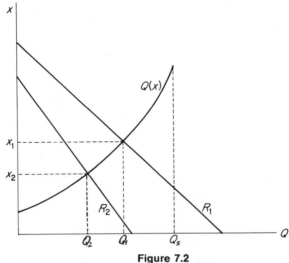

Figure 7.2

honest system suddenly transforms itself into a completely corrupt one. In cases where the family of $J^j(x)$ curves resemble the one depicted in Figure 7.1a, then, beyond some minimum x, the total corrupt supply increases as x increases. Since this supply relation, depicted in Figure 7.2, is analogous to that of standard price theory, I call this the *standard* case. By calling this case standard, however, I do not mean to imply that it is empirically the more common one. Instead Figure 7.1b may hold, and the supply curve may resemble the backbending curve familiar to labor economists and illustrated in Figure 7.3. In this case $Q(x)$, the quantity supplied corruptly as a function of x, reaches a

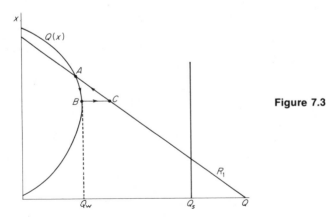

Figure 7.3

maximum for some Q_w which may be less than the total available. In the increasing portion of $Q(x)$, fixed costs are becoming less and less important. Eventually, however, the increase in the marginal expected penalty dominates the increase in the bribe for all bureaucrats, and $Q(x)$ falls back to zero.

4. THE CORRUPT MARKET

In examining the behavior of the corrupt market, the cases where every official is corrupt or where no one is corrupt can be dealt with quickly. If everyone is corrupt, then x will be determined by the intersection of the level of output mandated by the legislature, Q_s, and demand.[10] If the curve representing the corrupt supply of goods is discontinuous at some x, then the equilibrium quantity supplied corruptly, Q, equals either zero or Q_s, depending upon whether the market-clearing price is above or below the discontinuity. An increase or a decrease in Q_s can eliminate corruption entirely. The more realistic situations, where bureaucrats have different penalty functions, require more extensive analysis.

A. The Standard Case

Consider first the case where each bureaucrat's $J^j(x)$ resembles Figure 7.1a. This means that the supply curve of corruptly supplied output is nondecreasing in x. Now suppose that this supply curve intersects the demand curve, R_1, at some interior point where $0 < Q_1 < Q_s$. To determine whether or not this intersection (illustrated by x_1 in Figure 7.2) is an equilibrium, one must know how suppliers behave who are unwilling to accept x_1. If these $Q_s - Q_1$ suppliers provide no services at all,[11] the corrupt market will then clear at x_1. If, however, all units of service must be dispensed either honestly or dishonestly, then x_1 will be an equilibrium only if honest suppliers allocate all of their q to those with $x_1 + D^i(x_1) > p_i$ who are unwilling to pay a bribe of x_1. If, as will often be the case, some of those who receive the service would have been willing to pay x_1, then clearly the initial intersection is not an

[10] This case is similar to a black market where government officials appropriate the difference between the legally established price and the black market price. Schmidt (1969) stresses the close analogies between corruption and black market transactions.

[11] For example, exemptions from a regulation may not be permitted without payment of a bribe.

equilibrium. Assume a nonatonement adjustment process where all of those supplied without bribes are given their unit of q. Then the demand curve facing the corrupt firms falls to R_2, in Figure 7.2, which excludes the customers supplied honestly, x falls to some x_2, and more suppliers give up corruption for honest allocation procedures. These new honest suppliers may then allocate their units of q to some demanders who were not previously supplied by honest bureaucrats and who would otherwise have been willing to pay x_2. If this occurs, the corrupt demand for q falls still further. Thus the end result is either the elimination of corruption, $Q = 0$, or an internal equilibrium at some Q where a marginal increase in the ranks of the honest bureaucrats has no impact on the demand for corruptly supplied services.[12]

B. Corruption and Random Selection

To be more definite about the relationship between decentralization and corruption, it will be necessary to specify the principles under which honest bureaucrats allocate the scarce benefit under their control. Fortunately, a good deal of progress is possible without undertaking a concrete analysis of every conceivable allocation formula that honest bureaucrats may employ. For one can identify a broad class of allocation criteria that can be treated in a common analytic framework. Under these criteria, applicants are assigned the good on the basis of attributes that are not correlated with their willingness to pay bribes. While the existence of such a correlation is, of course, an empirical matter, there are many cases that may well approximate this pattern. For example, there is no reason to think that a system of assigning units in public housing that favors veterans or old people will be systematically related to the applicant's willingness to bribe. In all such cases, we may for present purposes simply treat the honest bureaucratic process as if it chose beneficiaries randomly.[13]

Suppose that the bureaucratic allocation procedure operates sequentially. I begin by assuming that some level of bribe–prices, x, prevails with its associated corrupt supply, $Q(x)$, and then find the probability, $\theta(x)$, that this x will support an equilibrium. Under this regime, the

[12] The corrupt marketplace in this case is analogous to the market for "lemons" described by Akerlof (1970). In Akerlof, low quality products may drive out high quality products until no market exists. In the case in the text, honest bureaucrats can drive out dishonest ones until the corrupt segment of the market is eliminated.

[13] In order for bribery to persist the agency head must be unable to identify corrupt transactions with certainty. This means that corrupt bureaucrats must convince superiors that they too have assigned benefits randomly.

probability that an equilibrium will be established for any $x, Q(x)$ combination with a mix of honest and dishonest bureaucrats will often be quite small, but will be positively related to the excess demand at the legal price. (See the appendix to this chapter.) If, in fact, no equilibrium is generated at the initial level of x, then consider what happens in the next round. If, in the first round, honest officials have chosen a few applicants willing to pay bribes, the possibility of an equilibrium being established in the next iteration may fall. In particular, I show in the appendix that θ falls as x and $Q(x)$ fall for $Q^* < Q(x) \leq Q_s$ but rises as Q falls for $0 \leq Q(x) < Q^*$ where $Q^* = \frac{1}{2} Q_s$. This relationship depends upon $Q(x)$'s dual role. On the one hand, a low $Q(x)$ implies that a great many units must be distributed without bribes. Thus the chance that at least one unit is honestly assigned to a potential briber is increased, and this decreases the probability, θ, that x is an equilibrium bribe. On the other hand, a low $Q(x)$ raises θ because it implies that the set of those willing to bribe is small and therefore easy to miss in a system of random assignment. For any given initial x, the probability that equilibrium will be established only when bribes have fallen to zero is, of course, not $[1 - \theta(x)]$ but is instead a much smaller fraction that depends upon the whole path of subsequent xs and $Q(x)$s. However, it remains possible for a system with a large number of bureaucrats and applicants willing to engage in corrupt transactions to be completely honest if the allocation practices of those who do not accept bribes serve to destabilize the corrupt market place.

C. Backbending Supply

When $Q(x)$ has both an increasing and a decreasing portion, the results can be quite different. If the only intersection of $Q(x)$ and R_1 is in the increasing portion of $Q(x)$, the previous analysis applies: An equilibrium at $Q(x) \neq 0$ is possible but not certain. Suppose, however, that there is a single intersection and that it occurs at a point where $Q'(x)$ is negative (see point A in Figure 7.3). Whatever honest suppliers choose to do, this point cannot be a stable equilibrium. Since some *suppliers* prefer lower xs to higher xs, they will offer to serve customers for less, thus pulling down the market-clearing price and increasing the corrupt supply. The increase in supply will be, in general, less than the corresponding increase in demand.[14] Hence consumers will bid up the bribe–price. Instead of being pleased by their higher bribery receipts, however, some

---

[14] By chance the increase in total supply could equal the increase in demand if honest suppliers exactly filled the gap between demand and corrupt supply.

suppliers will lower their prices. The result will be a continual cycle of varying xs (see Figure 7.3), unless suppliers refuse to accept the higher bribe offers and simply ration the corrupt output.[15]

5. CONCLUSIONS

I have, then, demonstrated the importance of distinguishing between discretion and monopoly power in discussing the corrupt incentives generated by bureaucratic tasks. The officials in this chapter's competitive model have discretion, since they can provide the service to anyone they wish. They do not, however, have monopoly power.[16] Competition between officials thus keeps the level of individual payments relatively low and may eliminate bribery entirely.[17]

In order for the incidence as well as the volume of corruption to fall, however, legal and administrative sanctions must operate effectively. Nevertheless, competition can push bribes to zero even if the sanctioning strategy only deters small bribes. If competition for payoffs lowers the level of prevailing bribe–prices, then some officials may drop out of a corrupt system because bribery returns are too low. Their honesty may push the market-clearing bribe–price still lower, inducing other officials to give up corruption. A sanctioning strategy which deters only small bribes, while ineffective in the monopolistic case, can now, when combined with interofficial competition, prevent the routinization of corrupt payments. To consider a simple case, imagine that a number of competitive bureaucrats are each given a fixed number of units of public housing to allocate to worthy applicants. Imagine further that the penalty function has the standard form, which deters only small bribes. In this case, the presence of honest officials will, in general, lower the

---

[15] The supply and demand curves need not intersect. The demanders' willingness to pay may be so high that excess demand always prevails or so low that no one pays any bribes. Furthermore, multiple intersections are possible.

[16] Hence in this case it is impossible to justify the common prosecutorial practice of granting immunity to bribers and directing law enforcement activity against officials. In the "competitive" cases analyzed here, neither briber nor bribee is more guilty than the other. It is impossible to view the official as the initiator and the applicant as the victim.

[17] Examples of petty monopoly power are found in Heidenheimer (1970), Palmier (1975), and Scott (1972). In many of these situations low-level corruption could be eliminated or substantially reduced by permitting low-level officials to compete. Of course, the cost of this reform might outweigh its benefits. If a small volume of government business is transacted in an outlying community, it might be very costly to use more than one official.

corrupt returns to others who insist on payment. The benefits of illegality may then be so low that acceptance of the risks of detection is not worthwhile and no one will take bribes.

Even under a different penalty function, which deters only high bribes, $(J'' > 0)$, corruption may also fail to become a stable routinized feature of bureaucratic allocation. The amount supplied corruptly and its bribe–price might constantly oscillate. This oscillation may itself deter corruption by making it difficult for bribers and bribees to predict the terms of a corrupt deal. While a preference for stability among applicants and officials was not part of the above analysis, when it is included corruption may destroy itself in this case as well.

The analysis suggests that a competitive bureaucracy may be an important reform tool. Indeed, if distribution costs were zero, a single honest official offering to serve all customers would destroy a corrupt system. Since there are always administrative costs, however, this solution is unrealistic. Officials who stand ready to serve all who apply will often find queues developing. When this happens, corruption can still survive with the equilibrium bribe–price equal to the cost to the marginal customer of honest service minus this customer's $D^i(x)$.[18] Similarly, if queues are eliminated by increasing the number of officials, the agency will still be limited by budgetary appropriations in the level of services it can supply. Only if scarcity is entirely eliminated will corrupt incentives necessarily be zero. Nevertheless, the introduction of interofficial competition can still reduce both the level[19] and incidence of bribery. In this context, one partial response would be an overall limit on supply, Q_s, without any individual assignment of quotas to officials. The agency head would keep track of the units of q issued and halt their distribution when Q_s have been given out. This method may often deter corruption—at least if honest officials are efficient and try to process requests speedily.

Of course, competition is not always a viable strategy. Giving officials monopoly power may have other benefits which outweigh the risks of

---

[18] See Chapter 5. Just as in the case where congestion costs allocate the use of roads (Edelson, 1971), the bribe that results from the decentralized choices of bribers and bribees may not equal the true marginal cost of increased supply.

[19] The size of individual bribes may, however, be a poor measure of the importance of the corrupt transaction if those who pay bribes are not the intended beneficiaries of the government program. In the recent scandals involving the bribery of Federal Housing Administration appraisers in return for inflated appraisals of subsidized units, the overlapping jurisdictions of appraisers appear to have held down the level of bribes. While bribe payments were relatively low, the impact on low income households was very large, with houses sometimes selling at two to three times market value. (*New York Times*, December 4, 1971, January 2, March 29, 1972, June 26, 1974).

corruption. Their contracting or licensing tasks may simply be unsuited to interofficial competition. A more serious objection to the competitive model presented here, however, is its oversimplified picture of bureaucratic operations. While the model captures some essential features of many bureaucratic procedures, it is a poor description of others which coerce individuals, examine qualifications, or perform other more complex tasks. Therefore, in the next chapter I extend the analysis to include other functions characteristic of government bureaucracies in both modern and developing states.

APPENDIX

The chance that any given bribe–price, x, will support a stable equilibrium can be expressed as follows. Given any x, the proportion of bureaucrats willing to accept bribes is some fraction, $\alpha(x)$. Thus $[1 - \alpha(x)]Q_s$ is the number of units of output that will be randomly assigned by honest bureaucrats. Letting M be the number of applicants in an honest system when no prices are charged (i.e. $p_s = 0$), and writing $\alpha(x)$ as α, the number of ways $(1 - \alpha)Q_s$ customers can be chosen from the pool of M customers is,

$$\binom{M}{(1 - \alpha)Q_s} = \frac{M!}{[(1 - \alpha)Q_s]![M - (1 - \alpha)Q_s]!} . \tag{a}$$

This is the standard formula for combinations. Those unfamiliar with this formula should consult any standard statistics text (for example, Mood and Graybill [1963:19–24]). A bribe of x will be an equilibrium if all of the $[1 - \alpha(x)]Q_s$ customers are drawn from the pool of people who are unwilling to pay x, i.e., those with $x + D^i(x) > p_i$. At any point where $Q(x)$ intersects some R_k, this pool contains $M - \alpha Q_s$ customers. Thus for x to have any chance of being an equilibrium, the number of people unwilling to bribe must exceed the quantity supplied honestly, i.e., $M - \alpha Q_s > (1 - \alpha)Q_s$ or $M > Q_s$. Given this condition, the number of combinations which make x an equilibrium is

$$\binom{M - \alpha Q_s}{(1 - \alpha)Q_s} = \frac{(M - \alpha Q_s)!}{[(1 - \alpha)Q_s]![M - Q_s]!} . \tag{b}$$

Letting $\theta(x)$ be the probability that everyone who is willing to pay a bribe of x is, in fact, required to bribe, divide (b) by (a) to obtain:

$$\theta(x) = \frac{[M - \alpha Q_s]![M - (1 - \alpha)Q_s]!}{M![M - Q_s]!} . \tag{c}$$

The probability, θ, that x is an equilibrium depends upon the size of the market, M, the number of units supplied, Q_s, and the proportion of the total supplied corruptly, α. Since θ is not continuous, it has no derivatives, but if M falls by one unit, θ decreases, i.e.,

$$\text{sign}[\theta_M - \theta_{M-1}] = \text{sign}[\alpha(1 - \alpha)Q_s^2] = \text{positive}. \qquad (d)$$

In short, any bribe x is more likely to generate a mixed equilibrium the larger the pool of customers.

Similarly, if the output quota is cut by one unit

$$\text{sign}(\theta_{Q_s} - \theta_{Q_{s-1}}) = \text{sign}[-(M - Q_{s-1})(M - 1) - \alpha(1 - \alpha)Q_{s-1}^2] = \text{negative}. \qquad (e)$$

(Since α is not an integer, the expressions for αQ_s and $(1 - \alpha)Q_s$ may have to be rounded down or up.) Expressions (d) and (e) together imply that θ increases as Q_s/M falls. The greater the level of excess demand at the legal price, the greater the chance that any given x will produce an equilibrium with $\alpha > 0$.

To develop an expression for the relationship between α and θ, consider the case where α falls by an amount just sufficient to reduce αQ_s by one unit, i.e., taking α_0 as given, $\alpha_1 = \alpha_0 - 1/Q_s$. The sign of the change in θ is then:

$$\text{sign} [\theta_0 - \theta_1] = \text{sign}[M - (1 - \alpha_0)Q_s - M + \alpha_0 Q_s - 1]$$

$$= \text{sign}[(2\alpha_0 - 1)Q_s - 1].$$

Thus θ falls as α falls if $\alpha Q_s > \frac{1}{2}(1 + Q_s)$. Since the expression $(1 + Q_s)$ is an artifact of the combinatorial formulas which require integer values for Q_s, the inequality can be written $\alpha > \frac{1}{2}$ with no important loss of generality.

8

COMPETITIVE BUREAUCRACY: VAGUENESS, COERCION, AND MARKET STRUCTURE

1. INTRODUCTION

This chapter extends the analysis of the way a competitive bureaucratic structure can reduce corrupt incentives. As before, the main questions are whether overlapping jurisdictions can reduce corruption and whether, in this "competitive" context, a few devoted and honest officials can make bribery unprofitable for their more opportunistic colleagues. Now, however, these issues are framed in terms of more realistic models of the bureaucratic process.[1]

Thus, Section 2 expands the model to include the costs of making a second application and assumes that bureaucrats are charged with determining who is qualified to receive official approval.[2] If the decision

---

[1] Only Section 2 will be difficult for the reader with no mathematical training.

[2] Many examples of corruption in government programs involve cheating on quality specifications. In a major scandal, United States grain companies and inspectors were reported to have substituted and approved lower quality grains than were called for in contracts (*New York Times*, November 30, 1975). Federal meat inspectors have been bribed by meat packers (Schuck, 1972; *New York Times*, November 10, 1976, June 3, 1977). Federal Housing Administration appraisers have been charged with taking bribes in return for inflated appraisals of houses sold under federal subsidy prorgrams (*New York Times*, December 4, 1971, January 2, March 29, 1972).

to approve any particular beneficiary is unlikely to be noticed either by superiors or by the media, a corrupt official can certify clearly unqualified applicants.[3] Even if unqualified beneficiaries are rigorously eliminated by higher level review, however, corruption may still exist if the rules setting qualifications are vaguely stated. In this case, even honest bureaucrats may differ in their assessments of an applicant's worth. A wide range of applicants may be willing to bribe their way onto the rolls since they will be uncertain of their success with honest bureaucrats.[4] An official's bargaining power is, of course, futher enhanced if it is costly and time consuming to reapply to another official after being initially turned down.[5] Indeed, the vagueness of rules may increase corruption in a second way by increasing the time an honest official needs to make a decision. Conscientious behavior by some officials will then increase the costs of reapplication, and so increase the bargaining power of corrupt officials. Thus, even an applicant who clearly qualifies will often trade off the net benefits of immediate approval against the benefits of searching for an honest official. The maximum bribe that the official can obtain is the difference between the benefits of immediate corrupt approval and the expected gain from additional search.

Section 3 turns to a broad class of coercive programs whose distinctive feature is that clients do not want to be served by the agency. Housing code inspectors do not ask landlords if their services are desired, and the police do not ask suspects whether or not they want to be arrested. Instead, clients try to avoid law enforcers and may pay

[3] The approval may be either fraudulently granted or not recorded at all. The official can simply let an unqualified applicant sneak in. Corruption in the United States Immigration Service along the Mexico–United States border, for example, apparently took both forms. Entry documents were sold, and people were allowed into the United States without proper papers (*New York Times,* May 21, 1973).

[4] In India, applications for licenses under the Industrial (Development and Regulation) Act of 1951 can be made at any time during the planning period. Monteiro (1966) states that

> Persons whose applications have once been rejected are not precluded from making fresh applications in the expectation that at some time or other they will succeed if the officers concerned are suitably "persuaded." It is well known that the presentation of any application is followed by visits and letters to the applicant with the offer of "fixing up" the license for prices depending on the nature of the application [p. 33].

[5] Summer employment programs for disadvantaged youths in New York City fit this model reasonably well. A number of different sponsors were each allocated money for a fixed number summer jobs which they were to fill with qualified applicants. Although applicants could apply to more than one sponsor, the cost of approaching another sponsor may have been high and the expected probability of success low. Therefore, sponsors were sometimes able to demand kickbacks on the wages of job recipients (*New York Times,* March 28, 1977).

bribes to avoid consuming the bureau's services. Bureaucratic discretion in picking targets for enforcement activity creates corrupt incentives even in the absence of arrest quotas. Here the effectiveness of a system with overlapping jurisdictions depends on the nature of the offense. Criminals will pay little or nothing to be excused from arrest by one police officer if they expect either to be shaken down repeatedly or arrested by honest officers. If, however, the corrupt police officer can suppress the evidence of the crime before the arrival of other officers, the existence of officials with overlapping jurisdictions will not check peculation. The presence of victims may be a second important check. Organized tenant groups and complaining victims may keep even an isolated inspector or police officer honest.

Turning from the behavior of corrupt suppliers to the demand of corrupt beneficiaries, here too the earlier analysis was oversimplified. Thus Section 4 broadens the analysis of consumer behavior by considering the possibility that applicants themselves may cartelize to obtain a better bargaining position vis-à-vis corruptible suppliers.

2. CHOOSING THOSE WHO QUALIFY

Assume that bureaucrat j, dealing with applicant i, wants to determine the maximum bribe that can be imposed on i. There are also minimum and (perhaps) maximum bribes that bureaucrat j is willing to accept, but I ignore these limits and merely assume that i's maximum is acceptable to j. Assume that the applicant, i, does not bargain with the bureaucrat, j, but that if the bribe requested is too high, the applicant will refuse to pay and approach another official. Although no one has information about the characteristics of particular officials, both official and applicant believe that if i continues to search,[6] i has a probability β in period 2 of once again confronting a corrupt official who demands an expected bribe of x_2. So far as any individual applicant or bureaucrat is concerned, x_2 is assumed to be exogenous. Alternatively, the applicant has a probability $(1 - \beta)$ of finding an official who will not accept a bribe. Within this class of officials, however, only a proportion, α, will accept

---

[6] Shopping around for an official who will accept a lower bribe does occur in practice. Seeking a certification for the cleanliness of his grain-carrying ship, an owner rejected the demand for a $5000 payoff from the first inspector and later was able to find a second official who provided the required certification for $2500 (*New York Times*, May 20, 1975).

i's application. Thus $\alpha(1 - \beta)$ is the probability that i's application will be approved without a bribe, and $(1 - \alpha)(1 - \beta)$ is the probability that an honest official will turn the applicant down. Letting $D^i(x)$ be i's penalty function, c the transaction cost of filing a second application, p_i the value of an approved application, and r the constant rate of discount, the official j, if he wishes to receive payment, must set x_1 so that:[7]

$$p_i - [x_1 + D^i(x_1)] \geq \left\{ \frac{(1 - \beta)\alpha p_i}{(1 + r)} \right.$$

$$\left. + \frac{\beta}{(1 + r)} [p_i - x_2 - D^i(x_2)] - \frac{c}{(1 + r)} \right\} \quad \text{(1a)}$$

$$+ \frac{(1 - \beta)(1 - \alpha)}{(1 + r)} \left\{ \frac{(1 - \beta)\alpha p_i}{(1 + r)} \right.$$

$$+ \frac{\beta}{1 + r} [p_i - x_3 - D^i(x_3)]$$

$$\left. - \frac{c}{1 + r} + \frac{(1 - \beta)(1 - \alpha)}{1 + r} \right\} \ldots .$$

and

$$p_i \geq x_1 + D^i(x_1). \quad \text{(1b)}$$

The right hand side of the inequality (1a) is the expected gain to the applicant from further search under the assumption that other corrupt officials set x_j to discourage further search once the applicant has approached them. Following the convention that if equality holds in (1a), the applicant chooses to pay x_1, official $j = 1$ will set x_1 where equality holds so long as the official's penalty function is nondecreasing in x.[8] The critical question, therefore, is the official's estimate of $x_2, x_3, \ldots$ In one simple case, the x_j are easy to calculate. Suppose the official believes that all other officials have nondecreasing penalty functions. Then anyone who is willing to accept bribes will face the same set of calculations. Thus all corrupt officials will charge i the same bribe, $x =$

---

[7] Customers are assumed to be risk neutral, and α and β remain constant throughout the applicant's search. This latter assumption implies that applicants can return to those who refused to service them in the past. It is an unrealistic assumption, but it simplifies the mathematics and does not seem to introduce any important biases into the qualitative results.

[8] That is $J'(x) \geq 0$ and $J''(x) < 0$. See Chapter 7 for a discussion. This assumption implies that officials will accept all bribes greater than some minimum $\bar{x} \geq 0$. At this point in the discussion, I assume that $x_1 > \bar{x}$. Later I discuss how β depends on x.

$x_1 = x_2 = x_3 = \cdots$. Using this reasoning, the official can solve for x:[9]

$$x + D^i(x) = \frac{c + rp_i}{r + \alpha(1 - \beta)},$$ (2)

$$\text{s.t. } p_i - x - D^i(x) \geq 0 \quad \text{or} \quad (1 - \beta)\alpha p_i \geq c,$$

i.e., the official can set x at the level that solves (2) so long as the applicant's net returns are positive. Holding α and c constant, the level of x chosen by a corrupt official using (2) can be represented by $x = g(\beta)$. If α varied across applicants, the official would try to set a different x for each type of customer. To simplify, assume that every applicant values the benefit equally at p and that the $D^i(x) = k$. When there are no other corrupt officials except j, $\beta = 0$, and $g(0) = (c + rp)/(r + \alpha) - k$, so long as $\alpha p \geq c$. As the proportion of corrupt officials increases, x increases at an increasing rate[10] up to $\hat{\beta}$, where $\hat{\beta} = 1 - (c/\alpha p)$. At $\beta \geq \hat{\beta}$ the applicant's returns are zero, not only relative to opportunities elsewhere, but in absolute terms as well. For $0 \geq \beta > \hat{\beta}$, $x = (c + rp)/(r + \alpha(1 - \beta)) - k$. For $\beta \geq \hat{\beta}$, x simply equals $p - k$. A typical $g(\beta)$ function is illustrated in Figure 8.1.

The discussion so far has assumed that the corrupt official could choose the level of the bribe, x, under the assumption that the probabil-

---

[9] Under the assumption that all xs are equal and that equality holds in (1a), then (1a) can be written as:

$$p_i - x - D^i(x) = \frac{1}{(1 + r)} \sum_{t=0}^{\infty} \left[\frac{(1 - \beta)(1 - \alpha)}{(1 + r)} \right]^t$$

$$\times \{(1 - \beta)\alpha p_i + \beta[p_i - x - D^i(x)] - c\}.$$ (i)

Using the standard discounting formula, $\sum_{t=0}^{\infty} [1/(1 + a)]^t = (a + 1)/a$, we have $a = \{(1 + r)/[(1 - \beta)(1 - \alpha)]\} - 1$. Thus (i) becomes:

$$p_i - x - D^i(x) = \frac{(1 - \beta)\alpha p_i + \beta[p_i - x - D^i(x)] - c}{(1 + r) - (1 - \beta)(1 - \alpha)}$$

$$[(1 + r) - (1 - \beta)(1 - \alpha) - \beta][p_i - x - D^i(x)] = (1 - \beta)\alpha p_i - c$$

$$x + D^i(x) = \frac{c + rp_i}{r + \alpha(1 - \beta)}$$ (ii)

[10] Thus,

$$\frac{dx}{d\beta} = \frac{\alpha(c + rp_i)}{[r + \alpha(1 - \beta)]^2} > 0,$$

where

$$\frac{d^2x}{d\beta^2} = \frac{2\alpha^2(c + rp_i)}{[r + \alpha(1 - \beta)]^3} > 0.$$

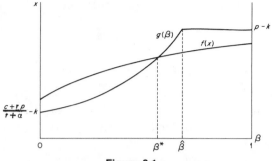

Figure 8.1

ity of finding a corrupt official, β, was a constant. In fact, however, the fraction of dishonest sellers, β, may depend upon the level of bribery receipts. To see this, consider a simple case where converts to corruption are drawn from honest officials so that α, the proportion of honest officials who will approve the application, remains constant whatever the level of β. The supply of corrupt officials can then be represented by $\beta = f(x)$, assuming[11] that $f'(x) \geq 0$. Figure 8.1 illustrates this situation with representative curves showing x as a function of β, $g(\beta)$, and β as a function of x, $f(x)$.

Despite the bargaining power that the approval of qualifications gives to officials, a partially corrupt system may not persist. The shape of penalty functions and the expected costs and benefits to applicants of further search may combine to push β to 0 or 1. If benefits, $p - k$, are low or if officials have high fixed costs of accepting bribes and if their expected penalties increase rapidly with x, $f(x)$ could be everywhere above $g(\beta)$ and β would equal zero. Alternatively, $f(x)$ might always be beneath $g(\beta)$ because the reverse conditions hold, i.e., corruption is relatively riskless to officials and relatively attractive to applicants. In that case, $\beta = 1$, but the actual level of x is indeterminate. If, as shown in Figure 8.1, $f(x)$ intersects $g(\beta)$ from above, the resulting equilibrium is unstable. A level of $\beta < \beta^*$ will move the system toward $\beta = 0$, i.e., no corruption occurs. For $\beta > \beta^*$ the system moves toward a situation where all officials are corrupt, $\beta = 1$. This situation is most likely if officials' marginal penalties fall rapidly as x increases; and if $\hat{\beta} = 1 - c/$ αp is large either because reapplication costs are low or because honest officials seldom approve petitions. In contrast, the inverse of these

---

[11] This condition holds if the $J^j(x)$ have $J'(x) \geq 0$, $J''(x) < 0$. In general, $f(x)$ need not have the shape illustrated in Figure 8.1. Even with $J''(x) < 0$, $f'(x)$ might be positive or might change signs as β increased. In addition, if all officials have identical $J^j(x)$ functions, $f(x)$ will shift discontinuously from 0 to 1 at the breakeven level of x. See Chapter 7.

conditions makes a stable equilibrium, where $f(x)$ cuts $g(\beta)$ from below, more likely.

If actual sanctioning strategies are not very sensitive to the size of the bribe received, the minimum acceptable x will be high and the curvature of $f(x)$ will be largely determined by the variation in penalty functions across officials. Thus a policymaker with control over nominal penalties may face a situation where marginal increases will have no deterrent effects at all while a massive increase could eliminate corruption entirely through a shift in the entire curve.

Of equal importance is the response of the system to reforms undertaken by top officials who are ignorant of the corruption beneath them. These officials simply observe that poorly qualified individuals are being approved by low-level bureaucrats, i.e., untrained individuals are practicing medicine or middle class households are inhabiting public housing. The response of top officials could then be a counterproductive increase in the stringency of honest procedures.[12] Reducing the likelihood that an honest official will approve an application, α, increases the relative benefits of paying a bribe. Thus, $g(\beta)$ in Figure 8.1 shifts to the "left" and $\hat{\beta}$ falls. In terms of (2), a fall in α implies that for any proportion of corrupt officials less than $\hat{\beta}$, the applicant's maximum willingness-to-bribe increases. Thus, if equilibrium were originally at the unstable point, β^* in Figure 8.1, the fall in α would induce all officials to become corrupt. Although the new intersection of $g(\beta)$ and $f(x)$ would be at a lower β and a lower x, this point could not be reached from β^*. If, instead, the existing equilibrium were stable, with $f(x)$ cutting $g(\beta)$ from below, then the fall in α would induce an increase in *both* β and x, unless x were already at its maximum level. More officials would become corrupt and the level of individual payoffs would increase.

3. COERCIVE PROGRAMS

Coercive programs are similar to the qualification programs discussed in Section 2, except that applicants are not free to decide whether or not

[12] The high incidence of corruption in securing a certificate of occupancy for a new building in New York may be partially attributable to the near impossibility of actually satisfying all of the detailed specifications in the city's 843-page building code. *New York Times* (June 27, 1972). In Europe, the regulations governing drug sales have led to corrupt attempts to get around the law. Most countries, however, are tightening their regulations in response to abuses. Several sources pointed out to the *New York Times* (March 21, 1976) that "with more exacting pricing and registration surveillance, there will be more and more incentive for companies to press their favors upon officials . . . in order to get through the labyrinth of regulations."

to approach an official. Honest officials apprehend those violators of the law whom they notice[13] but there is some probability that no honest functionary will observe the illegal behavior. To emphasize the points of contact with the preceding analysis, assume that bureaucrats are permitted to require eligible individuals to consume one unit of q apiece.[14] Each bureaucrat can, however, impose one unit of q on any number of different individuals. Each individual is willing to sacrifice a maximum of p_i to avoid this burden,[15] i.e.:

$$q_i = 0 \qquad x + D^i(x) \le p_i,$$
$$q_i = 1 \qquad x + D^i(x) > p_i.$$

The most distinctive feature of these programs is the inability of customers to choose which official to approach. Bureaucrats have extortionary power, i.e., once they have threatened to force a person to consume q, the individual cannot seek out another bureaucrat willing to be deterred more cheaply. So long as the arrest or imposition of a cost is not frivolous, the customer is at a disadvantage vis-à-vis the official. A person threatened with arrest cannot generally report a kickback demand without explaining why he or she should have been the object of it.[16] While bureaucrats have the ability to shop around and to price

---

[13] This description of honest bureaucratic behavior is oversimplified. Even incorruptible police officers do not apprehend all those they observe violating the law.

[14] For example, q might be a traffic ticket or a gambling raid.

[15] For numbers operators and bookmakers, Rubinstein and Reuter (1977:151, c-4) report that the major components of $D^i(x)$ are not expected criminal punishments but the disruption of business which a gambling raid entails.

[16] Honest officials might try to generate bribe offers in order to refuse them and gain a bargaining advantage. Blau (1963) reports this type of behavior in his study of agents charged with enforcing two federal laws applicable to business firms. "Being offered a bribe constituted a special tactical advantage for an agent. An employer who had violated one law was caught in the act of compounding his guilt by violating another one. He could no longer claim ignorance or inadvertence as an excuse for his violation. Agents exploited this situation to strengthen their position in negotiations. Refusing but not reporting bribes enabled agents more effectively to carry out their duties, which they considered important and on the basis of which they were evaluated. Since bribe offers helped agents in their work, there existed a perennial temptation, consciously or unconsciously, to provoke employers to make such overtures. Of course, we do not know, and neither do these agents, to what extent their attitudes invited the many offers of bribes that they, according to their own statements, received. In any case, to preserve the advantageous position into which such an offer had put an agent, he had to reject it outright rather than appear hesitant in anticipation of reporting it for prosecution (p. 191)." This situation, in which the person who makes the initial offer is at a bargaining *disadvantage* should be contrasted with first-mover *advantages* discussed by Williamson (1975) in legal bargaining situations.

discriminate not present when they are providing positive benefits, customers have little freedom of choice, even when the other competitive assumptions hold. The relatively stronger position of the official will, however, erode over time as the official grants several exemptions in return for bribes. Thus drug dealers and gamblers often keep evidence of bribes paid as a way both of preventing police officers from changing their minds and of lowering the required payoffs by threatening blackmail. For example, Moore (1977:35–36) explains how New York City heroin dealers gained over time at the expense of corrupt police officers involved in long-term payoff arrangements.

The anticorruption potential of competitive officials or "honest cops," however, cannot be assessed unless q is specified with more care. At one extreme, bureaucrats can demand payment of x_i where $x_i + D^i(x_i) = p_i$.[17] Criminals will be willing to pay this maximum if they know for sure that if they do make a payoff, then the arresting officer will destroy the evidence, and it will be impossible for them to be arrested by anyone else.[18] It is irrelevant whether other officials, honest or dishonest, have formal authority which overlaps that of the officer who demands the payoff. For example, sporadic speeders or barroom brawlers are unlikely to be apprehended by a second police officer if the first permits them to escape. The monopoly power of individual law enforcement officers is high since the episodic nature of the offense deprives the offender of market power.

Criminals subject to the short-run monopoly power of particular officials, however, may in the long run simply change jurisdictions. In most illegal benefit contexts, an official's monopoly power is temporally and spatially limited. Thus, although a drug dealer whose operation has been raided by the police cannot refuse to make a payoff on the ground that he knows of a less greedy police officer, the dealer can, in the future, move to the latter's district. Officials seldom have long-term monopoly power over particular individuals. They only obtain their extortionary positions by being in the right place at the right time. In short, those law breakers who are able to choose where to locate can foil

---

[17] Of course, they will only demand x_i if it maximizes their net gains over the set of bribes, $x \leq x_i$, which are acceptable to bribers. This condition is certain to hold if $x_i + J^j(x_i) > 0$ and $J'' < 0$. If bureaucrats maximize their gains at some finite bribe, x_j^*, then they demand either x_j^* or x_i, if $x_i < x_j^*$.

[18] Andreski (1970) reports that if a murderer "can pay a big sum, [African] police may even help him to erase the traces of his crime by framing up somebody quite innocent but helpless, and getting him hanged [p. 250]." The practice is similar to that of corrupt American police who arrest "ghosts" or stand-ins instead of major organized crime figures (Moore, 1977).

an anticorruption drive that focuses on only a portion of the responsible officials (e.g., the police department of a single city in a metropolitan region). These bribe payers can respond to a limited clean-up effort by moving to a more hospitable environment.[19]

At the other extreme, the presence of numerous competitive officials can reduce the willingness to pay of an individual gambler, drug dealer, prostitute, or slum landlord. An individual engaging in continuing illegal activity who pays off a police officer or inspector to prevent arrest may be approached later by another official who seeks to impose the same sanction.[20] The greater the probability that another official will soon appear, the lower the bribe that the first can obtain. Indeed, overlapping jurisdictions may eliminate corruption in the same way as they did in the model in Chapter 7. If the expected penalties facing a corrupt official deter small bribes but not large ones, then the lower the willingness to pay of individual law-breakers, the less likely it is that law enforcement officials will accept bribes. Thus, a system of free-lance competitive corruption, where someone who breaks the law expects to be shaken down by a succession of officials, may push the level of bribes so low that police officers choose to make arrests instead of collecting payoffs. A "competitive" police structure may reduce both corruption and the underlying illegal enterprise so long as the crime is an ongoing activity.

"Competition" is not a panacea, however. If the expected penalty falls as the number of corrupt officials increases, then smaller bribes may be acceptable as the incidence of corruption rises. Police officers know that while some of them may be made scapegoats, the whole force cannot lose its jobs. Thus if the introduction of competitive pressures implies that *more* officials will be exposed to corrupt opportunities, larger numbers of police might take bribes.[21] However, a shift from a system with ten corrupt officials in monopoly positions to ten with overlapping jurisdictions would still have a deterrent effect so long as

---

[19] Gambling operations have moved from central cities to nearby suburbs in response to crackdowns in the central cities. Salerno and Tompkins (1970) write that "the Syndicate has often changed its local domicile so that the incumbent can claim that his city or state is 'clean' [p. 150]." They cite the examples of Cicero, Illinois, outside Chicago, Halls Corners near Youngstown, Ohio and Covington and Newport, Kentucky, near Cincinnati. In addition, "similar patterns have been followed successfully by relocating gambling operations outside the city of Detroit, by moving certain New York City activities across the river to New Jersey, and by headquartering Syndicate operations in the New Orleans area in Jefferson Parish or across the river in Algiers [p. 151]"

[20] Moore (1977:31–32) discusses this issue as it arises for heroin dealers and argues that dealers will be more likely to payoff narcotics agents than police officers on the beat because of the greater monopoly power of narcotics agents.

[21] Peter Reuter made this point to the author in private correspondence.

high bribes are preferred to low bribes after taking account of the number of other corrupt officials.

The fact that many officials may be able to threaten to impose q_i (e.g., a gambling raid) on an individual (a gambler) suggests why "customers" will often prefer a centralized bureaucracy to a more competitive one. Since their bargaining power vis-à-vis any particular official is low, they may prefer a single high-level demand for a bribe payment from an official capable of guaranteeing protection to a series of low-level extortionary demands.[22] This preference for centralized bureaucratic power is characteristic of those whose criminality can easily be detected by any of a large number of officials over an extended period of time. While representatives of organized crime will certainly be in this category, legitimate businessmen in heavily regulated industries may have a similar point of view if they expect to break the law repeatedly in the normal course of their operations.

4. CUSTOMERS WITH MONOPOLY POWER

Having described two important ways in which the characteristics of a government service will affect the nature of corrupt dealings, I turn to consider a case where the demand for government services has special features. The last chapter used a competitive model of demand in which applicants were unable to form cartels for the purpose of improving their bargaining position. However, if demanders care about the number of other beneficiaries or the overall level of benefits, they have an incentive

---

[22] For example, the police commissioner of Suffolk County, New York has testified that the gambling syndicates were particularly happy with the consolidation of the nine police departments in Suffolk into a single county Police Department. See President's Commission on Law Enforcement and Administration of Justice, *Task Force Report: Organized Crime* (Washington: U.S. Government Printing Office, 1967) in Gardiner and Olson (1974:358).

Police officers have also sometimes organized themselves into corrupt groups to give them the monopoly power to extort payoffs from gamblers. Thus two major scandals in the New York City Police Department, the Gross and Koutnick cases, involved police initiative in organizing large-scale protection operations (Rubinstein and Reuter, 1977:80–83).

Those engaged in illegal businesses prefer centralized corruption not only to prevent their own arrest but also to eliminate competitors. The police may be induced to raid new entrants, and this possibility provides a way for a gambling syndicate to induce entrants to join with them or leave the "industry" (Kornblum, 1976). While Reuter and Rubinstein (1977:82) cite a similar example in their study of the numbers racket in New York City, they have not found any major change in the numbers business since the end of organized corruption following the Knapp Commission (p. ii).

to collude with others to increase their gains and to lower the level of bribe payments. Recognizing the benefits that can flow from cartelization is not, of course, sufficient to produce a cartel. Cartels may be difficult to organize, since all applicants want speedy service and high benefits as well as low bribes. Just as price-fixing cartels must allocate market shares, so bribe-lowering cartels must allocate both speed of service and the level of individual benefit. If the firms remain competitive in the output market, attempts to organize may break down. Each firm has an incentive to exceed the cartel's bribe offer in return for somewhat better treatment from officials. Similarly, if the cartel does not include all potential beneficiaries, it must be able to prevent bureaucrats from dealing with outsiders or else run the risk that nonmembers will exceed the cartel's offers. In order to preserve their favorable position, cartel members must therefore be able to establish prohibitive legal qualifications for new entrants or use fear and intimidation against officials and outsiders.

In some situations, however, the presence of corruption in the granting of licenses may itself facilitate organization by restricting the number of potential entrants and perhaps the number of firms actually operating in the industry. Entrepreneurs with high D^i functions will not enter industries that require bribes, and hence those with low D^i may earn excess profits, even after deducting bribes paid. The number of firms in the industry may then be small enough to lower the cost of organizing a cartel. Just as in limit-pricing behavior, the cartel might then try to "limit bribe," i.e., pay bribes that are as low as possible consistent with the goal of deterring entry. Similarly, even if corruption itself does not deter entry, other entry barriers may imply that the beneficiaries are few enough in number to give them bargaining power vis à vis the official. Hence in a concentrated industry bribes may be lower and the level of each firm's benefits higher than in a more competitive industry where each firm operates independently and the official can extort high payments.[23] In short, the relationship between

---

[23] Schelling (1967) argues that criminal enterprises that require long-term corrupt relations with the police or must undertake substantial investment to cultivate a market will also tend to become highly organized. Bilateral monopoly may therefore characterize corrupt relations between police and regular clients such as gamblers. Criminal activities that are geographically mobile and require no regular contact with the police are less likely to be organized.

The President's Commission on Law Enforcement and Administration of Justice, *Task Force Report: Organized Crime*, excerpted in Gardiner and Olson (1974), notes that independent gamblers are induced to join gambling syndicates through both fear and

oligopoly and administrative corruption can change over time. Corruption may help create oligopoly, but oligopoly can then lower the volume of bribe payments.[24]

---

promises of greater profits. The higher profits arise both because the organization "creates greater efficiency and enlarges markets and also provided a systematized method of corrupting the law enforcement process by centralizing procedures for the payment of graft [p. 357]." New York City Commission to Investigate Allegations of Police Corruption and the City's Anti-Corruption Procedures (Knapp Commission), excerpted in Gardiner and Olson (1974), reports an instance of monopoly behavior by Queens numbers operators in the face of increased bribery demands from plainclothes officers.

When borough plainclothes squads were eliminated in February, 1971, Queens division plainclothesmen reportedly demanded in addition to their own monthly share, the entire monthly share that had been going to borough plainclothes. Queens numbers operators held a meeting to discuss the demand and present a unified front. It was agreed that they would increase the monthly payment by an average of $200 to $300. According to one source, this meeting of numbers operators to resolve a common problem was most unusual in Queens, which the source stated was the only borough where policy operators did not have some sort of unity [p. 176].

Rubinstein and Reuter (1977), however, cast doubt on the proposition that cartel activity is widespread. In their study of the numbers racket in New York City, they found little evidence of collusive activity. Similarly, Moore (1977) in an analysis of the heroin industry found that the industry was fragmented in spite of economic forces encouraging the development of a few large suppliers.

[24] Some bureaucratic services are not provided individually to firms but are instead a public good to the industry. An oligopolistic industry structure facilitates corruption in this case since the fewer the number of firms the easier it is likely to be for them to overcome free-rider problems and organize as a group. Since the collective nature of the benefit implies that the bureaucratic decision must also be centralized, the competitive market analogy breaks down entirely, and is replaced by a bargaining environment like the bilateral monopoly case in Chapter 6. An excellent example of a bilateral bargaining situation arose in the milk marketing orders program of the United States Department of Agriculture which permits the secretary of agriculture to issue federal orders establishing minimum wholesale prices for milk. High levels of milk prices set by the government are an alternative to an attempt to monopolize a local market completely. Dairy farmers' cooperatives provide the organizational tool, and limitations on entry make it desirable for existing farmers to obtain prices set above marginal costs. The fact that former secretary of the treasury, John Connally, was acquitted on bribery charges does not undercut this example. Connally was accused of accepting bribes from a lobbyist for a large dairy farmer cooperative. The prosecution's case hinged on the question of whether the lobbyist actually gave $15,000 of the cooperative's money to Connally. The fact that the cooperative provided $15,000 to the lobbyist in 1971 is not in doubt. A former assistant to the general manager of the cooperative testified that the organization was "obligated" to Connally for having helped win an increase in federal milk price supports. (New York Times, June 30, 1974; April 8, 9, 18, 1975).

6. CONCLUSIONS

The analysis here, like that of the preceding chapter, lays the theoretical foundations for practical bureaucratic reform. Once again economic theory permits us to move beyond a simplistic reliance upon the criminal sanction to consider the possibilities of structural reform. The most important conclusions involve the anticorruption potential of competitive bureaucratic structures. While competition does not check corruption so powerfully in the more realistic models considered in the present chapter, nevertheless there remains good reason to think that it is an important reform tool.

This result contrasts sharply with conventional bureaucratic practice. Even in bureaucracies where officials have identical responsibilities, each is usually given a monopoly over a particular clientele based on geography, needs, or some such characteristic. This places qualified applicants who are unable to change jurisdictions at the mercy of corrupt officials, though it may not prevent unqualified applicants from seeking out bribeable officials.[25] These points have been ignored, however, by those students of public administration who advocate the creation of these petty bureaucratic monopolies on efficiency grounds.[26] Although a careful division of responsibility does prevent some wasteful duplication, the neat organizational solution may not be the honest one.

Restraining corruption through law enforcement and administrative oversight may, however, be incompatible with a policy of increased interofficial competition. Giving officials overlapping jurisdictions will be of most value in reducing corruption if other competitive market conditions hold. In particular, information about the bribe–prices charged by various officials should be easy for customers to obtain. The threat of legal and administrative sanctions, however, is likely to encourage secrecy and may convert corrupt transactions into bilateral bargains (Schmidt, 1969). Shopping around will often be costly because bureaucrats will need to develop trusting relationships with customers before making payoff requests. Nevertheless, even an imperfectly operating competitive bureaucracy will often be desirable on anticorruption grounds, given the high costs of monitoring the multitude of face-to-face transactions characteristic of many decentralized bureaucratic tasks.

[25] If they cannot legally change jurisdictions, they may bribe corrupt officials to misrepresent their locations as well as their other characteristics.
[26] A classic statement of this view is Weber (1947:337).

9

BUREAUCRATIC STRUCTURE
AND CORRUPTION

---

1. INTRODUCTION: FOUR MODELS
OF BUREAUCRACY

The bureaucrats described in the preceding chapters did not operate within a complex organizational environment. They were either at the bottom of the agency, dealing directly with contractors and clients and constrained by criminal laws and the guidelines of superior officials, or they were agency heads with no problems of internal organization and with monopoly power vis à vis the outside world. To enrich our view of the incentives for corrupt bureaucratic behavior, however, I need to move beyond these models to ask how the structure of the bureaucracy and an official's place in it will determine both his or her discretionary power and the expected costs of accepting a bribe.

While this chapter concentrates upon organizational reform, agencies can often use other techniques to control corruption. Thus an agency may increase the use of outside and inside auditors and inspectors, or appeal for the help of law enforcement agencies. The increased risk of detection which these methods entail may be coupled with stiffer disciplinary actions against those caught taking bribes. Furthermore, it may be possible to redefine bureaucratic tasks so that corrupt incentives are reduced simply by removing discretion or increasing the publicity of agents' actions. Finally, the bureau may seek individuals who have high standards of personal honesty or who subscribe to codes of professional conduct. If such individuals are unavailable, the government department might seek to create them through an educational and indoctrination program. Superiors may try to instill norms of honesty and attempt to control corruption through peer pressure.[1] Changing norms is likely to be difficult, however, and peer pressure can promote as well as retard corruption. Discussions of police corruption, for example, show that a willingness to take bribes may be a way to earn the friendship of fellow officers (Broadus, 1976; Rubinstein, 1973; Sherman, 1974b). Clearly, in any actual reorganization proposal, the personal scruples of employees and the relative merits of the other strategies would have to be weighed in an evaluation of the organizational possibilities presented here. This chapter, however, neglects these tradeoffs and considers instead how alternative bureaucratic structures will themselves affect the incidence of corruption.

In attempting this task, it would be desirable, of course, to draw upon a well-developed theory of bureaucracy, modifying standard models to capture the peculiarities of my subject. Unfortunately, however, a powerful positive theory of bureaucracy simply does not exist.[2] As a consequence, I have had to develop my own models of bureaucratic organization as part of the analytic effort. Instead of constructing an exhaustive theory for all bureaucratic structures, however, I examine four organizational forms which describe many situations in which corruption has been observed. For simplicity, I shall label these forms: the *fragmented,* the *sequential,* the *hierarchical,* and finally, the *disorganized.* In order to concentrate upon organizational features, I stylize the interaction between government agencies and the private sector. Since the incidence of corrupt transactions is my main concern, each official is envisaged as approving or rejecting an application for a "license" or "exemption"—and not as negotiating over the terms of the agreement.

[1] Ward (1967:108) shows how indoctrination into group norms is used as a control device in the Jesuits and the U.S. Navy. Janowitz's (1960:125–149) study of the professional soldier discusses the United States military academies' efforts to develop a commitment to the military profession and a sense of "military honor."

In some applications nepotism may be a substitute for indoctrination. Agency heads might hire their relatives because they can be trusted to carry out orders. Relatives, however, may be otherwise poorly qualified for government jobs. In fact, nepotism aside, honest high-level officials may often have to trade off the objective skills of job applicants against their level of personal honesty.

[2] For a review and critique of recent work, see Nadel and Rourke (1975) and Warwick (1975, Chapter 10).

Turning to the four formal constructs, the fragmented and the sequential models lack the hierarchical process of delegation and review that is often assumed to be a necessary prerequisite for bureaucracy to exist at all. In a search for positive models of government, however, these cases must be considered because many actual procedures seem closer to these models than to a hierarchical one. The fragmented case is the simplest to describe. An applicant must have each of several parts of an application approved; but each approval procedure is independent of the others, and the applicant can have the portions approved in any order. Each bureaucrat has particular powers, unreviewable except by law enforcement agencies,[3] and each decision-making node may be organized differently.

The *sequential* model is identical to the *fragmented* except that applicants must have the portions of their petition approved in a particular order. No bureaucrat in the sequence, however, ever reviews the choices made by officials who have already acted. These two models, then, best describe procedures in which each functionary behaves like an independent, specialized expert.

The *hierarchical* model is a traditional bureaucracy where the behavior of low-level officials can be reviewed by higher level ones. Authority over some portions of the approval and implementation process is delegated to bureaucrats at different hierarchical levels, but any low-level decisions can, in principle, be overruled by a higher official. The scarce time and imperfect information available to top bureaucrats, however, limits their ability to review subordinates' actions.

While distinguishing these three models facilitates analysis, it is nevertheless true that many actual application approval procedures combine several types. Thus businessmen operating in a regulated industry must often obtain approval from several independent government agencies, each of which is organized hierarchically. In other circumstances, however, it is impossible to characterize the organizational structure of the government. Consequently, the chapter concludes by considering a *disorganized* model, where the official chain of command is unclear and constantly shifting and the decision-making criteria are similarly arbitrary and unknown.

In explaining and comparing these bureaucratic models, I shall locate the opportunities for corruption in each and consider the extent to which

---

[3] This model is closest to the model of legislative behavior presented in Chapters 2 and 3 where no representative was responsible to any hierarchical superior. The model could also be extended to a discussion of federal government structure, where each level of government has independent unreviewable authority over certain issues. (Riker, 1975, defines federalism as a system where this condition holds for at least some issues).

reforms in bureaucratic organization have potential as anticorruption devices. Section 2 locates the corrupt incentives in models without centralized direction, and Section 3 considers whether hierarchical forms have greater potential for controlling corruption. Section 4 develops the contrast between hierarchical and nonhierarchical forms by using some simple formal models to compare the corrupt incentives under alternative systems. Finally, Section 5 examines a question that has concerned students of corruption in other disciplines—what is the role of disorganization and uncertainty in fostering or deterring bribery?

2. THE FRAGMENTED AND SEQUENTIAL MODELS

High-level review is missing from many government procedures. Different bureaucrats are tied together simply by the requirement that each gives approval to a particular part of an application before the entire proposal is permitted to proceed. For example, a developer seeking to build a structure in an urban region must obtain approval from the zoning board,[4] the building code administrator, and the fire marshal, to name only the most obvious.[5] Any portion of the approval process may be either competitive or monopolistic, i.e., several officials may be able to grant approval, or a single bureaucrat may be in charge of some portion of the application procedure. When bureaucratic tasks have been fragmented in this way, even obtaining honest bureaucratic approval may be a costly and time consuming activity for clients, requiring them to "walk their applications through" in order to avoid delay and caprice.

While Chapters 7 and 8 showed that the presence of competitive officials at some point in a *fragmented* process may sometimes deter corruption at that stage, granting officials monopoly power over other aspects of the application may permit them to extort bribes.[6] Thus the

---

[4] Zoning boards are, of course, composed of more than one official. Therefore, some of the considerations raised in Chapters 2 and 3 would apply to this stage in the application approval process.

[5] The example in the text is actually a mixed system, since the officials at most decision nodes are each at the bottom of an independent hierarchical system.

[6] Gardiner's (1970:7–12) discussion of Wincanton, Pennsylvania suggests that the fragmented model was a reasonably accurate paradigm for much of the town's corruption. No group exercised overall control, and the graft itself was not used to enforce centralization. Wolfinger's (1972) description of a decentralized political machine is also similar to the fragmented model, except that many of the officials in his analysis are politicians who face a reelection constraint.

applicant may face a situation similar to that of a developer seeking to assemble a large parcel of land. Some officials may wait until others have acted and then try to extort a large portion of the client's surplus. In situations where a holdout can make large corrupt gains, moreover, each official may try to be the last one to give approval. As a consequence, fragmented bureaucracies may suffer from long delays, generating pressure on bureaucrats to cartelize to present a united front to applicants.

This result obtains, of course, only in the fragmented case—where the order in which bureaucratic tasks must be performed is not specified by law. Quite often, however, the *sequential* model applies, and applicants must approach bureaucrats in an ordered sequence. If applicants must follow a predetermined path, with no competition between officials at any particular level, then only one corrupt official in each path is needed to produce a situation in which a high proportion of the program's benefits to the applicant can be appropriated by bureaucrats. If several in the sequence are willing to take bribes, the corrupt official who must be approached first has an inherent advantage. Corrupt officials who follow, however, might attempt to obtain bribery receipts by threatening to turn down anyone unable to bribe them.[7]

In other situations, applicants may be able to choose to approach any one of several different officials at a particular stage in the ordered sequence. The choice of a particular official may, however, also determine the future list of officials the applicant must approach, with the sequence of subsequent contacts differing from official to official. Each competitive official is, then, associated with a different, uniquely specified chain of other officials who must also grant approval. The choice of an initial bureaucratic contact thus can lead to a series of subsequent bilateral monopoly situations.[8] Given this structure, competition between corrupt officials may not do much to reduce the level of bribery receipts, since, unlike the officials described in Chapter 7, these bureaucrats are selling a differentiated product. Thus if the competitive stage is fully corrupt, applicants who are *legally* qualified will pay more to be served by officials with honest bureaucrats behind them than to be served by those where the officials next in sequence will also demand payment. This result stands in sharp contrast to the case where

---

[7] In New York City, the prevailing bribe–price for a certificate of occupancy, the final permit required for a new building was higher than the bribe required on various intermediate permits (*New York Times*, June 26, 1972).

[8] A similar situation exists when an applicant can choose what jurisdiction to apply in. For example, the unique chain of officials one must deal with may be important in the locational decisions of firms.

applicants want *illegal* services at each step in the organizational sequence. Those who want illegal benefits at each official decision-making node will pay more to a competitive official if subsequent contacts are also corrupt since the likelihood of a successful final outcome is greater. Cleaning up corruption at the final stages of the application approval process will therefore only deter corruption at earlier stages if bribes are paid to obtain illegal government benefits.

A bureaucratic situation where low-level officials assign applicants to one or another higher level bureaucrat is closely related to the sequential case—so long as higher level officials have no authority to review low-level choices. For example, clerks may be able to assign building plans to particular examiners or cases to particular judges. If honest officials are also competent, then applicants who want an honest evaluation from higher level officials may bribe clerks for favorable assignments. Similarly, those with poor claims will pay to be assigned to dishonest officials.[9] If, however, speed is the service being purchased, even those who have done nothing illegal may pay clerks to assign them to officials willing to provide expedited service in return for bribes.[10] This variant of the sequential model thus has two distinctive features. First, the low-level clerks' assignment responsibilities gives them the power to extract bribes from all applicants, whatever the legal status of their claims. Second, the elimination of corruption at the later stages *does* eliminate it in the earlier stages as well if the honest high-level bureaucrats are all equally competent. If some are honest but lazy, however, clerks may still be bribed to send applications to those high-level officials who work quickly.

Therefore, in assessing the normative significance of these positive models, neither the fragmented nor the sequential model of bureaucratic organization appears to be a very promising organizational means of deterring corruption. On the one hand, if applicants can approach officials in any order, corrupt holdouts can cause delays in their attempts to appropriate the program's surplus. On the other hand, competition at some stage in a sequential process may not deter corruption, even in that stage, if each official is linked to a chain of others with monopoly power. Thus, while a distribution of authority to a series of expert agencies may be justified by other objectives, it

---

[9] For example, maneuvering by New York lawyers to obtain particular corrupt judges has been alleged (*New York Times*, March 26, 1974 and January 28, 1976).

[10] In New York City an expediter hired to get building plans approved indicated that his initial strategy was to get the plan assigned to an examiner whom he knew was corrupt. This could be arranged by bribing the clerk who assigned plans to particular examiners (*New York Times*, June 27, 1972).

does not generally seem to have independent benefit in terms of the speed or honesty of the procedures. Furthermore, if those first in the sequence can assign applicants to particular officials at the next stage in the sequence, then corruption of the later stage creates corrupt incentives at the earlier stage. As we shall see, however, more centralized systems of bureaucratic control create different possibilities for abuse. The task for reform, then, is not to search for a universal remedy but to prescribe an organizational form that seems least subject to abuse, given the facts of particular cases.

3. THE HIERARCHICAL MODEL

A. Corruption and the Right to Appeal

The critical difference between a hierarchical bureaucracy and the first two models is the existence of internal review procedures distinct from the outside investigative and prosecutorial powers of the criminal law. Low-level officials are nominally delegated the power to approve applications but may be subject to high-level review. While agency heads have ultimate authority, they may choose not to exercise it.[11] Honest high-level officials can use their power to ferret out corruption. Dishonest ones can use it to buy off subordinates.

Corrupt incentives in a hierarchical bureaucracy depend upon the procedures under which low-level decisions are reviewed by superiors. If applicants have the right to appeal an unfavorable decision, those who are *legally* entitled to benefits will pay little or nothing to low-level officials with *honest* superiors, unless appeal is costly or superiors are lazy and unpredictable. This result contrasts with the sequential case where an applicant seeking a legal benefit would pay *more* to a corrupt official if subsequent officials were honest than if they were dishonest. The market power of low-level officials is enhanced, however, if applicants have no right to appeal or if the probability of appeal can be affected by the actions of low-level bureaucrats.

If superior officials are *dishonest,* however, then legally qualified applicants may be willing to pay high bribes to inferior bureaucrats. Subordinate officials can use the greater greed of their superiors as an

---

[11] Moore's (1977:33–35) description of the organization of the New York City police who enforce the drug laws implies that their department is a hierarchy of this type where superiors have only imperfect control over lower level police officers.

argument for paying off at a low level. Naturally, this threat of subsequent higher payments will succeed only if the bribe buys both approval and a lowered probability of appeal. Applicants will pay little to dishonest low-level officials if the likelihood of review is equivalent for both positive and negative decisions and if the next level's decision is independent of subordinates' recommendations.

Turning to applicants who are *not legally qualified,* however, the honesty of superiors now has an ambiguous impact on low-level corruption. On the one hand, it increases the risk of the corrupt transaction, since even if high-level review does not detect corruption, it may detect the bureaucrat's approval of an illegal application. On the other hand, the honesty of potential reviewers gives subordinates some monopoly power, since only they will accept bribes. Their power to extort bribes is further enhanced if they can also reduce the probability of appeal. The result once again contrasts with the sequential model when the honesty of subsequent officials *lowers* the bargaining power of the first official approached.[12] Thus while *dishonest* superiors may give low-level bureaucrats bargaining power over qualified applicants, *honest* superiors give them bargaining power vis-à-vis the unqualified.

B. High- and Low-Level Corruption: The Pitfalls of Reform

When corruption is uncovered at one hierarchical level, reformers often recommend a change in structure to give that level less discretion. Piecemeal reform will often fail, however, since reducing corrupt incentives at one level in a hierarchy may simply increase them someplace else. Thus, much has been made of the fact that police officers on the beat, and on-site inspectors of housing, construction, grain shipments, restaurants, etc.,[13] operate essentially alone without

---

[12] This conclusion, of course, depends critically upon the assumption that illegal applicants demand illegal services from everyone in the sequence. If, instead, they are able to request illegal services of corrupt officials and legal services of honest ones, this distinction breaks down.

[13] The National Advisory Commission on Criminal Justice Standards and Goals, *Community Crime Prevention,* (Washington, D.C.: U.S. Government Printing Office, 1973), excerpted in Gardiner and Olson (1974:236–246), attributes administrative corruption to decentralized and poorly supervised procedures. In particular cases, the incentives for low-level corruption are documented in Sherman (1974b) and Wilson (1968), for the police; *New York Times,* May 20, June 25, 1975, for grain; *New York Times,* June 26, 1972, November 5, 1974, for the New York City construction industry; *New York Times,* December 3, 1971, for housing inspection; *New York Times,* December 7, 1977, for restaurant inspections.

direct supervision by superiors. These jobs are conducive to corruption both because bribes can pass unobserved and because officials have broad discretion to make case-by-case determinations that cannot easily be checked by superior officials. Restricting the discretion of inferior officials may not, however, reduce corruption. Instead, its locus may simply shift to higher levels of the organization.[14] In fact, high-level bureaucrats in a tightly supervised hierarchy may have just as many unsupervised contacts with applicants as low-level employees have in organizations that allow considerable discretion to those at the bottom.[15] Moreover, personal friendships between high-level officials and clients are common, especially if officials are former employees of the clients' firms. The practice of bureaucrats and regulatory commissioners accepting jobs in the industries they regulate further links the two groups.[16]

[14] Broadus (1976) argues that the lack of enforcement of the Kentucky strip-mining law can be blamed, in large part, upon the coal companies' influence on high-level state politics. While some low-level corruption occurred, large payments were unnecessary because of the companies' influence over the central organization.

Students of American municipal government have found that the shift from centralized political machines to more decentralized forms does not necessarily reduce corruption (e.g., Wolfinger, 1972). Edward Costikyan, in *Behind Closed Doors* (New York: Harcourt, Brace and World, 1966), excerpted in Gardiner and Olson (1974:205–215), contends that today's civil servants are no less corruptible than past political bosses.

The New York City Police Department, however, seems to have realized that centralization was not sufficient. In response to the Knapp Commission's revelations of corruption, they centralized vice enforcement but also instituted other reforms. They engaged in corruption control activities and reports, reduced personnel in the vice division, and instituted a policy of making fewer arrests and giving vice enforcement low priority (Rubinstein and Reuter, 1977:67–68).

[15] The close relationship between top regulatory agency personnel and executives of the industries they regulate has been frequently documented. See, for example, Wilson (1974).

The informality of regulatory agency processes can be contrasted with the formality of judicial proceedings, where explicit limits are placed on the contact between decision makers and those with whom they deal. The contacts are formal and public, and both life tenure for judges and the random selection of juries are designed to isolate these individuals from the interests of petitioners. All contact is part of the public courtroom record, and strict rules limit the types of information and the kinds of statements lawyers are permitted to present. Judges and potential jurors are expected to refuse to hear cases in which they have a personal interest. The major exception is plea bargaining, which sometimes involves the judge (for example, in the case of Spiro Agnew, *New York Times,* October 11, 1973). Criticism of plea bargaining, in fact, concentrates upon its departure from judicial norms of formality and publicity.

[16] Defense contractors employ many former military and civilian Defense Department workers. Over 2,000 retired military officers with the rank of colonel and above worked for the 100 largest defense contractors in 1969 (Yarmolinsky, 1971:60). In a recent example, a high level Defense Department official in the Ford administration, accepted a

The main difference between high- and low-level officials, then, appears to be neither the amount of discretion nor the opportunity for private, personal contact, but the greater visibility of decisions at higher levels of government. The decision of a cabinet secretary is often newsworthy, that of a low-level civil servant is seldom so. When the cost of organized opposition is high, however, publicity may not in and of itself be much of a deterrent to officials. In fact, regulatory commissions and government agencies may not even need outright bribes in order to favor clients. Previous arguments for the superior bargaining power of clients vary (see Noll, 1971; Wilson, 1974) but do not depend on outright bribery, although implied job offers are often cited to explain official behavior. Bribes may be less important at high bureaucratic levels because clients dealing with top government officials generally have a plethora of legal means of influencing the officials' decisions, means not open to the individual facing an isolated police officer or inspector. (Compare the discussion of campaign contributions versus bribes in the legislative context of Chapter 3.)

Furthermore, centralization of authority may not deter corruption if it produces a bottleneck at the top. When low-level bureaucrats simply pass data and applications upward without a conscious attempt to sort and evaluate information, the agency head often faces a tradeoff between a speedy decision and an informed one. Larger and larger quantities of data may make a decision harder instead of easier. Corruption can then become a substitute for thought. The greater the volume of work the agency head faces and the poorer the quality and the larger the volume of the information available, the greater the incentive

---

position with Hughes Aircraft and received offers from two other defense contractors (*New York Times,* February 15, 1977).

Noll, Peck, and McGowan (1973:123) report that while many commissioners and high level staff officials of the Federal Communications Commission "have had experience in the communications business, the data mainly demonstrate that for most a high-level FCC job is an entry into a career in the industry." Common Cause reports that 75% of the top employees of the Energy Research and Development Administration were formerly employed by companies holding ERDA contracts. A study of regulatory agencies showed that 48% of regulatory commissioners who left government between 1971 and 1975 went to work for regulated companies or their law firms. Of commissioners appointed during that time, 52% were previously employed by regulated companies or their law firms. (*In Common,* Winter, 1977, vol. 8) A U.S. Senate study (1977:40) concluded that: "In our detailed considerations of appointment and reappointment of thirty-eight regulators in four agencies over a fifteen year period, we uncovered few instances of an actual financial conflict of interest. The single, most serious situation concerned negotiations for future employment while in office."

to let bribes determine outcomes.[17] The organization of the bureaucracy may mitigate or exacerbate this tendency. On the one hand, if in the journey up the hierarchy an application is competently interpreted and simplified at each stage, then the taller the hierarchy the easier the top bureaucrat's job and the lower the incentive to accept bribes. On the other hand, if each layer loses and distorts information,[18] then the taller the hierarchy the more difficult the agency head's job, and corruption may then be used to simplify the bureaucrat's decision-making tasks. Of course, an agency head may not know which type of hierarchy lies beneath, since even incompetent and corrupt underlings may pose as competent technocrats. Whatever the truth of the matter, if a top official does not trust subordinates to behave competently, he or she will be unwilling to delegate authority and will therefore also be likely to face strong incentives to take bribes.[19]

Thus far the analysis has assumed that centralization was imposed on a bureaucracy by an honest legislature concerned with corruption. It is also possible, however, that honest top bureaucrats may take a similar course of action when they think that inferiors are incompetent or corrupt and providing poor or biased information. Paradoxically, however, the centralization that results from this initial distrust may produce a situation where once conscientious bureaucrats succumb to the corrupt opportunities they have created. For a decision must somehow be made, and while flipping a coin may be one response to untrustworthy information provided by subordinates, bribery is a more lucrative option.

Moreover, on the other side of the potential corrupt transaction, the longer the delays and the more unpredictable and arbitrary the top official's choices, the greater the incentives for applicants to pay bribes to the agency head. Even if the top decision makers do not succumb to the temptations of corruption, however, there is a final difficulty with centralization that is often ignored in the standard anticorruption reform.

---

[17] As noted earlier (Chapter 6), foreign officials who lack technical expertise have sometimes relied on competitive bribery as a decision-making device when purchasing defense products.

[18] Montias (1976:178) writes that "whether information has been obtained from samples or aggregated from exhaustive reports, in transferring it from each tier [in the hierarchy] to the next losses and distortions in content and delays remain unavoidable."

[19] J. M. Montias, in a private communication, has also stressed the importance of geographical distance and poor communications as factors reducing the efficiency of a hierarchy and increasing the incentives for using extrabureaucratic means of expediting decisions.

With the agency head overloaded with work, any lower level official with the power to channel the flow of petitions or to select information is automatically in a powerful position.[20] The "gatekeeper" increases in power the less room there is for applicants inside the gate. The very scarcity of the agency head's time implies that, like it or not, some authority must be delegated even if it is only the power to fill in an appointment calendar or pile up papers in some order on the top official's desk. In some systems, however, the priviledged gatekeepers may not be bureaucrats at all but outside expediters,[21] lobbyists or agents[22] who are well connected with top officials. Their ability to obtain access can be used to earn high fees.

C. Implementation of an Agency Head's Decision

In the discussion thus far, low-level officials either made decisions on their own, subject to high-level review, or else passed information up to the ultimate decision maker at the top of the hierarchy. This view of bureaucracy, however, is only a partial one, since once a top official makes a decision, it must be implemented by low-level officials. Therefore, corrupt agency heads may have to share their bribery receipts with numerous subordinates. The potential deterrent effects of having multiple underlings depends on whether the bribe is paid to obtain a benefit to which the petitioner is legally entitled or to obtain an illegal service. In this second case, the higher level official must use some of the bribe money to buy silence from subordinates if their assistance is necessary to deliver the illegal benefit. A police sergeant, for example, may have absolute power to assign officers to particular beats, but may be incapable of inducing them to protect gamblers without offering a cut of the graft.[23] In this case, the smallest total bribe required to obtain the

---

[20] In India, Monteiro (1966) and Palmier (1975:579) both report that clerks who send files up for decision by senior officers are bribed to ensure that a case goes forwardly rapidly or is not forgotten.

[21] Expediters are commonly employed, for example, by managers of Soviet enterprises. Some of their work is similar to lobbying, but a certain amount of outright bribery and gift giving is indicated by journalistic reports of their activities and by data on their high levels of "travel" expenses (Berliner, 1952:356–358; 1959:361–362, 366–376).

[22] The use of sales agents by American firms in overseas sales, is reported in *New York Times*, June 22, July 6, 27 (Section 3), 1975; "Payoffs: The Growing Scandal," *Newsweek*, February 23, 1976, pp. 26–33; and Jacoby, Nehemkis, and Eells (1977).

[23] Gambling syndicates commonly bribe police officials at many levels. Gardiner (1970) reports that in Wincanton (Reading) the head of the gambling syndicate used two basic strategies: "to pay top personal as much as necessary to keep them happy (and quiet)

government service will be higher than when only a single official must be bribed, since subordinate officials will demand an amount that covers their moral costs and the expected costs of arrest and conviction. Moreover, the existence of corrupt practices will be difficult to conceal from outside investigators as the number of conspirators increases. Of course, if subordinates can be kept in ignorance, bribery may still be costly if top officials can hold out for most of the private surplus generated by their administrative power. However, the amount of surplus open to negotiation between the applicant and the top bureaucrat is larger, and more likely to be positive, the fewer the number of other people that must be bought off, ceteris paribus.

D. The Impact of High-Level Corruption on Bureaucratic Structure

Since bureaucratic structure will help determine the volume of corrupt gains available to agency heads, corrupt top bureaucrats will often have strong incentives to alter bureaucratic structures in order to facilitate corruption. On the one hand, they may try to have as few people as possible administering a program.[24] On the other hand, they may create a tall hierarchy to produce delays and then sell favorable positions in the queue to high bidders. When corrupt incentives are not generated by bureaucratic *procedures* (red tape) but by bureaucratic *outputs* (exemptions from law enforcement), corrupt agency heads will wish to have a short hierarchy to minimize the number of middlemen who must be paid off. Similarly, in making hiring decisions, top officials will stress loyalty to superiors rather than competence, efficiency, or honesty. Indeed, where delay produces corruption, inefficiency will be valued positively; and where the corrupt service is illegal, low scruples will be a strong recommendation. In short, corrupt high-level bureaucrats not only may distort their agencies' purposes by allocating benefits on the basis of

---

and to pay *something* to as many as possible, thus implicating them in the system and keeping them from talking [p. 24]." Low-level officials had little recourse against the gambling syndicate, however, because of its close ties with high-level politicians and the lack of effective outside law enforcement activity by the state or the F.B.I. In other cases, say the police department in a large city where other portions of the city government are not corrupt, lower level police officers may have more bargaining power. See also Rubinstein (1973) and Rubinstein and Reuter (1977).

[24] Thus state politicians in Maryland apparently centralized the disbursement of capital funds for public works projects as a means of centralizing the graft (Edsall, 1974).

willingness to pay, they may also organize their agencies inefficiently in an effort to maximize their own income.[25]

4. CHOOSING THE LEAST CORRUPT
FORM OF BUREAUCRACY

We are faced, then, with an unattractive range of choices. A fragmented bureaucracy may generate extensive delays as corrupt officials hold out for large bribes, a sequential bureaucracy may be permeated with corruption even though officials have overlapping jurisdictions, while a corrupt bureaucrat at the top of a hierarchy may transform the entire administrative structure into an engine for the maximization of corrupt receipts. However, it should be clear that the control of corruption is only one of the goals of bureaucratic design. Considerations of cost and expertise often imply that one form is preferable to another. The analysis can then suggest the corrupt incentives to be anticipated as a result of the pursuit of these other policy objectives. Nevertheless, there are times when the control of corruption *is* a central policy goal, and one would like to compare the differing organizational forms systematically. This section, then, considers how a policymaker concerned with minimizing the expected proportion of corrupt transactions might analyze the choice of bureaucratic form in very simple situations. While any real-life applications would, of course, be much more complex, nonetheless even a few simple cases will allow me to make some basic points. Abstracting from the possibility that corruption may be reduced by increased monitoring or law enforcement activity, this section concentrates on the interaction between personnel policy and structure.

Assume, then, that an organizational designer can classify job applicants on the basis of the probability that they will be corrupt, β_i, and that the β_i are given exogenously. Job applicants can be classified so that $\beta_1 < \beta_2 <, \ldots, < \beta_n \leq 1$. Only one individual of each kind exists.[26] In contrast to Chapters 5 through 8, the size of the bribe has no

---

[25] Corrupt agency heads would also consider the impact of corruption on their honest returns. Thus, Chapter 4 argued that agency heads would take legislative responses into account in deciding on the level of bribery receipts. Organizational structures that facilitate bribery will be rejected, even by a corrupt bureaucrat, if they imply too great a sacrifice of agency performance.

[26] Instead of a fixed applicant pool with known β_i one might assume that the executive branch believes that there is a function, $\beta = f(w)$, where w is the wage rate and $f'(w) < 0$. This function can be interpreted in either of two ways. Either it implies that as w increases more honest people apply for government jobs or it implies that the more civil servants are paid the less likely they are to be corrupt.

role in the analysis. If an official is corrupt a briber can always find a satisfactory positive bribe. The β_i are given independently of the size of the bribe paid. My task will be to show how the designer might think about the choice among three simple organizational options under the assumption that the level of expected sanctions is independent of the bureaucratic form. The baseline is a bureaucratic structure in which each official is given monopoly power over a certain share of the applications, without any effort being made to review the flow of low-level decisions. This *independent* structure is then compared to the *sequential* and *hierarchical* alternatives already discussed.

To keep the problem simple, suppose the designer decides that two officials with corruption probabilities β_1 and β_2 must be hired to handle the agency's work and that if these two officials are honest, it is equally efficient either to give each of them *independent* power over half the workload or to give them *sequential* decision-making authority over all the applications. For example, if the policymaker is charged with designing a system for issuing building permits, then if everyone is honest it makes no difference whether one official enforces the building code and the other the fire regulations or whether each carries out complete inspections. Furthermore, corruption has no direct impact on efficiency. Unlike the queuing models in Chapter 5, bribery neither slows down nor speeds up performance.

Assume, finally that the policymaker is concerned only with the problem posed by an official forcing applicants to pay for a benefit to which they are *legally* entitled. In this case, the use of independent officials is always superior to the sequential alternative. While this can be demonstrated formally,[27] the basic intuition is simple. In the case of an independent official, even if one official is corrupt, some applicants will not have to pay bribes if the other agent is honest. In contrast, in the *sequential* case, all applicants must pay bribes so long as one corrupt official exists. If, in addition, independent officials can compete with one

---

[27] The probabilities of the four possible alternatives are

	one	
two	corrupt	honest
corrupt	$\beta_1\beta_2$	$\beta_2(1 - \beta_1)$
honest	$\beta_1(1 - \beta_2)$	$(1 - \beta_2)(1 - \beta_1)$

The expected proportion of corrupt transactions with two independent bureaucrats is $(\beta_1 + \beta_2)/2$, and with a sequential system it is $1 - (1 - \beta_2)(1 - \beta_1)$. Thus, $(\beta_1 + \beta_2)/2 \gtreqless \beta_1 + \beta_2 - \beta_1\beta_2$ or $2\beta_1\beta_2 \gtreqless \beta_1 + \beta_2$. Dividing by $2\beta_1$, $\beta_2 \gtreqless 1/2[1 + (\beta_2/\beta_1)]$. Since $\beta_2 > \beta_1$, this implies $1/2[1 + (\beta_2/\beta_1)] > 1 \geq \beta_2$. Thus, a system of independent officials is superior.

another, the presence of one honest official may eliminate all corruption (see Chapter 7).[28]

When the bureaucracy is organized *sequentially,* the results are different when *illegal* benefits must be provided at *each* stage in order for an unqualified applicant to succeed. Since an application cannot be divided up into independent legal and illegal sections, corruption at the first stage is useless unless both officials are corrupt. Similarly, an illegal application will never get to the second stage unless the first official is corrupt. Thus, the conclusions must be reversed. If bribery buys illegal benefits, a sequential system is superior to one with independent officials,[29] since no corruption occurs unless *both* officials are corrupt.

Turning now to a hierarchical organization, let us compare it first to an independent bureaucracy, where corruption is used to obtain a *legal* benefit. Assume that the highest level of the agency reviews all decisions. Hierarchical review thus eliminates low-level corruption. If a bribe is demanded by the low-level official, the applicant resists the corrupt pressure and appeals to the agent's superior. Of course, the conclusions here would have to be modified if, as is often the case, review is not certain or if low-level bureaucrats can use the information under their control to skew higher level outcomes. Nevertheless, if these difficulties are not important, the expected proportion of corrupt transactions is β_1 so long as the most honest official is placed at the top. This is obviously superior to a system of independent officials where the expected proportion is $(\beta_1 + \beta_2)/2$.[30] Similarly, it is easy to see that hierarchy is also superior to independence in the *illegal* benefit case. So long as inferior officials are not able to turn their superiors in, the probability that an illegal application will be approved is β_1. This is less than the chance, $(\beta_1 + \beta_2)/2$, in the independent official case.[31]

[28] This result depends upon how congested the honest official becomes. If the presence of one honest official prevents the other from obtaining any bribes, then the expected proportion of corrupt transactions is $\beta_1\beta_2$, which is less than $(\beta_1 + \beta_2)/2$.

[29] The chance that an illegal application will be approved is $(\beta_1 + \beta_2)/2$ for an independent system and $\beta_1\beta_2$ for a sequential method of organization. Since $\beta_1\beta_2 < (\beta_1 + \beta_2)/2$, the sequential organization is preferable.

[30] If independent officials can compete, and if no congestion exists, then the expected probability is $\beta_1\beta_2 < \beta_1$, and the independent case is preferable.

[31] The minimization of the expected proportion of corrupt applicants is not the only plausible objective function, however. For instance, if applicants are obtaining benefits to which they are legally entitled, the policymaker might want to maximize the chance that at least one applicant obtains the service honestly. (If the benefit is illegal, this alternative objective function is, of course, not a very sensible one.) The policymaker might be willing to sacrifice something in terms of the *proportion* of transactions decided corruptly in order to reduce the chance of having a *completely* corrupt system. Given

The last comparison to be made is between hierarchy and sequence. When the benefit is *legal,* the superiority of hierarchy follows immediately from the previous arguments showing that hierarchy (H) is superior to independence (I), and that independence is superior to sequence (S). Therefore, H is preferable to S. When bribes are paid in return for *illegal* benefits, a sequential system dominates a hierarchical one, however, since illegal applicants, turned down at the first stage, cannot appeal to the next level.[32] This conclusion, of course, depends critically upon the assumption that honest officials never approve illegal applications and that low-level bureaucrats do not report the illegal actions of their superiors. In short, for legal benefits, H is better than I which dominates S; while for illegal benefits, S is better than H which dominates I.

Before turning to the final, disorganized, case, it is worthwhile to suggest an interesting way to extend the present analysis. One of the most restrictive assumptions was the exogenous nature of β_i, the probability of taking a bribe. In the preceding chapters, however, the official's willingness to be corrupted was not exogenous but depended upon the size of the bribe and the expected penalties levied. For example, if no official will accept bribes lower than some minimum determined by the fixed and variable costs of corruption,[33] this fact will work in favor of a sequential organization in the illegal benefit case. If illegal benefits are provided at each stage in the sequence, then the minimum total payoff equals the sum of the reservation prices of each official. The longer the sequence, the higher the minimum payoff and the greater the possibility that it will exceed the briber's maximum willingness to pay.

5. DISORGANIZED BUREAUCRACIES

Thus far, I have been dealing with ideal types. Under each model, the route to bureaucratic approval was clearcut, even if neither the probability of a successful outcome nor the length of procedural delays was known. Even in a fragmented bureaucracy, a land developer knows that official X is in charge of granting building permits, official Y must

---

this objective, an independent system will dominate a hierarchy, since the probability of one honest applicant getting through is $1 - \beta_1$ with a hierarchy, and $(1 - \beta_1\beta_2) > (1 - \beta_1)$ with independent bureaucrats.

[32] In symbols, $\beta_1\beta_2 < (\beta_1 + \beta_2)/2$, by the argument in note 27.

[33] Chapters 6 and 7 distinguished between this case and others where only low bribes were acceptable.

approve the sewers, and so forth. Some actual bureaucracies, however, can only be described as chaotic: Members of the public have difficulty discovering which officials are legally authorized to deal with their problems or what kind of bureaucratic review they are entitled to demand.

This pervasive uncertainty has two very different impacts upon corrupt behavior. First, the uncertainty of legal procedures makes applicants willing to pay bribes in return for a higher probability of actually obtaining the government benefit.[34] Therefore, the payment of bribes may be undertaken more readily by risk-averse applicants than by those who like to take chances. The probability of arrest on charges of corruption may be so low that the risks associated with following honest procedures are greater than the risks associated with paying bribes. In fact, the very disorganization of the bureaucracy may lower the risk of detection since there may be no clear standard of honest behavior. This first effect of chaos, however, may be offset by a second. While corrupt bureaucrats may be willing to accept bribes, applicants cannot be sure that officials have the power to perform their side of the bargain.[35] Chaotic legal procedures increase the *demand* for more certain illegal ones, but if the disorganization of government is far advanced, no bureaucrats may be able to *supply* the requisite certainty even when offered a monetary incentive.

Curiously, past writing on this subject has failed to distinguish between supply and demand in a disorganized bureaucracy. Thus one group of authors associates chaos with corruption by concentrating upon the demand for illegal bureaucratic services in a disorganized government.[36] V. O. Key (1936), for example, links corruption to a world in flux—where rapid changes in society overwhelm an outdated government structure so that only cash has any chance of accomplishing

---

[34] The Italian bureaucracy provides an example. Jacoby, Nehemkis, and Eells (1977) write that "within the vast bureaucracy, no one knows for certain which laws are valid and what some of them really mean [p. 77]." Only expediters with plenty of bribe money can overcome "the chronic chaos, buck-passing, indecision, and extortionate rulings [p. 37]."

[35] Wraith and Simkins' example (1963:24–25) of the Nigerian tailoring contract cited in Chapter 3, note 34 also applies here. Examples can also be drawn from recent Western experience in Saudi Arabia where firms often do not know who has authority to make decisions. One prominent agent has amassed a fortune handling the affairs of multinational companies who wish to deal with the Saudis (*New York Times*, July 3, 1977).

[36] Ford (1904), Key (1936), Huntington (1967), Jacoby, Nehemkis, and Eells (1977), and LeVine (1975:96). Jacoby, Nehemkis, and Eells also mention that in a chaotic regime bureaucrats may wish to supply more corrupt benefits but fail to note that they may be incapable of doing so.

anything and there is no trust and no set of established institutional procedures. In contrast, a second group emphasizes the *supply* side and advocates the introduction of uncertainty as a means of preventing bribery.[37] Proponents of this latter position, however, do not go so far as to advocate chaos. Instead they generally envisage a basically stable, well-organized bureaucracy within which personnel are constantly rotated, e.g., rotating the beats of police officers, given an honest and well-run police department, or electing a reform mayor who is willing to institute controls on bureaucrats and police officers. The aim is to prevent the development of close, trusting bonds between bureaucrats and clients. Both sets of authors tend to draw overly strong conclusions. Those who advocate the introduction of change stress the impact of this policy on *supply,* forgetting that *demand* may increase. In contrast, observers of corruption in underdeveloped countries notice the high level of *demand,* often neglecting the frequently low levels of *supply.*

Instead of taking the degree of disorganization as fixed, consider also the possibility that corruption itself can play a role in transforming a chaotic bureaucracy. These changes may not be desirable from the perspective of organization theory, but they may have important consequences for both legal and illegal government operations. Paradoxically, corruption, arising in response to the disorganization of the bureaucracy, may generate clear hierarchies where none existed before.[38] Low-level

[37] The Pennsylvania Crime Commission (1974) recommends that in enforcing drug laws the Philadelphia Police Department should "rotat[e] undercover personnel so that undercover assignments last no longer than 18 months or a certain number of arrests [p. 839]." The New York City Police Department rotated police officers every four years in a special gambling control unit and frequently changed the unit's organizational form "to keep people off balance [Kornblum, 1976:11–12]." Rotation does not always work, however. In the New York City Police Department, corrupt clerical officers of plainclothes units checked on the "reputation" of officers who were transferred in order to maintain the corrupt system in spite of rotating assignments (Rubinstein and Reuter, 1977:66). Police involved in drug traffic in Latin America sold lists of corrupt contacts when they were transferred (*New York Times,* April 21, 1975).

[38] The government would then be similar to that analyzed by Johnson (1975). Waterbury (1973), for example, describes Morocco as a place where "corruption is manipulated, guided, planned and desired by the regime itself [p. 534]." Corruption in Indonesia has come under attack, in part, because of its increasing concentration at high levels. A local observer is quoted as saying "Corruption by itself may not be so bad, but corruption without sharing is selfish (*Wall Street Journal,* December 8, 1977)." Banfield (1975) explains that a "boss" who has gained control of a previously decentralized agency "will invest heavily in the dependability of his principle subordinates (one 'comes up through' a machine by demonstrating loyalty over time), regulate the breadth of their discretion, maintain an incentive system that motivates machine workers (especially job patronage, legal fees, the purchase of insurance, construction contracts, etc.), and monitor then to check unauthorized corruption [pp. 601–602]."

officials who try to collect bribes may find that higher bureaucrats, who would have ignored their honest behavior, now try to exert authority over them to appropriate their corrupt gains. This possibility depends, of course, upon a theory of bureaucratic organization in which the officials themselves play a critical role in establishing an agency's structure. Under this hypothesis, individuals in nominally superior positions do not bother to assert their authority over those below them unless given an incentive to do so. If the usual legal incentives—such as the desire for promotion, the love of power, or personal devotion to the agency's goals—do not operate in a disorganized world, only the hope of extracting some of another's corrupt receipts can induce one bureaucrat to exercise authority over another. It is possible, of course, that once corruption creates *some* kind of bureaucratic order out of chaos, the resulting structure might be more easily reformed than its disorganized counterpart. A shift in personnel may be sufficient to establish legal routes to bureaucratic approval and hence, over time, reduce the demand for corrupt benefits.

6. CONCLUSIONS

One of the most common responses to a scandal is piecemeal institutional reform in which new bureaucratic structures are proposed to guarantee that the scandal will not be repeated in the future. However understandable this response, the basic lesson of this chapter is that policymakers who concentrate on a single stage of the bureaucratic process are unlikely to achieve lasting reform. Thus, perhaps the most common response to the corruption of low-level officials—such as building inspectors or cops on the beat—is the creation of a stronger hierarchy with more review and less delegation of authority. Yet in a given organizational context, this step may simply push the corruption upstairs. Similarly, the reaction to a high-level scandal may be a call for the decentralization of authority. Yet this may only lead to different abuses that will generate a call for more centralized control. Thus both *independent* and *hierarchical* organizational forms place great pressure on personal honesty; *fragmentation* breeds hold-outs, and *sequences* may sometimes permit a few strategically placed corrupt officials to benefit from others' honesty. Furthermore, if central control is really abdicated, the whole system may degenerate into the disorganized case.

All these scenarios, of course, are not equally likely under all conditions. The analysis does suggest, however, the necessity for a hard-headed scrutiny of alternative systems with an awareness that each one is vulnerable to exploitation by unscrupulous officials. Moreover, having identified the critical points in each system, reformers must move on to propose more particularized structures—closer monitoring, higher pay, nonvested pension rights, and so forth—that will increase the expected costs of peculation at the critical soft spots.

Beyond providing a general framework for reform, the chapter also generates some more specific lessons. The most important point emphasizes the existence of a previously ignored tradeoff in institutional design. On the one hand, one may take institutional steps to prevent bureaucrats from forcing applicants to pay bribes for benefits to which they are *legally entitled*. On the other hand, one may prevent *legally unqualified* applicants from bribing their way onto the roles of beneficiaries. But it will not generally be possible to design institutions which achieve both goals at once.

My task is not to resolve such tradeoffs but to demonstrate that they must be confronted by serious reformers. Thus I have specified a set of conditions under which a *sequential* system will dominate a *hierarchy* as a means of reducing corruption if bribes are paid in return for *obviously illegal* actions. In contrast, if officials provide *legal* services in return for bribes, I have specified a simple model in which *hierarchy* dominates both a series of *independent* officials and a *sequential* system. This means that a policymaker will generally be forced to ask some hard questions before recommending a particular institutional structure. Which, for example, is more important—eliminating the bribes paid by legally qualified public housing tenants or making it impossible for unqualified people to obtain subsidized units?

The analysis also permits a refinement of the proposal—developed in Chapters 7 and 8—to introduce competition between officials as a check on corrupt incentives. In both the *sequential* and *hierarchical* models, if subsequent bureaucratic contacts vary in their willingness to accept corrupt payments, competitive officials are really selling a highly differentiated product, and one that is valued differently depending upon whether or not the applicant is seeking a legal or an illegal benefit. In a *sequential* bureaucracy, those who are legally qualified will pay more to an official who gives the applicant access to a sequence of honest officials, while those who want an illegal service will pay more to those who provide access to corrupt officials. In contrast, in a *hierarchical* system, legally qualified applicants will pay only relatively small sums to officials with honest superiors. Nonetheless, even imperfect competition will tend to reduce the dollar value of bribery and, less surely, its incidence as well.

Aside from its use as a tool for reform, the analysis also reveals a reciprocal relation between structure and corruption. Just as structure may influence the level of corruption, so the desire for corrupt returns will influence structure. Corrupt top bureaucrats in public agencies will seek to replace disorganized procedures with rationalized ones that centralize authority. Once in control of an agency, however, corrupt bureaucrats will wish to establish arbitrary and slow-moving legal procedures, either by hiring incompetent underlings or by promulgating complicated regulations. Their ability to use these devices to extract bribes will, of course, depend upon the existence of private market substitutes or alternatives in other areas of government. Thus a corrupt agency head might also try both to outlaw private substitutes and to absorb competing public agencies or independent government jurisdictions. Chaos will be replaced by order, yet this organization may produce, not speed, but agonizing deliberation.

10

CORRUPTION AND THE PRIVATE SECTOR

1. INTRODUCTION

While political scientists have not hesitated to use moral convictions, patriotism, and devotion to duty to explain the behavior of government officials and private citizens, economists have often assumed that the behavior of private firms can be explained without appeals to "higher" values. Even economists who recognize serious market failures and inequities in the distribution of income and wealth tend to seek structural solutions or changes in government taxing and spending policies, rather than reforms of the educational process or modifications of cultural values. My study of corruption, for example, has been concerned with corrupt *opportunities* and with ways to change structures to reduce *incentives*. More generally, economists are uncomfortable with public programs that exhort consumers to make private sacrifices for collective goals or call on businessmen to recognize their social responsibilities.

Despite this discomfort, the profession commonly works with models that assume that law abiding behavior is the norm. Although the aresponsibility of profit-seeking organizations has long been recognized in the literature of industrial organization and public finance, it is generally assumed that if a law is passed regulating behavior, no one will violate

189

its provisions (for exceptions see Buchannan and Tullock, 1975; Roberts, 1976). Government intervention may distort behavior, but the simple expedients of corrupting the inspector or juggling the books are seldom part of the analysis.

Research on crime (Becker, 1968; Stigler, 1970), fraud (Darby and Karni, 1973), smuggling (Bhagwati, 1974), organized crime (Schelling, 1967), and corruption make clear, however, that illegal behavior will often be in the interest of both individuals and profit-making firms. Similarly, it will not always be in an individual's interest to follow the rules laid down by superiors. Research on the problems of control in large organizations has emphasized the frequent conflicts of interest between managers and employees or principals and agents (Alchian and Demsetz, 1972; Leibenstein, 1966; Williamson, 1967). Thus it is only necessary to juxtapose research on the economics of crime with analyses of the problems of organizational control to generate an inquiry that threatens the legitimacy of the private business corporation. It is easy to see that corporations single-mindedly concerned with profit maximization will choose an "optimal" amount of fraud or corruption (Banfield, 1975; Darby and Karni, 1973). Some illegal behavior will be encouraged because it increases profits, and other behavior will be tolerated because it is too costly to eliminate. Furthermore, since the illegal behavior of agents, employees, or top management will generally impose external costs on others, it is unlikely that the firm's optimizing decision will be socially optimal under anyone's definition of social welfare. If the opportunities for illegal behavior are widespread in modern business firms, the corporation may only be justified if peopled by individuals who do not take advantage of all opportunities to benefit at the expense of shareholders, top managers, or the public. It follows that economists cannot afford to look askance at those social scientists who are concerned with individual values. The economist's own models are deeply embedded in a set of often unstated assumptions about human values, and many of the normative claims for the market are fundamentally dependent upon the assumption that economic actors will not break the law.

Fortunately, I can discuss the limits of market institutions without having to develop a completely new analytic structure. My models of organizational behavior and of the opportunities for corruption in government can be modified to apply to a study of the private sector. To see this, I look at two aspects of corporate behavior. First, in Section 2 I will consider cases where, unlike high-level government officials, executives in private business firms face situations in which low-level corruption will further the aims of both top management and shareholders. Executives and owners may want to save face and escape legal liability by avoiding direct knowledge of corruption, but they may wish to organize their firms to facilitate its occurrence. Second, Sections 3 and 4 consider other forms of private-sector corruption that involve a conflict of interest between owners and directors or managers, or between high- and low-level employees. These cases are much more analogous to the legislative and bureaucratic corruption discussed in the preceding chapters. There are, nevertheless, some important differences caused by the fact that stockholders and voters do not have identical means of controlling officials whom they elect and by the distinction between competitive pressures and the accountability of bureaucrats.

2. PRIVATE FIRM ORGANIZATION AND CORRUPTION

Beginning with the first theme of "profitable" corruption, one can easily see that although a company's stockholders and managers will wish to prevent situations where employees or agents *accept* bribes in return for price discounts on sales or price premiums on purchases, they may not wish to know about cases in which their sales personal *pay* bribes to obtain lucrative deals.[1] This corruption, of course, need not necessarily involve the bribery of government officials. As Section 4 demonstrates many wholly private activities produce corrupt incentives analogous to those which exist in the public sector.

A firm's internal organization may reflect the desire to facilitate low-level corruption. Executives may delegate responsibility and avoid close monitoring in order to create an environment hospitable to corruption.[2]

---

[1] Jacoby, Nehemkis, and Eells argue that the stock prices of firms which disclosed "political payments" abroad did not suffer a long-term decline (1977:51–57). Shareholders, however, may prefer to be uninformed about these payments particularly since it is generally illegal for them to approve such actions (Henn, 1970:380). Thus in one company 99% of those stockholders who voted said that they did not want further information on questionable payments (the case is from a speech by Roderick Hills reprinted in *Yale Law Report* 23 (Fall 1976): 4–5, quoted in Jacoby Nehemkis, and Eells, 1977:57).

Gulf's current top management and board of directors denied knowledge of Gulf's political payments (McCloy, Pearson, and Matthews, 1976:8–15; 224–276). Of course, as the report points out, the actual extent of their knowledge is difficult to document.

[2] This practice is not limited to legitimate business firms. Rubinstein and Reuter (1977:20) report that individuals high in the numbers racket in New York City have organized their operations to facilitate low-level payoffs to the police.

They may satisfy legal mandates by issuing directives that exhort employees to obey the law,[3] but fail to follow these orders up with surveillance activities or with promotion policies that reward law-abiding behavior. Instead of monitoring the day-to-day activity of subordinates, managers may simply use output measures such as sales, market shares, or profit margins to evaluate their inferiors.[4] Indeed, a firm may go further and purchase the services of independent entrepreneurs to do the firm's dirty work rather than hiring them as employees. The outsider provides specialized contacts with decision makers or expedited service through a government bureaucracy, and the seller asks no questions about how the service was performed. The use of agents illustrates the role of market transactions in *reducing* information flow, a factor ignored in standard economic discussions, which typically assume that managers always benefit from more accurate information.[5]

Agents are commonly used as buffers in international business (Jacoby, Nehemkis, and Eells, 1977; Weiss, 1975:66–67). For example, the Northrop Corporation used the Economic Development Corporation [EDC], established by a Northrop consultant, to promote the sales of Northrop aircraft to Iran. "Northrop agreed to pay EDC a commission equal to a percentage of all aircraft sales to Iran, and later extended the agreement to cover sales to other countries. According to a report

[3] See the codes of conduct reprinted in an appendix in Basche (1976). Basche gives no evidence, however, on companies' enforcement policies.

[4] There is a close analogy here to executives who use similar output measures to evaluate division managers in a competitive environment in which antitrust violations can improve a division's performance. See Herling (1962) and Smith (1963) for a discussion of top management's role in the electrical equipment price fixing conspiracies of the 1950s. Company presidents combined a high pressure drive for profits with moves toward decentralization of the company hierarchy. Divisional managers were given authority to set prices for the products they produced, and they responded to the pressure for profits by engaging in illegal collusion. Top management appears to have been ignorant of these illegal activities for a decade (Smith, 1963, Chapters 5 and 6).

Although the courts have not taken a clear position, top management cannot always escape criminal liability through this device. Kriesberg (1976) writes that

> The courts have failed to delimit precisely the "responsibility" of corporate employees. . . . Frequently . . . there is no evidence of explicit direction to transgress the law, and the liability issue is whether a corporate employee who assented to, acquiesced in, or failed to halt illegal conduct by others is criminally responsible. In these situations of passive participation, courts usually have approved penal sanctions only when the applicable statute imposed an affirmative managerial duty and the employee charged was a corporate executive [pp. 1097–1098, footnotes omitted].

[5] For a modern discussion of the internal organization of the firm which assumes that information always has positive value see Williamson (1975).

prepared by Northrop's auditors, 'the company is not interested in knowing how EDC operates, and who they are in touch with, but can only measure the benefit of EDC by sales that occur' [quoted in Weiss, 1975:67].'' Similarly, in New York City the construction industry uses agents as expediters to obtain government permits and inspections (*New York Times,* June 27, 1972); and shipping company executives avoid knowledge of payoffs made to the International Longshoremen's Association by using outside agents. The president of a shipping company told a reporter "We have no direct dealings with labor at all. We have a contractual price with certain companies to load and unload our cargoes. What they do with the money is their business, not ours [*New York Times,* September 1, 1977].''

The use of outsiders can also be beneficial for reasons unrelated to their ability to isolate businessmen from unpleasant truths. Professional middlemen are likely to have more bargaining power vis á vis bureaucrats than individual firms. Indeed, individuals engaged in what is often called organized crime are sometimes used as middlemen because of their willingness to use violence if politer forms of criminal behavior are unsatisfactory.[6] The level of bribes may be reduced by threats of violence while legitimate businessmen isolate themselves from both the corruption and the violence and earn high profits as a consequence. The cost in this case is the fear that the threats may be turned against businessmen who try to extricate themselves from their underworld connections. Even more genteel outside agents, however, may be superior to employees. Officials who demand high bribes can be told by the middlemen that they will bring no further business if concessions are not forthcoming, and a bureaucrat who threatens to report a corrupt offer can be deterred by the professional's threat to expose the official's previous indiscretions. Thus there appear to be "economies of scale" in bribe paying that favor its production by a few specialists.[7]

A firm which isolates itself from its salesmen by making them independent entrepreneurs rather than employees, however, may increase a second type of risk—the risk that agents will not serve their client's interests. On the one hand, the salesman may demand high fees, claiming that they are needed to pay bribes, when in fact these payments

[6] For example, in New York City doctors processing large numbers of Medicaid patients are reported to use underworld figures both to collect bills due them from the city government and to prevent the entry of competitors (*New York Times,* June 3, 1977).

[7] The benefits to specialization will be particularly large in societies where the government bureaucracy is especially large, complex, and hard to understand. See the discussion of disorganized bureaucracies in Chapter 9.

are simply pocketed by the middleman.[8] On the other hand, the salesman may sell out to the firm's customers through reverse bribery, agreeing to a low selling price for the firm's product in return for a direct payment from the buyer. Empirical work is needed, however, to determine whether outsiders are in fact more difficult to control than insiders. One suspects that the nature of a firm's business will be more important than its formal relationship with its salesmen in determining the ease of monitoring.

Because of the costs of control, business executives will often be placed in the awkward position of trusting agents to engage only in those illegal activities that benefit the company. Yet in order to assure performance of the corrupt bargain, agents on both sides may well develop close personal relationships, especially if they meet frequently to transact business. Thus agents might, under these conditions, decide to collude to favor themselves at the expense of both principals. Firms may have to put up with some counterproductive cheating in order to avoid having to monitor and punish corruption which benefits the organization.

There is one important case, however, where firms will not have to worry about corruption that damages their profit position. When a firm faces a monopolistic seller or a monopsonist buyer, it knows that an honest transaction will be on terms unfavorable to the company. Management expects that honest transactions will imply high input prices or low output prices. Since honest transactions are likely to be costly to the firm, corruption has at least some chance of improving the firm's position. Firms in this situation are therefore very similar to those trying to obtain a favorable place in line from a single official in Chapter 5 or seeking government contracts in Chapter 6. The firm's agents have nothing of value to provide except for a bribe or kickback which can induce the monopolist's agents to soften their demands. It follows that in this situation *competitive* firms have a stronger incentive to facilitate low-level corruption than those with market power.[9]

---

[8] Milbrath (1963) in his study of Washington lobbyists cites one lobbyist as saying: "They [a client] came to me with the idea that we had to do something under the table or something dirty to get what they wanted. They asked, 'Where do we put the fix in?' Such persons are often taken in by unscrupulous lobbyists who probably pocket the money they have been given to bribe officials [p. 282]." Similarly, firms dealing with Saudi Arabia through agents have little idea how much of their payments are passed on to government officials and how much agents keep for themselves (*New York Times,* July 3, 1977, Section 3).

[9] Banfield (1975) makes a similar point. He writes that "One would expect the tendency to corrupt other organizations to be the strongest among those profit-maximizing businesses which must depend upon a small number of customers or suppliers . . . and whose profit margins in the absence of corruption would be non-existent or nearly so [pp. 594–595]."

A striking case, which illustrates this point as well as the danger that agents will exploit their positions for personal gain, came to light in the New York City supermarket industry. The industry faces a monopsonistic supplier of labor—the Amalgamated Meat Cutters and Retail Food Stores Employees Union. Supermarkets are reported to have made payments to a middleman who in turn paid union officials to assure labor peace.[10] Some unknown proportion of these funds was kept by the middleman. More important, however, this agent apparently used his influence within the union as a way of inducing supermarket chains to use him as their meat wholesaler. Those who did not buy meat through him were threatened with labor troubles. His ability to blunt the monopoly power of one input (labor) permitted him to obtain monopoly power over another input (meat). He further cemented his monopoly position by paying kickbacks to supermarket executives who bought meat through his company. Finally, his control over meat wholesaling in New York permitted him to obtain payoffs from suppliers of beef. One large Middle Western beef processor paid large sums to this agent in return for being able to sell in the New York area without incurring union opposition. The company wished to carry out many butchering activities in the Middle West, thus reducing the shipping costs of the beef but also reducing the work available to New York butchers. While this might seem a classic case of compensating those who lose from a technological innovation, there is no evidence that the butchers themselves received any benefits (*Wall Street Journal*, September 10, 11, 1974; *New York Times*, March 14, 26 and October 8, 1974).

Such complex systems of kickbacks and payoffs, however, appear to be relatively uncommon. Instead, in a wide range of situations, management is likely to believe that the possibility of disloyal agents or the risk of scandal is high. They may then respond to the problem of corruption in a radically different way: They may try to reorganize their business so that no corrupt incentives exist. Chapter 6, suggested that bribery in government contracting could be eliminated by direct public production of a good or service that had been purchased corruptly in the past. This strategy of vertical integration can also be used by private firms. They may do this by merging with corruptible organizations or by hiring the individuals offering corrupt inducements or demanding bribe payments. Thus nursing homes have eliminated the kickbacks paid for pharmaceuticals by merging with druggists (U.S. Congress, Senate, 1975), and firms can hire people with inside information about competitors (Henn, 1970:460) instead of paying for their services. Labor union demands, such as those faced by supermarket owners, cannot be solved by

---

[10] Similar payments by the building trades industry at the end of the nineteenth century are reported by Hutchinson (1970: 26–27).

merger, however. The only alternative for a firm may be to move to a part of the country where corrupt unions are not as powerful. This is, of course, not possible for industries dependent upon large concentrations of population (like supermarkets) or particular geographical or geological features (like ocean shippers or the mining industry).

Many instances of corruption by business firms, however, involve payments to government officials in return for favorable regulatory treatment, tax relief, or direct transfer payments or loans. Full legal merger between a firm and a government agency as a substitute for obtaining special favors amounts to nationalization of the company. So long as the firm's owners can affect the level of compensation paid by the government, mergers of this type may be sought by unprofitable business firms.[11] In other cases, however, less extreme strategies that amount to a partial and short-run merger of a firm and a government are possible. Thus there are many examples of key executives holding political offices that help them aid their firms' fortunes. In Latin America, some politicians are directly involved in the illegal drug trade, and in the early days of railroading, executives obtained government financing and assistance for their firms by serving as public officials.[12] Today it remains common in the United States for local politics to attract building contractors and merchants with a stake in city decisions.[13] Similarly, executives may seek to establish friendships with key bureaucrats either by having friends or relatives appointed or by establishing personal ties with those already in office. This strategy could be so successful that officials perform favors out of friendship rather than for monetary gain. Conflict-of-interest laws and civil service reforms prevent the most flagrant examples of mergers of this type, but cases can still be found of federal contracts awarded to firms that have members of Congress as part owners or of politicians favoring family business interests.[14]

---

[11] Before the bankruptcy of the Penn Central Railroad, its executives were seeking not only loan guarantees but also nationalization of passenger service (Daughen and Binzen, 1971:259). The authors report that a finance committee member told them, "We believed that although the reports of losses would scare some investors and might dry up private sources of credit, it would hasten government help. We wanted to alert the government so that it would stay in and help us and maybe even take over the railroad, or at least the unprofitable parts of it [p. 261]."

[12] *New York Times*, April 21, 1975 and Cochran (1953).

[13] For a discussion of this phenomenon, see Margolis (1974).

[14] Representative Robert Sikes, for example, had an interest in a Florida land development project when he pushed legislation beneficial to an adjacent project (*New York Times*, July 27, 1976).

3. THE CORRUPTION OF CORPORATE BOARDS AND TOP MANAGERS

Section 2, assumed that a firm's managers wished to maximize profits and that toleration of low-level corruption might be one way to accomplish that goal. There is no need, however, to assume that managements and boards of directors are single-mindedly interested in furthering stockholder interests. Just as legislators may sell out voters, corporate directors may sell out stockholders; just as corrupt top bureaucrats may exploit the discretionary power given them by nonmarket forms of regulation, so too may private managers exploit imperfections in the market mechanism that generate corrupt opportunities. Thus, many of the factors that were important in explaining legislative and high level bureaucratic corruption may have close parallels in the activities of private firms and nonprofit organizations.

To begin at the highest corporate level, boards of directors are often elected by a group of voters more numerous than many political constituencies. It is generally believed, however, that the election of directors by shareholders is not much of a constraint on board behavior.[15] There are several reasons for this. First, most shareholders have little incentive to amass large amounts of information about corporate performance. Any individual with a diversified portfolio will not be damaged much by the poor performance of a single company. Second, even if a shareholder did uncover evidence indicating that the board was not furthering shareholders' interests, obtaining support from other owners is likely to be costly and difficult. It will usually be a better strategy to keep one's knowledge secret and sell the stock before anyone else finds out. Third, even if shareholders are willing to act, the legal rights of shareholders to control directors' actions appear to be fairly limited. In fact, current doctrine holds that directors should not be thought of as agents or representatives of shareholders but rather as "fiduciaries" whose duties are primarily to the corporation itself.[16] The

---

[15] Eisenberg (1969) cites a number of authors who share this viewpoint. Among these is Manning (1958), who writes: "Managements are almost never reprimanded or displaced by the shareholder electorate; shareholders remain stubbornly uninterested in exerting control [p. 1487]." Eisenberg also mentions some evidence to the contrary; some institutional investors, in particular, take shareholder voting seriously. Empirical work on the separation of ownership from control and its consequences for performance began with Berle and Means (1932). While the phenomenon is well documented, its consequences for firm performance have not been clearly demonstrated empirically. See Clark (1977) for a summary of recent work.

[16] Henn (1970: 415–416).

meaning of this responsibility has, however, never been carefully defined.

From the perspective of corporate democracy, then, the incentives for corruption[17] appear to be high except in closely held corporations where a few shareholders have a major stake in company performance.[18] While accepting kickbacks and profiting personally at the expense of the corporation are clearly not proper actions for a fiduciary,[19] it may be difficult for shareholders to detect such behavior, and very few have an incentive either to undertake the search or to reveal their findings.

There is, however, a second critical check on the corruption of corporate boards not present in government legislatures. Stockholders, unlike voters, need not rely on the ballot box if they are dissatisfied with company policy. They can simply sell their stock; and if potential buyers can also evaluate company performance, the price of the stock will fall. Corruption may be deterred not by the threat of electoral defeat but by the fear of a fall in the market value of the firm followed by a takeover bid from a new group of investors.[20] While similar factors are at work in the public sector, e.g., the fall of New York City bond prices in the face of a threat of bankruptcy,[21] the pressures imposed by fiscal constraints

---

[17] Many private sector transactions that are analytically similar to illegal corruption are not, in fact, illegal; and those which are illegal are often not treated as criminal offenses. A law journal note (Anonymous, 1960) documented the fact that in 1960, 25 states had no statute making commercial bribery a crime. The author also presents a table summarizing state law at the time. Thirteen states had general statutes and 17 (including 5 of the original 13) had special statutes making it a crime to bribe particular people such as purchasing or hiring agents or common carrier personnel (pp. 849, 864, 866). There is no general federal statute making commercial bribery a crime (p. 849). The Federal Trade Commission is authorized to prevent "unfair methods of competition," a phrase which includes commercial bribery, but their enforcement powers are limited to cease and desist orders (pp. 849–850). This legal situation apparently continues to the present day. In New Jersey, a state listed in 1960 as having no criminal statute, commercial bribery is a misdemeanor and does not carry a prison sentence (New York Times, November 30, 1976). In Pennsylvania, the offense is a misdemeanor and carries a fine of up to $500 or a jail term of up to 1 year or both (Pennsylvania Code, Vol. 18, Sec. 4667, 1963).

[18] Clark (1977), however, argues that even in closely held corporations the incentives for managers to benefit at the expense of owners may still be high.

[19] Henn (1970) lists six ways in which fiduciary duties can be violated: "(a) competing with the corporation, (b) usurping corporate opportunity, (c) having some interest which conflicts with the interest of the corporation, (d) insider trading, (e) oppression of minority shareholders, and (f) sale of control [p. 458]." These categories are not, however, meant to be exhaustive.

[20] Takeover bids however, can be costly. Clark (1977) cites several studies that estimate these costs.

[21] See Gramlich (1976).

appear generally to be lower for elected representatives than for board members.

In both cases, however, a well-informed public is a critical check on corruption. The major difference here is the ability of legislators and board members to control the flow of information for corrupt purposes. Recall that if politicians had some control over the information provided to voters, they might present blurred and ambiguous stands on the issues, even in the absence of offers of financial support from special interest groups. Creating a rhetorical fog could be the vote-maximizing strategy of an honest legislator, as well as that of one who accepts bribes or campaign contributions from wealthy groups. The same point does not apply in the private corporate sector. The basic reason is that investors do not have widely varying preferences with respect to firm performance. While they may weigh the factors differently, ceteris paribus, everyone wants higher profits, more capital gains, and higher dividends. Thus the board of a firm operating in competitive input and output markets cannot be seriously corrupt since the firm's performance can always be evaluated by comparing it with that of others in the industry. Any loss produced by corruption will cause investors to transfer their money to more profitable operations. And if a corporate board tries to hide corruption by revealing few facts about company operations, it is unlikely to gain investors, since the suppression of data will be taken as an indication of poor performance. To be successful, then, corruption in a competitive industry may have to be associated with fraud in a way which is often unnecessary in the political sphere.[22]

Turning from private, quasi-legislative bodies like corporate boards, I continue the search for private analogues by looking briefly at the corrupt incentives faced by top executives. Their position is similar to that of the agency heads described in Chapter 4. High-level managers are restrained from building up personal fortunes, not by the budgetary choices of a political body but by the profitability and growth of the firms under their administrative control. Managers may be fired by corporate boards and their future careers jeopardized if their actions either are illegal or can be associated with a deterioration in the firm's profits. The ease with which corporate boards can evaluate managers' performance conditions the directors' ability to check executives' be-

---

[22] In failures of banks and insurance companies, a combined strategy of corruption or self-dealing and fraud has frequently been uncovered. Fraud is less often given as a cause of regular business failures. The evidence is presented in Clark (1976:12–13), who mentions the difficulty of interpreting these results (p. 77). Bank failures may, for instance, often be associated with fraud simply because there are so few other reasons why banks might fail.

havior.[23] Managers will have considerable freedom of action in just those industries where corporate boards are relatively immune from the oversight of market investors. Of course, just as in the political case, the board and the firm's executives may be able to collude for their mutual benefit in the face of a generally poorly informed public. Many cases exist, for example, in which executives and board members have siphoned off funds from failing companies into other business ventures in which they had interests, and bank failures are often caused by risky loans made to bank officials or to their families and friends.[24] A similar situation prevails in the nonprofit sector. If the public has difficulty evaluating the performance of a nonprofit organization, then the board of trustees is likely to have a similar difficulty controlling their executive appointees. Alternatively, collusion between managers and trustees is also possible and seems at least as difficult to control as the analogous problem arising in profit-making businesses.

4. MARKET FAILURE AS A CAUSE OF CORRUPTION

While the delegation of authority creates corrupt incentives all the way from boards of directors down to low-level salesmen, some firms will be more corruption prone than others because of the nature of their products. The familiar market failure categories provide a useful way to organize a discussion of how a firm's business produces corrupt opportunities. Thus, scale economies, products which are heterogeneous and technically difficult to evaluate, production or consumption externalities, as well as government regulations can all produce corrupt incentives.

A. Scale Economies

Simple monopoly power caused by nothing more esoteric than scale economies may provide corrupt incentives. In this case, if corporate boards or managers make deals that benefit themselves at the expense of

---

[23] Even if a manager's performance can be quite easily evaluated, Clark (1977) points out that executives might still engage in corruption or other forms of illegal behavior if they are close to retirement and do not care much about their future career prospects. The opportunity for private gain could be so large that the possibility of losing one's pension rights might not be an important deterrent. The executive close to retirement is similar to the corruptible lame duck legislator discussed in Chapter 2.

[24] See Henn (1970:465–470) and Clark (1976) for examples.

stockholders, profits do not fall to zero. Returns may still be high enough to attract investors. For example, although evidence is cloudy on the profitability of the Credit Mobilier, the construction company for the Union Pacific Railroad in the 1880s,[25] one of its purposes may have been to divert railroad profits from the Union Pacific to railroad executives (and key politicians) who owed a controlling interest in the contruction company (Smith, 1958; White 1895:22–23). Furthermore, if the firm's rate of return is controlled by a regulatory commission, corruption or self-dealing which inflates the rate base will simply increase profits. This may take the form of the purchase of inputs at inflated prices from companies controlled by executives or from firms who pay bribes (cf. Chapter 6). Since the inputs must be ones whose true market value is difficult to calculate, real estate rentals and design or research contracts are obvious sources of corrupt incentives. Similarly, large firms under surveillance by the Justice Department for possible antitrust violations may try to avoid prosecution by keeping profits down. While this may easily lead to inefficient and stagnant operations instead of more vigorous competition, it could also give board members an incentive to convert some of the firm's profits into kickbacks or personalized benefits.

B. Vagueness, Access, and Inspections

Products are often either one of a kind or of uncertain quality. Here corruption can flourish because no one has a reliable way of measuring a firm's performance. This general characteristic ties together all those who, for instance, do classified work, carry out research, provide artistic or creative products, or run job training programs or nursing homes. Vague standards can also generate corruption on the input side of the market, even for firms producing standarized outputs. A firm may delegate the task of choosing the "best qualified" workers to a personnel director or a trade union official. Those who want jobs may pay to receive employment, and an employee's receipt of a bribe may pass

---

[25] Fogel (1960) argues that promoters reaped profits "two to five million dollars greater than the 'reasonable' amount [p. 85]." He goes on to demonstrate, however, that "the charge that profiteering was the root cause of the financial enervation of the Union Pacific was based on a compound of errors that included the overestimation of the profit of the promoters, the underestimation of the cost of construction, and the omission of the element of risk. The railroad would have tottered on the brink of bankruptcy even if the promoters had scrupulously limited their profit to the amount 'justified' by the risk they had borne [p. 86]."

undetected if the rules are vague and general or if all applicants for jobs or access are, in fact, fungible. In the building trades, for example, "walking delegates" used to control the labor supply of their craft. Sam Parks, one such walking delegate, is quoted as saying to a union member in 1903, "I don't care a damn for the union, the president of the union, or the laws of the country. You can go back to work when you pay Sam Parks $2,000 [Hutchinson, 1970:30]." Furthermore, firms themselves may pay union officials to obtain labor at rates below the standard union wage (Hutchinson, 1970, Rottenberg, 1960). A 1952–1953 inquiry in New York showed that officials of the International Longshoremen's Association distributed jobs on the basis of kickbacks from men and payoffs from employers (*New York Times,* February 13, 1977).

Similarly, many employees—from private guards to executive secretaries—control access to a corporation's buildings and top personnel.[26] Other employees monitor the performance of lower level employees or franchisees. Their inspection tasks are little different from those of government housing code or meat inspectors. Thus, employees of Chervolet who distribute new cars to franchised dealers and oversee warranty work face numerous corrupt incentives. Dealers presented gifts of liquor, turkeys and gift certificates to establish good will and justified their payoffs as a way to obtain some freedom of action. "A guy who went strictly by the book could give you a hell of a time," one dealer lamented (quoted in the *New York Times,* June 15, 1975; the discussion here is based on this article). Other Chevrolet employees, also engaged in large-scale corrupt practices. Fictitious billings for warranty work were certified by Chevrolet inspectors, who were paid bribes or sold automotive parts at large discounts. When these activities came to light, Chevrolet fired all the employees involved. Most of them, however, were quickly hired by sympathetic dealers at increased salaries.

C. Vagueness and the Nonprofit Sector

In the private sector, corruption is not the exclusive prerogative of profit-oriented business firms. Many nonprofit organizations almost

---

[26] Individuals charged with determining access are more easily corruptible if the consequences of the bribe are not obvious. Ticket takers who let people enter baseball stadiums without tickets are unlikely to be caught, while executives are likely to notice if their secretaries schedule appointments on the basis of willingness to pay. Similarly, in admissions decisions, bribes, contributions to the alumni fund, or good connections can help borderline cases more than they can help those with poor qualifications.

perfectly fit the model of a firm whose outputs are vague and difficult to measure. Charity, hospital care, education, research, and culture all have poorly defined quality and quantity dimensions. It has been argued, however, that where information on outputs is hard to obtain the nonprofit label is used as a way of indicating that high-quality services are, in fact, being provided by a selfless, altruistic group of people.[27] There are two difficulties with this inference. On the one hand, altruism may not be sufficient to produce high-quality output. Benevolence can easily be associated with inefficiency or ignorance. On the other hand, the nonprofit form is not a guarantee that an organization's founders are altruistic. Whenever production functions are difficult to observe, those in control of an organization have an incentive to extract corrupt benefits. By taking advantage of a popular presumption that the nonprofit label implies benevolent trustees, an organization may instead permit kickbacks or self-dealing schemes that enrich individuals in charge of allotting the organization's funds.[28] The advantage of the nonprofit form seems to rest on the rather slim reed of trust and on the notion that entrepreneurs select profit-making firms if they are narrowly self-seeking and choose nonprofits organizations if they have altruistic temperaments.

Furthermore, nonprofit firms may also be susceptible to corruption since they are probably less likely to use market signals in choosing inputs or dispensing outputs. For example, admissions committees of private clubs, schools, and colleges determine which applicants to accept; and boards determine who is qualified to receive particular university degrees or occupational certifications.

D. Externalities

Firms that produce positive or negative externalities in their ordinary course of business may create corrupt incentives if the externalities impose high levels of costs or benefits on a small group or on a single individual or firm. Of course, in these small-numbers cases, where free-rider problems are not serious, we might expect a legal negotiated settlement. Even so, if a firm's low-level employees have some independent control over the level of externalities produced, then bribery of these individuals may substitute for a legal high-level approach. Further-

---

[27] The view is expressed in several of the articles in Phelps (1975) and Weisbrod (1977).
[28] Both nonprofit and for-profit nursing homes were involved in scandals arising under Medicaid and Medicare according to Mendelson (1974, Chapter 9).

more, in some businesses the alternative of reaching a high-level bargain may be explicitly prohibited by law or by managerial directives.

Excellent examples of situations where low-level bribery may be used to control externalities are found in the market for information. Although it is frequently bought and sold in private market transactions, information has many of the characteristics of services provided by governments. While the product is one whose technical characteristics cause extensive positive and negative externalities, it is nevertheless provided in private markets operating with widely varying amounts of government regulation. Private entrepreneurs have made a series of compromises in the production and sale of these information services that reflect its complex character. It is, however, not surprising that corrupt incentives are created whenever private firms either "privatize" a good with important external effects or refuse to sell a good for which others are willing to pay.

For example, employees in some portions of the information market are very similar to bureaucrats who control access to a benefit or who can impose costs on selected individuals. Information provided at minimal cost by journalists, disc jockies, and television reporters to the general public often imposes substantial private benefits and costs on small groups of individuals or firms. Both muckraking accounts of alleged corruption and the free favorable publicity given to some individuals and firms and not to others impose external costs. Nevertheless, the preservation of the freedom of the press implies that a public, negotiated settlement between the media and those they benefit or harm is out of the question.[29]

Some industries are peculiarly dependent upon free publicity to advertise their products. For example, the record industry relies upon the record-playing decisions of radio stations to promote its new releases. Record companies compete for scarce radio time just as customers of a government agency may compete for a bureaucratic

---

[29] The equal time doctrine applies only to legally qualified candidates for public office. Broadcasting stations are not required to provide equal time, however, if the publicity is part of a newscast, interview, news documentary, or on-the-spot coverage of a news event. However, these other activities are subject to the "fairness" doctrine which requires broadcasters "to afford reasonable opportunity for the discussion of conflicting views on issues of public importance." (See 47 U.S.C. 315 [1952]). In *Red Lion Broadcasting Co.* v *FCC*, 395 U.S. 367 (1968) the Supreme Court upheld a Federal Communications Commission regulation which gives individuals or groups the right to use a broadcaster's facilities to respond to "personal" attacks. This regulation, however, does not permit individuals or groups to respond either to favorable publicity given to a rival or a competitor, or to critical comments that do not reflect on their "honesty, character, integrity, or like personal qualities."

output. Recording studios therefore have an incentive to internalize the externalities of broadcasting by merging with radio stations. An alternative to merger, however, is the use of gifts and money to influence radio station employees directly. Thus, four record company officers have been given prison terms for a variety of offenses including payoffs to disc jockies, music directors, program directors, and other employees (*New York Times,* June 25, 1975, April 13, 1976).

Of course, much of the free publicity provided by the media and by individuals with access to the media is unfavorable. Hence corruption can be used to suppress critical stories. In fact, one could imagine unscrupulous journalists writing exposés in order to extort payoffs. This use of monopoly power is similar to that possessed by the police and administrators of coercive programs described in Chapter 8. Alternatively, the risk of offering a bribe may be high in these situations because of the risk that the bribe offer will be made part of the unfavorable publicity. Hence, the option of attempting to implicate the muckrakers themselves in scandals in order to discredit their information may be the chosen alternative. Of course, the fear of extortion might here serve the useful purpose of deterring scandalous activities just as effectively as the actual release of news stories. False news may, however, be nearly as damaging as true reports. Since controls on the veracity of news in the United States must confront constitutional guarantees of freedom of the press, extortion can only be effectively checked by the professional ethical codes of journalists.[30] In fact, the failure of journalists to take advantage of the corrupt possibilities offered by their jobs may be a sine qua non for the preservation of the constitutional guarantee.

Secret inside information is analytically close to free publicity. In both cases, an employee of one organization has access to information which can benefit or harm outsiders. While media employees are not supposed to provide information to the *public* on the basis of third party payments, employees with access to research data and trade secrets are not authorized to sell their information to *competitors*. In this latter situation, however, the firm's managers could decide that it was in their interest to license their patents to other firms. Legal, high-level agree-

---

[30] While many individual journalists undoubtedly have strong ethical beliefs, "there is no universally accepted code of professional ethics to guide and judge the behavior of newsmen or their editors [Kampelman, 1975:91]." Kampelman reports on a proposal by the Twentieth Century Fund to create "a newspaper council to receive and air complaints against the press by aggrieved persons [p. 91]." The proposal, modeled after a similar British institution, was opposed by the *New York Times* and the *Washington Post*.

ments are possible, but are likely to be expensive for licensees. Furthermore, even if licenses are either unavailable or very costly, a firm can avoid outright bribery by hiring employees with inside information. Nevertheless, even given these alternatives, firms may choose to pay insiders for expert knowledge without asking them to change jobs. The hiring alternative will be preferred if the information is not simply a page of formulas but requires knowledge gained from on-the-job training. Corruption may be favored, in spite of its illegality, if the bribing firm expects to use their spy over and over again to communicate the new discoveries of their competitor.[31]

E. Government Regulation

Finally, payments from one private individual or firm to another can be used to circumvent government regulations. No public official is involved, but the existence of legislation which restricts private transactions creates payoff opportunities. The most common examples of these practices are the black markets and kickbacks which typically accompany price controls and rationing (Schmidt, 1969). It will often be important to distinguish between payoffs to a firm for favored treatment and payoffs which are given to the firm's agents. Thus, on the one hand, government regulation of shipping rates has led shippers with excess capacity to offer illegal rebates to customers. The kickbacks were paid directly from one corporation to another and were equivalent to a price cut (*New York Times*, September 14, 1976). On the other hand, kickbacks paid to purchasing agents are apparently common in the beer and liquor industries. Laws that forbid retailing and wholesaling practices common in other business are circumvented through payoffs. Here agents have often pocketed the payoffs instead of their employers (*Business Week*, March 8, 1976).

The first case has few direct parallels in the public sector and is not even *corruption* under my definition (see Chapter 1), since no agents are involved. It is equivalent to a situation where a firm pays the government treasury for the privilege of supplying a good at a legislatively determined price. The second, is similar to the low-level corruption of government bureaucrats analyzed in Chapters 5 through 8. The main difference is the attitude of the agent's superiors. In contrast to many public sector applications, the employer of the agent who takes a bribe

---

[31] Compare Schmidt (1969). Inside information is frequently used in stock market purchases. If the tip has been obtained through bribery, two crimes have been committed: corruption and the use of inside information to determine stock market investments. Henn (1970:470–474) provides examples.

will be no worse off with low-level corruption than if the agent had obeyed the law. Although the purposes of the government regulation are obviously being subverted, neither of the organizations directly involved in the transaction are damaged.

5. CONCLUSIONS: CORRUPT INCENTIVES IN THE PUBLIC AND PRIVATE SECTORS

In this chapter I have tried to break the link between corruption and government that mars even some scholarly analyses of the subject. Once this link is made, it is often easy to imagine that one may eliminate corruption simply by ending government involvement in one or another area of economic life. But this point of view idealizes the private sector in an entirely illegitimate way. While it is true that *perfect* competition in *all* markets will prevent corruption, deregulation will almost never lead to the resumption of a market resembling the competitive paradigm. Indeed, many of the market failures that justify government intervention are the very same conditions that generate corruption in the absence of intervention. Thus scale economies, externalities, and products which are unique or of uncertain quality all create incentives for employees to enrich themselves at company expense. Deregulation may simply mean the substitution of a corrupt private official for a corrupt public one. It is not at all obvious that this is much of an achievement.

Indeed, even if the destruction of a governmental program *will* produce a competitive industry, this will not necessarily lead to a reduction in overall corruption. Competition on only one side of the market will not be sufficient to eliminate corrupt incentives if either suppliers or customers have market power. While the discipline of the market will prevent individual employees from benefiting at the expense of the company, a competitive firm might organize itself to facilitate the corruption of the agents of buyers or sellers. In these circumstances, competition may create corrupt incentives that would be absent if the industry could merge into a single firm. The individual firms might bribe for the purpose of making a sale[32] or obtaining a scarce input while a

---

[32] The competitive oligopolists in the arms industry have frequently paid bribes to obtain contracts. For a Lockheed executive's attempt to justify himself in terms of the strength of the competitive pressures he faced see "Kotchian Calls Himself the Scapegoat," (*New York Times*, July 13, 1977, Section 3). He said, " 'I may have been wrong. But I thought I was doing it in the best interests of the company, its employees and its shareholders. I think any manager of a large enterprise has a responsibility to look after his employees, and the only thing you can do to keep them working is to sell your product, and that is what I tried to do.' "

monopoly firm could transact its business through legal market power without the need to pay bribes. In short, the results are in the general tradition of second-best analysis. If the economy is fully competitive, then no corruption can occur. If some of the competitive conditions are violated, however, then changing one condition to make it closer to the competitive ideal may increase the level of corporate bribery.

Market pressures, however, are not the only factors to consider in comparing corrupt incentives in the public and private sectors. Also important is the ability of top managers and agency heads to supervise lower level officials. While observers like Banfield (1975) argue that private oligopolistic firms will be much better at ferreting out bribery than government agencies, there is neither systematic empirical nor theoretical support for this view. Although Banfield asserts, for example, that firms have clear hierarchies, while government bureaucracies tend to be disorganized and fragmented, this difference cannot be clearly linked with anything essential to the nature of governments and firms. Indeed, many modern firms are very decentralized (Williamson, 1975) while many governmental units are exceedingly hierarchical. Furthermore, to the extent that decentralization is required by the nature of the government task—e.g. law enforcement, education—shifting these activities to the private sector would not importantly reduce corrupt incentives. Banfield, however, seems to be on firmer ground in emphasizing the threat of bankruptcy or takeover if corruption is carried too far. Similarly, disciplining corrupt employees may be more difficult for governments constrained by civil service regulations than it is for private firms, at least for those that need not deal with powerful unions (Banfield, 1975:597). Counteracting the profitability constraint and the more flexible personnel policies of private business, however, is the lesser effectiveness of legal remedies. Commercial bribery is not a criminal offense in many states and is seldom a major concern of prosecutors (Anonymous, 1960).

Even more important than the *ability* of high-level officials to oversee low-level employees is their *willingness* to engage in monitoring. While Banfield recognizes that private managers may have goals other than profit maximization for the firm (p. 591), he does not develop the possibility that they may seek instead to maximize their private incomes. Thus he envisions firms as balancing the costs and benefits of corruption and permitting only the amount of bribery that maximizes profits. In contrast, Banfield asserts that government officials generally have no clear organizational objectives and so are unwilling to engage in systematic efforts to end corruption. This contrast, however, lacks strong empirical and theoretical foundations. First, competitive pressures are not powerful enough in many industries to prevent high-level corruption by top executives and board members. Thus, many businessmen have incentives to structure the organization under them to facilitate personal payoffs. Similarly, in industries where slack is possible because of the absence of strong competitive pressures,[33] simple laziness may open the way for low-level corruption.

Second, many government bureaucracies are neither disorganized nor immune from legislative or public review.[34] While it is obvious that both voter and legislator oversight of executive agencies has often been weak and ineffective, the revelation of a scandal frequently leads to budget cutbacks, personnel reshuffles, and the termination of programs. Politicians in many political jurisdictions do react strongly, if sporadically, to evidence of bureaucratic corruption, particularly if pressed by an active media campaign.[35] In short, rather than talking about the Public Sector and the Private Sector as if they were monolithic entities, a far more complex and disaggregated approach is needed to grasp the varieties of structure that generate corrupt incentives.[36]

[33] The problem of organizational slack is examined by Leibenstein (1966) and Williamson (1967).

[34] While Banfield recognizes the deterrent effects of monitoring and unfavorable publicity (1975:598–599, 600–601), he does not believe that they provide effective checks. In concluding his paper, he states that "every extension of government authority created new opportunities and incentives for corruption [pp. 603–604]."

[35] A redirection of housing aid occurred in response to the revelations in 1972 and 1973 of widespread scandals combined with high levels of defaults on subsidized mortages (*Business Week,* August 25, 1973). The troubled programs were suspended, and in 1973 President Nixon called for the development of new policies. The Department of Housing and Urban Development then carried out a National Housing Policy Review (U.S. Department of HUD, 1973). The report does not explicitly discuss corruption although it does mention "abuses and fraud" in homeownership programs Section 235 (p. 4–43). Instead, the authors locate other difficulties which limited the efficiency and equity of the suspended programs.

[36] Roberts (1975), in a study of public and private electrical utilities, confirms this general perspective. He was unable to find any important interorganizational differences that could be attributed to type of ownership.

Conclusion

11

CONCLUSIONS: ECONOMICS, POLITICS, AND MORALITY

1. CORRUPTION AND DEMOCRATIC THEORY

A. Competition and Information

Both economists and political scientists have, each in their own ways, harbored strangely idealized views of the modern state. The blind spots in each field arise in part from an imperfect understanding of the neighboring discipline. On the one hand, economists have often left the analysis of governmental structures to political scientists, contenting themselves with a study of the costs and benefits of substantive policy alternatives. On the other hand, political scientists have viewed the competitive relationship among political actors in a way which economists would find simplistic.

While political scientists often see great virtue in political competition as a way of assuring stability and preventing tyranny by balancing conflicting interests, economists' long confrontation with the concept of "market failure" cautions against making too facile a move from competition to the general welfare. The problem of corruption, of course, is an ideal way of making this point, since it indicates that competition of self-interested actors may sometimes be used to subvert democratic processes and prevent the implementation of legislative

211

decisions. This book's demonstration that widespread corruption can be consistent with even a grossly idealized version of representative democracy is an especially stark version of the general proposition that competition and decentralization in political life do not assure beneficial outcomes. This is perhaps the simplest and most far reaching implication of sophisticated economic models of government.

In saying this, I do not mean to suggest that a satisfactory analysis of corruption should consist simply of a massive transfer of the economists' conventional tools in a way that distorts the distinctive character of democratic political life. Instead, economic theory provides the motivation for integrating three strands of political analysis in a way that makes their interrelationship of fundamental importance. Under the first set of vote-maximization models, representatives are viewed as seeking reelection and therefore can be assumed to vote on legislative proposals so as to maximize their chances of winning.[1] Under the second set of pluralistic models, the emphasis shifts to organized groups which interact with legislators and bureaucrats to obtain government benefits.[2] Under the third set of institutionalist theories, the analysis concentrates upon the interaction of different parts of the governmental structure and stresses the importance of a system of checks and balances where legislature and executive restrain each other's tendencies toward self-seeking behavior.[3]

The main aim of this book has been to demonstrate that each of these analytic strands—and their interrelationships—must be specified clearly if we are to grasp the corrupt incentives inherent in a given political structure. Thus, in examining the relationship between governmental institutions and corruption, analysts must move beyond crude contrasts between autocratic regimes and the more decentralized and democratic types that are the major concern of this study. For I have shown (Chapter 4) that the opportunities for corruption remain high if bureaucrats and legislators can collude on a common strategy, despite an institutionalized system of checks and balances. Since my major purpose has been to examine the pathology of relatively healthy organisms, however, I have concentrated upon political systems in which legislative–bureaucratic collusion is not a central problem. For even when this

---

[1] The formal statement of this view of political behavior varies between authors. See Chapter 1, note 3.

[2] The classic statements are Bentley (1908) and Truman (1951). Olson (1965) criticizes those pluralistic theories which neglect the costs of organization. For a recent attempt to define *pluralism* see Dahl (1976).

[3] See James Madison in Federalist 10, 51 (Rossiter, 1961), Dahl (1956; 1961).

condition is satisfied, an attempt to integrate the insights of the vote-maximization and pluralistic theories reveals that a wide variety of corrupt possibilities remain.

To do this, however, it is necessary to endow politicians with a more complicated preference structure than that assumed by standard vote-maximization theory while retaining a level of rigor often lacking in pluralistic accounts. Politicians are not assumed to be merely vote maximizers, but they are not ideologists either. While they do not care about ideas or policies per se, they do care about their personal incomes. Under some conditions, they will trade off an increase in the expected percent of the vote, $\hat{p}$, in return for an increase in income, y. While income is easier to measure than personal beliefs, the reader should observe that much of the analysis of the corrupt politician can also be applied to the highly principled legislator.

With this model of legislative motivation, it is easy to show that an informed and issue-oriented electorate is not sufficient to assure honest politics (Chapter 2). Even when these conditions obtain, politicians may sell their votes on particular issues if they are either very confident of reelection or practically certain to be defeated (i.e., if $\hat{p}$ is either very high or very low). Indeed, an issue-oriented and well-informed electorate may channel interest group activity in corrupt directions, since bribery may be the only means of changing representatives' votes on legislative proposals. Of course, the income that will satisfy legislators will depend upon the chance they take that their changed votes will cost them reelection.

Thus, combining an informed and concerned electorate with a political process that regularly produces closely contested elections leads to a world in which corruption is limited by competition. It does not follow from this, however, that a poorly informed electorate will necessarily be a breeding ground for corrupt politics. For if the voters remain interested and "educable," organized groups may find it worthwhile to contribute to campaign funds or engage in educational efforts, rather than using bribery. This is not to say, of course, that campaign contributions are superior to bribes simply because they are legal. When voters are not well informed, politicians can accept campaign funds, vote in ways that favor contributors, and then use the money they collect to present other types of information to voters. Corruption may be unnecessary, yet the importance of wealth in determining legislative outcomes may be very large.

This consideration only serves to introduce the pluralistic elements of the analysis. For the prospect of minority interests spending themselves to victory may spur a countereffort by groups with majority support on an issue. Thus the most favorable situations for majority rule are, on the one hand, those where no interests are organized or, on the other hand, those where all interests are organized. It is important to realize, however, that the domination of majority groups may be associated with a system in which large amounts of money enter the pockets and campaign chests of politicians. Although the competitive organization of groups could deter anyone from making a first payment, the result could just as easily be a regime where large contributions are routine. Furthermore, the widespread organization of interests is not sufficient to assure the domination of groups supporting the majority. These groups may either have high organizing costs or low levels of resources and so be outbid by minority interests.

This close relationship between group organization and corruption or campaign money, moreover, permits an analysis of the normative claims made by many pluralists on behalf of interest group activity. According to this line of thinking, interest group activity is an important way in which minorities may protect themselves against the rigors of simple majoritarianism (Dahl, 1971). Of course, even pluralists recognize that their case is weakened in a world where many large and diffuse interests cannot overcome the high costs of political organization. My criticism, however, goes beyond this familiar point. For I have shown that in a partially organized world, minority interests may gain their way through corrupt payments that induce legislators to vote against the wishes of a majority of their constituents. Moreover, even if all groups were organized, the use of bribes and campaign contributions to obtain votes would often benefit wealthy groups.[4] This is a particular difficulty in a representative democracy, since those damaged by a program often will not be compensated for their losses. Even if the funds are chan-nelled into campaign funds or the provision of particularized benefits to voters, full compensation is unlikely both because legislators need only the support of a majority of their constituents and because citizens may not have very strong preferences for campaign messages. However, the benefits of wealth will be weaker if the voters either have a clear position on the issue or are at least educable, thereby tempting groups to spend their money on public relations rather than corruption. The productivity of money in buying persuasion is less clearcut than its ability to buy votes directly.

---

[4] It will not, of course, *necessarily* benefit them. First of all, the payment of a bribe is itself a cost that wealthy groups would like to avoid if they could. Second, the wealthy may be more costly to organize and less willing to pay for political benefits than the poor or middle class.

All this presupposes an institutional framework governed by the separation of powers in which bureaucrats are unable to collude with legislators to maximize the size of payoffs. Even within this general structure, however, institutional variation is of great importance. In particular, interest group influence will be conditioned by the amount of competition among the legislators themselves. While an individualistic legislature will not necessarily be less influenced by interest group activity than one with organized parties and influential politicians, there are nevertheless several reasons why competition among legislators for payoffs may facilitate majority rule (Chapter 3). Bribery and campaign contributions may simply be less expensive for most groups in a legislature where power is concentrated. First, in this type of assembly, groups need not expend resources discovering the reservation prices of numerous legislators. Second, political parties may be able to reward defeated politicians with government posts. Third, parties may have more staying power than politicians and so may be worth the investment of funds even if defeat is imminent in the short run. Fourth, party leaders or powerful individual legislators may have low reservation prices if power is associated with a comfortable reelection margin. Finally, a party leadership able to determine the fate of proposed legislation and the content of bills has considerable extortionary power. They can manipulate the legislative agenda so that groups will pay to avoid proposed harms as well as contribute to obtain benefits.

The self-interest of individual legislators may, of course, prevent a corrupt political party from maximizing net returns. Nonetheless, so long as politicians are unconcerned with anything other than income and reelection, maintaining competition will not be a simple matter. Seeing the gains of centralized authority, politicians may try to strengthen party discipline and change the rules of legislative practice to increase their power. Interest groups and politicians who perceive the constraint of voter opposition, may collude to pass unpopular legislation in omnibus bills in the last days of a legislative session. Bills that favor particular groups can be written so that they are complex and hard to understand or so that the costs are diffused broadly and almost invisibly over the population.[5] While an informed, issue-oriented electorate provides some check on this kind of behavior, its ability to perform this function depends upon the existence of an opposition party composed of challengers who can credibly claim that they will act more morally if elected to office.

---

[5] Thus programs that slightly raise the prices of privately produced goods or channel private capital toward a wealthy special interest group may be chosen over programs with immediate tax consequences.

We come, then, to a familiar moment in this essay. An effort to use economists' methods to synthesize political scientists' concerns ultimately forces us to recognize the limitations of the economists' approach itself. While information and competition may often reduce corrupt incentives, they cannot completely substitute for the personal integrity of political actors. If one wishes to understand the functioning of a democracy, it will not be possible to follow the conventional economist's inclination to ignore moral constraints upon self-seeking behavior. I shall return to this point in the final summing-up.

B. The Corruption of Top Bureaucrats

Thus far, I have been dealing with a set of institutions that conforms to a simple version of the American idea of the separation of powers. Up to the present point, the legislature was the only institution making laws, while the bureaucracy was insulated in the executive branch and could be trusted to administer the laws honestly, efficiently, and impartially. It followed that legislators had no incentive to pass laws that could be administered corruptly and no need to look for inefficiencies in the operation of government agencies. As soon as one admits the possibility of bureaucratic corruption, however, the necessity for a more sophisticated understanding of the separation of powers becomes apparent (Chapter 4). There are three important cases. At one extreme, it is possible to hypothesize an aggressive, honest legislature that actively ferrets out cases of bureaucratic dishonesty. At the other extreme, there is the case of legislators who actively collaborate with bureaucrats to maximize illicit receipts and generate large campaign contributions. The intermediate case is presented by legislators who wish neither to share in the returns of bureaucratic corruption nor to monitor the honesty of the administrative process. This passive legislature, however, does enact a set of budgetary appropriations each year, and this simple fact has important consequences for the top-level bureaucrat's freedom to engage in corrupt manipulation.

When the legislature is honest but passive, top bureaucrats may succeed in subverting public programs for their own benefit while providing biased data to the representative assembly. Free of the risk of legislative review, agency heads need not work within existing structures but can increase corrupt receipts by changing organizational forms to eliminate competitors, centralize power, keep information secret, and prohibit the discretionary behavior of underlings. These powerful administrators are not autocrats, however, since they must consider the impact of their peculation upon the budget the legislature will approve. The nature of the corrupt possibilities will then determine the ultimate impact of corruption on government operations and spending. While corruption will, in some cases, produce bloated agency budgets; under other plausible conditions, the size of a budget will fall, thereby constraining the bureaucrat's ability to obtain illicit benefits. For example, when corruption takes the form of kickbacks that raise the price of government purchases, budget appropriations will increase if the public has an inelastic demand for the government program and fall if their demand is elastic. The reverse conclusion holds if corruption lowers costs through a speed-up of processing and a reduction in legal salaries.

But, of course, the legislature need not remain passive while the bureaucracy lines its pockets. If voters are indifferent or poorly informed, politicians can force the bureaucracy to share its corrupt gains in return for legislative actions that facilitate extortion. If legislators fear that their corruption will be punished, they may prefer to use their influence over agency decisions to generate campaign contributions rather than to obtain direct bribes. In either case, politicians will favor programs that require discretionary case-by-case administrative and contracting decisions so long as legislators can obtain bribes or campaign funds by intervening with an agency on behalf of contributors. Legislators' choices will thus be biased against both open-ended programs using inputs that can be obtained in competitive markets and programs with standardized outputs. The incentives for collusion can be very high in a world with massive government budgets and few clear standards of good performance. In contrast, creating realistic incentives for aggressive honesty in the legislative process is not an easy matter. Indeed, favorable publicity seems the only important political benefit that follows upon a corruption probe; and there are other, simpler ways of getting into the newspapers.

Given these alternatives, it seems sensible to seek structural remedies that discourage legislative–bureaucratic collusion without making it impossible for legislators to carry out the oversight functions essential in a democracy. To some extent, Niskanen's (1971) proposal to force legislators to change committees after a limited time is responsive to this need.[6] Unfortunately, while this reform may prevent collusion, it will also prevent legislators from acquiring the necessary expertise to evaluate an agency's budget requests. Similarly, Niskanen's proposal that agencies compete for government programs is limited by the difficulty of

---

[6] Niskanen (1971, Chapter 20) makes a series of related proposals to reduce the tendency of committee members to favor the agencies they oversee.

measuring the output of many public services. Perhaps it is more useful to open up the bureaucracy to the oversight of groups other than the legislature. Some of these groups might be permanent governmental entities, like the General Accounting Office; others may be loose collections of journalists, interests groups, and the general public. Needless to say, this increase in oversight has its costs as well as its benefits. Indeed, journalists and interest groups may take advantage of their newfound access to obtain special benefits for themselves rather than to expose embarrassing facts to public view (Chapter 10).[7] Nevertheless, the usefulness of these public oversight strategies seems greater than direct reforms of bureaucratic–legislative interaction of the kind suggested by Niskanen.

2. LOW-LEVEL CORRUPTION

A. The Range of Policy Options

The second half of the book confronts a set of problems that permits an economist to employ more familiar tools and generate more realistic and practical proposals. It must be emphasized, however, that this surface clarity has been achieved only by assuming that the fundamental problems discussed in the first half of the book have somehow been resolved so that high-level decision makers are concerned with something other than the size of their corrupt receipts. This point dramatizes both the power and ultimate limits of economic analysis. While economics can isolate structures that make it easier for politicians to act honestly, it also makes clear the importance of personal honesty and a devotion to democratic ideals in preserving representative government. A similar pattern is revealed in the second half of the book. While low-level bureaucratic structures may be easier to change, institutional incentives cannot be expected to substitute entirely for morality; indeed, there are many occasions in which morality must bear a weight that will often be too heavy for it. Economics does have a central role, however,

---

[7] Since agencies are likely to retain some power to control information on their operations, they may be able to discipline critical reporters by refusing to supply any new leads. A prominent Capitol Hill reporter explained why he preferred congressional reporting to covering an executive department. He reported to Matthews (1960) that in executive departments, especially the State and the Defense departments, "they can really punish a critical or unfriendly reporter who needs more than routine hand-outs to meet his obligations to his paper [p. 200]."

in clarifying those situations where extraordinary appeals to personal integrity are not necessary for effective administration.

Starting with fundamentals, it is plain that all corrupt incentives cannot be eliminated. Neither perfect hierarchical control nor perfectly competitive markets are realistic goals for social organization. On the one hand, authority must be delegated in large organizations because of scarce time and expertise. On the other hand, even when markets can be established, they will generally lack the optimality properties of perfect competition and so will not be clearly superior to nonmarket alternatives even on efficiency—let alone distributional—grounds (see Chapters 5 and 6). Given the costs of monitoring, agents will generally have some independent discretion requiring them to balance opportunities for private gain against loyalty to superiors, to the institutions of which they are a part, or to the public.[8]

Of course, if the incentives for corruption are too pervasive, the sensible solution may be to eliminate the program entirely. Less drastically, if corruption occurs because demand exceeds supply at a legal subsidy price, bribery can be reduced or eliminated by expanding the scope of the program or reducing the level of subsidy. When these steps are not feasible, however, changes in organizational structure or law enforcement strategy may be helpful in reducing corruption and improving government behavior.

Turning first to the legal system, I have shown (Chapter 6) that the existing pattern of penalties is a very inadequate deterrent to corruption. The common practice of setting maximum fines and jail terms may deter only petty corruption. Furthermore, while penalties are sometimes tied to the volume of bribe money which changes hands, they are not systematically related to the level of the briber's benefits. Thus potential bribers generally face only a fixed cost of engaging in corruption. The actual size of their bribe offers is determined by bargaining between them and government officials with expected legal penalties playing no role except to determine the minimum acceptable bribe.

Two reforms are therefore critical if the legal system is to play an effective deterrent role. First, expected penalties must depend upon the gains of corrupt transactions to bribers as well as to bribees.[9] For

[8] This point has been made by other authors, e.g., Loveman (1972), Williamson (1975).

[9] While this point may seem obvious, it has been overlooked—even in recent legal reforms. For example, in response to growing evidence of corruption in subsidized nursing homes, the Medicare and Medicaid Act was amended in 1972 to include penalties both for making false statements in order to obtain benefits and for accepting or paying kickbacks or bribes (U.S. Senate, Congress, 1975). The penalties as defined in the law are merely upper limits ($10,000 or 1 year in jail or both). Nowhere are they explicitly

example, a firm that pays to obtain a contract should face penalties geared to the excess profits a bribe makes possible. Second, to avoid situations where only small bribes are prevented, marginal expected penalties must exceed marginal expected benefits, at least for large bribes. Expected penalties however, depend upon the probability of arrest and conviction, as well as the sanctions actually levied upon convicted white collar criminals. Therefore, policies that give the individual receiving a corrupt offer a financial incentive to report the solicitation will have a deterrent effect. One difficulty with bounty schemes, however, is that many individuals involved in corrupt deals cannot report a bribery offer without also admitting other misdoings of their own. Furthermore, the difficulty of proving guilt in corruption cases will discourage reportage unless the bounties are set at very high levels. A bounty scheme would have to be associated with an active prosecutorial response to reports of corrupt offers. However, if police and prosecutors continue to devote only a small proportion of their time to ferreting out corruption, even a sophisticated sanctioning strategy will have little deterrent effect.

Furthermore, the higher the penalties, the greater the incentive to corrupt the criminal justice system itself. Thus one weakness of using the law to prevent bribery is that the system itself provides many corrupt incentives. The discretion given to the police and to prosecutors or judges and the extortionary power inherent in any institutional position that gives one the power to arrest, prosecute, and punish others imply that using the law to fight corruption may simply corrupt the law itself.[10]

Given the inherent limitations of legal sanctions, structural solutions must play a central role. The most obvious institutional response (to an economist at least) is to legalize bribery by using the price system to allocate the bureaucratic service in question. After summarizing the serious limitations of this technique, I shall turn to the range of strategies that may be used where the existence of a nonmarket allocation scheme is a crucial feature of governmental policy. Responses fall into two rough groups. In the first group, the primary focus is on

---

tied to the gains of either bribees or bribers. Judges levying actual penalties can take the gains of the actors into account so long as they have a value less than $10,000 plus one year in jail, but judges are not required to follow this penalty strategy. If the risk of detection is independent of the size of the bribe, the law appears to be less of a deterrent to large bribes than to small ones.

[10] For an analysis of this case see Pashigian (1975).

changing official behavior through organizational reforms; in the second, the focus is on the incentives facing potential bribers.

In confronting the possibility of legalizing bribery, avoiding an enthusiastic embrace of the free market solution is as important as rejecting a simplistic and moralistic approach condemning outright the effort to replace corrupt payments with legal fees. The moralistic approach is misplaced in a society where countless services are in fact allocated through the price system. The advocates of a market approach, however, must keep in mind that even when their sights are limited to efficiency, public programs often lack two important features of a competitive market. First, in many cases the number of sellers (i.e., officials) or buyers (i.e., potential beneficiaries) is small. Thus oligopolistic behavior may result instead of an efficient competitive market. Second, substantial external costs are often placed on other groups in the population when high program levels are chosen by corrupted officials. High milk prices, for example, impose costs on consumers; hence corruption in the setting of government price floors cannot be said to promote efficiency. Granting zoning variances to the highest bidder may produce externalities for existing residents.

When corruption is used mainly to produce speedy outcomes in a program without redistributive or quality control goals, however, the case for legalizing bribery is very strong (Chapter 5). In order to succeed in their purpose, however, the fees should be paid directly to the bureaucrats rather than to the government treasury. Furthermore, to avoid monopoly behavior, officials must be able to compete with one other. However, while user charges will produce speedier service than an administrative regime with honest but lazy officials, bureaucrats cannot be expected to charge prices that produce a completely efficient system. Since those waiting in line impose costs upon others behind them, designing an efficient system of prices and priority queues is a complex issue that has only recently received the attention of economic analysts. Individual income maximizing officials will not generally choose efficient prices. Nevertheless, this system will often be superior to either corrupt payments or honest sluggishness.

Since legalized bribery will frequently be unacceptable on either efficiency or equity grounds, it is necessary to consider a wide variety of less drastic structural remedies. In the first broad grouping, the corrupt incentives facing bureaucrats are reduced by changes in administrative procedures. Some changes are obvious enough: Thus low-level discretion can be reduced by the use of clear, simple rules or by an increase in the number or thoroughness of inspections and audits. Both of these methods of checking discretion, however, have difficulties of their own. The former may require a change in a program's purposes, while the latter may simply induce clients to bribe inspectors and auditors as well as low-level functionaries.

Other situations, however, may be open to more sophisticated responses. The most important example involves the administration of licensing or social welfare programs. Here applicants may be permitted to apply to any of a large number of independent bureaucrats and allowed to seek out another official if the first turns them down. The introduction of a competitive relationship between low-level bureaucrats will often reduce the level of individual corrupt payments and may sometimes make corruption unprofitable within the system as a whole (Chapters 7 and 8). This change in procedures might, however, increase administrative and queuing costs. The benefits of honest administration would have to be weighed against the costs of permitting multiple applications.

The kind of job that government officials must perform limits the efficacy of this competitive solution. Government contracting officials cannot compete with one other in the same way as low-level officials charged with certifying people to receive government benefits. Their ability to provide benefits to contractors can, however, be eliminated by using sealed bids and requiring the bureaucrat to choose the low bidder. If the contracting official must either choose one of several identical firms or use discretion to locate the "best" contractor, the incentives for corruption are technologically impossible to eliminate by a sealed bidding process, and one must once more place greater emphasis on personal honesty rather than on institutional control. Similarly, if judgment is required to choose beneficiaries or if the program is coercive, then competition can not entirely eliminate the monopoly power of individual officials, although it can still be a useful device for reducing the level and incidence of payoffs.

In programs where competition cannot be used, however, appropriate personnel policies may be able to change official behavior. While job applicants can obviously be screened for reliability directly, the key question is whether pay and benefits packages can be used to improve the level of honesty. The issue has two parts. On the one hand, compensation can be designed to make the loss of a government job costly. Becker and Stigler (1974), for example, have suggested the use of liberal, nonvested pension rights as a means of tying bureaucrats to their jobs, and high legislative and bureaucratic pay is often justified on anticorruption grounds. On the other hand, the pay and working conditions of a job may have a systematic impact upon the moral fiber of those who seek various positions. For example, if certain positions were staffed entirely by volunteer labor, this could imply a group of workers morally committed to the institution's aims. Similarly, worker participation in the management of an organization might reduce low-level corruption and pilferage.[11]

Finally, in addition to marketlike solutions and changes in personnel policies, the bureaucracy's structure might be modified to reduce corrupt incentives. There is, however, no simple organizational reform that can eliminate bribery (Chapter 9). I have examined three models of bureaucracy, the *fragmented*, the *sequential*, and the *hierarchical* and have shown that corrupt incentives could not be eliminated by a shift from one to another. Furthermore, in any system, competition at one decision-making node may be a poor deterrent to corruption if each official provides access to a different group of superior bureaucrats. The honesty of one's superiors might then encourage lower level corruption if an applicant wants an illegal benefit and if the chance of review is not positively related to the size of the bribe or the illegality of the decision. In a complex organizational structure, then, reform at one level may be ineffective since corruption may simply reappear at higher or lower levels in the hierarchy. Reducing low-level discretion may lead to the corruption of top bureaucrats. Strict conflict-of-interest laws designed to improve the performance of agency heads may lead to a proliferation of petty bribery. The corrupt opportunities may simply be shifted down the bureaucratic ladder.

The role of unpredictability in organizational behavior is similarly unclear. On the one hand, a chaotic formal structure clearly increases the *demand* for corrupt alternatives. On the other hand, an agency's very disorganization will often reduce a bureaucrat's ability to *supply* a needed service. Thus reformers ought to exercise caution in recommending artificially created change as a device for reducing bribery. This policy might instead increase the level of illegal payments by reducing trust and making official procedures unclear. In fact, corrupt officials themselves might wish to provide vague information about bureaucratic procedures as a means of increasing their extortionary power.

The second broad class of strategies attempts to reduce the beneficiaries' incentives to pay bribes. Thus programs might be redesigned to place the incentives for corruption on a group with high moral scruples

---

[11] The use of self-management as a device for reducing the alienation of workers has been stressed in Yugoslav writing on the subject (Granick, 1975).

or high expected costs of corruption. If a particular industry is believed to be corrupt, benefits might then be provided to households directly rather than through contracts with private producers.[12]

More radically, one could modify the structure of the bribe-paying industry to make it either less able or less willing to organize for illegal purposes. An industry's *ability* to organize can be reduced by policies which increase the competitiveness of the industry. Alternatively, its *willingness* to pay can be reduced by the legal provision of benefits. To prevent an industry's managers from bribing government revenue collectors, for example, the industry's taxes could be legally reduced. Obviously, this type of policy will only be desirable if the government has independent reasons for wishing to benefit this segment of the economy.

Finally, one may eliminate the need for dealing with the industry by pursuing a policy of vertical integration. Under this strategy, the government develops an in-house capacity to produce a corruption-prone good or service, carrying its vertical integration to the point where it only needs to purchase standardized inputs in competitive markets. While this nationalization alternative will be useful in some situations, it does raise the possibility that corruption of outsiders may simply be replaced by internal payoffs, bureaucratic inefficiency, and time-consuming bargaining among officials.[13]

---

[12] The argument for placing corrupt incentives on households rather than suppliers depends upon the existence of fixed costs of corruption. If there are moral costs or costs of arrest and conviction not tied to the size of the bribers' gains, then ceteris paribus the larger the expected dollar gain from successful bribery, the more likely is an individual to make a payoff (For contrary cases, see Chapters 6, 7 and 8). Hence if private suppliers are few in number relative to the program's beneficiaries, direct government provision of the product may be preferable to a system where incentives for bribery rest with suppliers. This preference has nothing to do with the ease with which suppliers may be organized but rather with the fact that the fixed costs of bribery are more likely to be exceeded the larger the dollar gains from corruption.

This conclusion requires modification if entrepreneurs either have higher levels of moral scruples than households or if the fixed penalties, both formal and informal, levied on firms are higher than those levied on individuals. The latter possibility may well be a realistic one—in fact, if not in law—if the program is administered locally and if the individual beneficiaries are highly mobile. In that case, even if corruption is discovered, the individual household is likely to have left the region. Furthermore, even with a perfectly immobile population, enforcement of antibribery statutes against a large group of individuals will be very costly. Hence, corrupt applicants can, at most, anticipate an enforcement program that seeks bad examples.

[13] A practical difficulty in instituting an appropriate corruption-reducing strategy is the fragmentation of authority over law enforcement policies, personnel policies, changes in internal organization, and structural remedies. Hence the tradeoffs in anticorruption policy are seldom perceived, or if perceived, seldom acted upon. This often leads to a

B. Directions for Reform

Given this summary of the policy options analyzed at greater length in earlier chapters, it remains to provide a sense of their interrelationship by contrasting concrete settings that seem amenable to one or another practical remedy. Consider first two areas which look relatively intractable: police work and inspection processes. The structural reform of police departments is complicated by the nature of a police officer's job. So long as police patrol neighborhoods singly or in pairs, it will be almost impossible to supervise them closely. Discretion is inevitable and cannot be eliminated simply by increasing police department budgets. If an action is legally a crime, individuals cannot be permitted to purchase the right to perform it, as the pricing strategy proposes. Some of the more routine protective services provided to businesses and individuals could be legally sold, however, and might thus eliminate an entire class of petty corrupt incentives. The vertical integration alternative is irrelevant for most police work since the services of police officers are inevitably differentiated. Reducing the demand for corrupt services, which in this context implies the decriminalization of certain activities like gambling and the possession of drugs, is useful in some contexts but is clearly not a general solution. Redesigning programs to place corrupt incentives on scrupulous individuals and "market structure shifts" will be similarly ineffective. Lawbreakers are, almost by definition, unscrupulous; and the government can hardly be expected to work vigorously to modify the market structure of an industry that is not supposed to exist. Thus honest police chiefs have usually concentrated on nonstructural solutions as partial remedies for corruption. They may instruct officers not to enforce laws that are a particular temptation to corruption, indoctrinate employees with an ethic of honesty, rotate assignments, and increase the threat of legal sanctions by using informers and undercover agents and penalizing some bad examples.[14]

The analysis, however, suggests that there is one structural solution

---

strategy of "following the scandals" rather than a broader look at the range of alternatives available and a more fundamental reappraisal of the role of private influence and of quasi-market schemes on the whole range of government behavior.

[14] See Kornblum (1976) for an analysis of the New York City Police Department's response to the Knapp Commission's finding of widespread corruption. Rubinstein and Reuter (1977) discuss those reforms that bear especially on the numbers racket. In addition to reorganization and indoctrination, police officers are now unable to enforce certain laws vigorously. They are not permitted to arrest numbers runners (Rubinstein and Reuter, 1977:67) and restricted in their ability to enforce Sabbath laws and inspect bars and cabarets (Kornblum, 1976).

that will reduce police corruption in some types of law enforcement work. Even if most officers are willing to take bribes, giving them overlapping jurisdictions should lower the level of individual payoffs and may make bribes unattractive to both police officers and lawbreakers. Letting officers compete may reduce both corruption and crime. Although duplication of authority is not costless, it may nevertheless be worth the expense in a range of cases. It is not, however, a general solution since some crimes leave evidence that cannot be observed by a second policeman. The arresting officer may himself be the principal witness and can therefore destroy the evidence in return for a bribe (or threaten to fabricate evidence unless paid off).

Similar difficulties will affect the effort to control any administrative process that requires on-site inspections. Since a favorable inspection is supposed to be based on the quality of the housing unit, nursing home, meat packer, grain shipment, etc., certification cannot be sold to high bidders without undermining the purpose of the inspection. Furthermore, low-level discretion is inevitable so long as inspectors must go into the field to make assessments. Permitting inspectors to have overlapping jurisdictions would reduce their monopoly power over qualified beneficiaries, but unqualified applicants would still have an incentive to pay bribes. Alternatively, standards could be relaxed so that more of those inspected could legally qualify, but this action might vitiate the purpose of the inspections entirely.

There are other situations, however, where changes in either program design or the market structure of bribers, rather than in enforcement strategy, hold more promise of reducing corruption. Consider first kickbacks in the sale of drugs to nursing homes, and second, the federal government's home-ownership program for very poor families. The state formulas determining the prices that nursing homes can pay for particular drugs appear to be high enough in some areas to give druggists an incentive to seek nursing home sales. Since the prices are considerably above the marginal cost of these large sales, druggists sometimes compete for the business by providing kickbacks. While vertical intergration with druggists has sometimes been used by homes in order to eliminate corruption,[15] this device merely provides nursing home operators with higher profits at no benefit to the government. Two other structural remedies, however, appear workable and do promise some savings for the government. The first and simplest is to legalize the druggists' price competition, with the formulas serving as ceiling prices. Bids would need to be public and easily available to state officials,

---

[15] For documentation see U.S. Congress, Senate (1975).

however, since nursing home operators would still have an incentive to accept the bid of a high-priced bribe payer. The second possibility for reform is a market structure remedy designed to reduce the monopoly profits of druggists. In contrast to the situation in many states, price advertising for drugs could be legalized with state nursing home price lists based on the lowest advertised prices of drugs listed by generic title rather than by brand name.

Corruption in the provision of subsidized housing was a feature of the federal government's home-ownership programs for low-income families that were suspended in 1973. These programs were sometimes administered so that private entrepreneurs were the main gainers at the expense of both government bureaucrats and intended beneficiaries. Very low interest mortgages were provided to high-risk households who would have found credit either unavailable or very costly in the private market. In many cases, private entrepreneurs effectively appropriated this very deep subsidy by simply increasing the price of the housing sold under the program far above its private market value. The major profits accrued to the sellers, but federal officials were implicated because of the need to obtain inflated statements of the value of the housing.[16] Given the inherent risks of relying upon inspections to produce well-run programs, the most obvious solution here is an increase in supply or a

---

[16] *New York Times,* December 4, 1971, January 2, March 29, 1972, June 26, November 9, 1974. The large profits made by some corrupt developers were not competed away by new entrants because the size of the program was restricted by budget limitations and by the scarce time of the Federal Housing Administration appraisers. Some houses, however, were of such poor quality that they were quickly abandoned by their new owners. Where this abandonment was widespread, the program failed to increase the supply of housing in any significant way. Inflated profits could persist even with free entry so long as buyers had poor information about the risks of purchasing a subsidized house.

A stylized example will illustrate the case of supply restrictions. Suppose the government agrees to subsidize $\alpha\%$ of the selling price of eligible housing. Households pay $(1 - \alpha)p_0$, where p_0 is the total sale price of the house. If p_0 is set equal to the price of private substitutes and if only a limited number of houses qualify for the program, then excess demand may exist in the subsidized market. One way to clear the market is obviously to raise p_0 to p_1 such that at a price of $(1-\alpha)p_1$ no excess demand exists. (Of course, $(1 - \alpha)p_1$ must be less than or equal to the price of private substitutes.) In order for suppliers to succeed in setting prices of p_1, however, it will be necessary to prevail upon government officials supervising the program to accept price discrimination between the subsidized and unsubsidized markets. Since there is nothing, of course, to commend such a dual pricing scheme to a conscientious official, a bribe will be necessary. If this illegal technique succeeds, the subsidy will be divided between sellers and government officials. In this case, paying bribes to officials permits suppliers to allocate the good by raising their prices sufficiently in the subsidized market, i.e., reducing the effective subsidy, so that demand equals supply.

reduction in demand. Thus on the one hand, the number of houses in the program could have been increased so that dishonest developers would face competition from honest producers and so that subsidized supply would equal subsidized demand at a price close to the legal one. On the other hand, demand could have been reduced by lowering the subsidy level. Either solution would reduce corrupt incentives by reducing the profits of bribery. Of course, some households would be hurt by the latter strategy, but it seems unfair to give a very few of the poor very high benefits while leaving most dissatisfied.

Alternatively, the program might have been redesigned to make less use of the private sector. The government could have used old housing that owners had abandoned and purchased the relatively standardized inputs needed for rehabilitation. The government would then have faced the problem of assigning houses to families in the large pool of potential beneficiaries. These applicants would, of course, face corrupt incentives, but there could be a net reduction in corrupt payments if households are less likely to pay bribes than suppliers (see Note 12).

These cases and the other examples in the footnotes and text of this volume are all designed to illustrate the basic outlines of the analysis rather than to provide blueprints for specific reform. I have avoided becoming immersed in the details of particular programs and situations in order to concentrate upon features that characterize broad classes of public policies. The book will have fulfilled one of its most important purposes, however, if this perspective permits those with programatic goals to use its framework as an aid in designing or reforming both legal structures and governmental and private institutions.

3. MORALITY, CORRUPTION, AND ECONOMIC THEORY

One of the most distinctive features of neoclassical economics is its attitude toward the diversity of values. Rather than trying to judge the ultimate worth of a consumer's tastes, the traditional aim has been to demonstrate that a market system can generate socially efficient results from a population with diverse and conflicting preferences. Of course, two centuries after Adam Smith it is now clear just how unrealistic a set of conditions is required before a system of private markets can fulfill neoclassical aspirations. And when modern economic theorists turn from private markets to public choice, the results are even more unpromising. A discouraging series of impossibility results should alert the political economist to the difficulty of designing a mechanism that can translate every configuration of individual preferences into a determinate collective choice.[17]

Nonetheless, the belief that economics *must* take a completely neutral attitude toward the preferences of individuals remains a central element of the profession's creed. While this assumption has been challenged by others, I have tried to move beyond platitudes and use economic analysis itself to refine the understanding of the place of morality in social life. Positive economic theory, of course, cannot substitute for a normative theory defining desirable political behavior. Once these ultimate ideals are clarified, however, positive theory can play two essential roles. First, it can help economize on virtue by defining institutional structures to give people material incentives to behave ideally. While the notion of an ideal democratic government run by purely self-interested people is a fantasy, it is nonetheless true that political ideals may be realized through a variety of structures, some requiring more personal idealism than others. Thus economists can force normative theorists to confront a tradeoff between institutions and personal morality that they might otherwise ignore.

Second, and at least as important, is the aid economists can bring to the normative analysis of institutional malfunction. Here it is assumed that one group of political actors is *not* behaving ideally, and the question then is how to modify the behavior of other actors so that the system as a whole nevertheless approaches the normal. Economic theory is especially useful in this second-best analysis since it is designed to trace the way different people with different goals interact to generate an overall outcome.

To discharge either of these functions, however, requires a set of principles specifying an ideal political system. While there are obviously many candidates, I shall use a single one that permits me to build upon

---

[17] In proving his General Possibility Theorem, Arrow (1963) specifies that the social welfare function must satisfy every logically possible configuration of individual preference orderings. This condition of unrestricted domain has been retained in much subsequent work on social choice (see Sen, 1970). Some recent work has, however, built upon Black's (1958) notion of single-peaked preferences and sought to restrict individual preference orderings to obtain consistent social choice (Sen, 1970, 166–186, Sen and Pattainaik, 1969; Slutsky, 1977).

Others have attempted to derive social welfare functions by using more information than is provided by individual preference orderings. If "extended sympathy" allows one to make ordinal interpersonal comparisons of utility (i.e., I can say that "person 1 in state A is better off than person 2 in state B") it is possible to construct a social welfare function similar to that originally sought by Arrow (see Arrow, 1976; Hammond, 1976; Strasnick, 1976a, 1976b).

the earlier chapters while suggesting the utility of the general approach. Assume, then, a simple democratic political theory which stipulates that government policy should always reflect the preferences of the majority of citizens.[18] The interpretation of this democratic principle is, of course, beset with numerous technical difficulties: the possibility that majority rule will not generate a unique policy outcome,[19] and the question of whether the "majority will" should prevail on each individual issue or on the total package of public and private goods. Moreover, the simple democratic principle is open to a series of normative objections.[20] Nonetheless, I put aside these familiar problems to demonstrate the complex relation between positive and normative theory in understanding the operation of functioning political systems. Assume, then, a simple political system composed of an electorate, a representative assembly, and a bureaucracy. What kinds of personal commitments must be demanded of actors at each of these three levels before the system as a whole approaches the majoritarian norm?

The point is, of course, that there is no single way of answering this question—that the moral requirements to be imposed on one set of actors depends in part on the values and preferences of others in the political system. Let us begin, however, with a system in which individuals follow the classical conception of good citizenship. Assume first that a *technology* is available that provides voters with accurate information about the policy positions and personal honesty of elected representatives and challengers.[21] Even this is not sufficient, however,

---

[18] May (1952) has found a set of necessary and sufficient conditions for majority rule (see Sen, 1970:68–74 for a review of May). May's analysis, however, is only applicable to the case in which society must make a single choice concerning the allocation of bundles of goods and services. No actual majority rule system even remotely approaches this model. Instead, separate votes are taken on a range of different issues that are not mutually exclusive. Other activities are left to market forces or administrative decree. A political theory must then justify a particular process of issue definition and agenda formation as well as a procedure of sequential majority votes. It appears, in fact, that none of May's conditions would be satisfied under a plausible model of this more complex world.

[19] Condorcet's paradox illustrates the failure of majority rule to satisfy path independence, i.e., the winner of a sequence of votes is not independent of the order in which alternatives are paired (Sen 1970:38).

[20] The most obvious are majority rule's indifference to minority rights and its inability to take into account intensity of preference. Furthermore, the technical difficulties noted above may also have normative significance. Many of these issues are discussed in Dahl (1956). Schumpeter (1950) expresses a common sentiment when he writes that democracy, although it has instrumental value, is "incapable of being an end in itself, irrespective of what decisions it will produce under given historical conditions [p. 242]."

[21] Alternatively, information costs can be reduced if only a few clearly understood issues are raised in each legislative session.

to induce citizens to take the trouble to learn about the issues and go to the polls. Since an individual ballot is almost certain to be irrelevant to the electoral outcome, economists find it very difficult to explain voting without an appeal to democratic ideology.[22] While economics may be unable to explain why people prefer to be good citizens, it can work with this assumption to specify the way politicians and bureaucrats should respond if the system as a whole is to reflect the majority will.

Given good citizens, the ideal politician is easy to characterize. Suppose that politicians' preferences fall into three broad groups: they wish to (a) add to their personal wealth, (b) further their ideological positions, and (c) attain and remain in office. In a society of good citizens, then, the ideal of majority control can be achieved if politicians are *single mindedly* devoted to this third objective. Otherwise, as the analysis has shown, politicians may sacrifice popular support to further their nonmajoritarian goals. Thus a system with ideal citizens operates best with a group of professional politicians who have no goals other than office seeking. Of course, this ideal system can operate even if some politicians are willing to sacrifice votes in return for monetary or ideological gain, so long as there are enough professional outsiders seeking office to produce active challengers in all districts. Incumbents can then be reelected only if their legislative voting records satisfy at least a majority of voters more than any other possible mix of policies proposed by a challenger.[23] Even if incumbents seek to hide their legislative records on some issues, challengers can be expected to expose these votes. Given voters who seek information on political candidates, electoral competition produces good data on voting records; and no one can be reelected who does not follow constituents' prefer-

---

[22] Economists and political scientists with an interest in economic models of human behavior have puzzled over the question of why people vote, given the small probability of being decisive. Barry (1970) finds economic theories of voting particularly unsatisfactory. Downs (1957) has admitted that voters must be "motivated to some extent by a sense of social responsibility relatively independent of their own short-run gains and losses [p. 267]." Riker and Ordeshook (1968) also assume that voters may derive utility by conforming to an ethic of voting, or by supporting the democratic system.

[23] Maximizing one's chance of reelection is not necessarily the same as following the wishes of the majority on every issue. See Chapter 2, note 15, Dahl (1956), and Downs (1967). In addition, the principles of constituency definition can affect the closeness of the relationship between the vote-maximizing behavior of politicians and the wishes of the majority of the nation's population. Furthermore, if logrolling is important, citizens may judge politicians in terms of legislation actually passed instead of the way they vote on each issue. The discussion also assumes that the agenda is fixed from session to session and that cycles are unimportant. These assumptions are needed to give legislators who seek reelection a reason to follow their constituents' wishes (see Chapter 2).

ences. The only role for organized groups in this idealized system is to inform legislators about citizens' preferences. Minority interests can gain nothing from organization. Their only hope for obtaining influence is to lie about the public's preferences. Their lies will be uncovered at election time, however, when a challenger defeats the incumbent by refusing to subscribe to the minority group's position.

The passage of a law is only the first step in assuring that governmental actions are determined by majority preferences—everyone can think of examples where a popular law has been gutted by poor administration.[24] In examining bureaucratic behavior, however, it is clear that the ethical predispositions of bureaucrats must be different from those of legislators or citizens. Unlike ideal voters, who have their own opinions on all political issues, bureaucrats who wish to remain in government must be willing to carry out legislative mandates no matter what they think of a program's merits. This professional ethic contrasts strikingly with the requisite ethic imposed on professional politicians in this model. Of course, if citizens could monitor bureaucrats costlessly and had some costless mechanism for removing unsatisfactory officials from office, bureaucratic devotion to duty would not be required. Placing this additional requirement on voters, however, stretches the ideal of citizenship far beyond the bounds of credibility.[25]

I have, then, developed a first simple model of majoritarian democracy—consisting of good citizens with well-defined preferences, professional office-seekers, and dutiful bureaucrats. It is clear, however, that none of these groups need act in the way this particular system requires. The task, then, is to see how a change in the moral dispositions of one group requires a change in the moral demands made upon the others if a

---

[24] A law may also be mooted by a poorly operating legal system. Although the judiciary has been omitted from the analysis, much of the discussion of bureaucrats would apply to them as well.

[25] Those bureaucratic behavioral norms which further majority control with the least policing, however, present a subtle difficulty for the preservation of democracy. Some scholars (e.g., Pateman, 1970) have argued that a high level of participation in political life is dependent upon a high level of democratic participation in the decision-making processes at one's workplace. Therefore, if a sizable part of the labor force is employed by the government, the hierarchical organization of the bureaucracy may lower the amount of citizen participation in politics. Rule-bound civil servants, trained to follow orders, may not be able to be independent minded voters with clear policy preferences. However, bureaucratic democracy, in which officials make fundamental policy decisions, is inconsistent with the separation of powers and the notion that citizens, through their elected representatives, should determine government policy. Voters will have little interest in participating in politics if all the critical decisions are made by government employees.

majoritarian system is to be approximated. Consider, then, a citizenry that responds to the costs of information in a less idealistic way. While they continue to vote, they are unwilling to spend their own resources to obtain independent political intelligence, contenting themselves with the information purveyed by candidates. In a political system of this kind, politicians who are interested only in being elected may collect campaign funds from wealthy groups in exchange for votes that further the groups' interests.[26] Hence legislative outcomes may be very far from what a majority of citizens would have chosen in a world with perfect information.

Therefore, politicians can no longer be professional office-seekers if we are to achieve the majoritarian ideal. Instead, politicians must believe that they have a duty to vote in a way that would have gained the majority support of ideal citizens. Since this may not always be the way to win elections, incumbents must be willing to tradeoff possible defeat against their belief that responsible legislators vote to further their understanding of their constituents' interests. Moreover, before this second-best system can operate according to the majoritarian principle, all politicians must act as responsible legislators. For if some are professionals, then they may exploit voter ignorance by developing those superficial characteristics the electorate associates with responsibility.

This concept of responsibility is obviously a difficult one for legislators to live up to. Its costs, however, should not be exaggerated. In particular, I do not mean to suggest that responsible legislators must be completely unconcerned with reelection. They will, however, spend campaign money for different purposes than their professional rivals: They will try to educate voters about the issues, inform them of voting records, and find out what citizens think. Under this model, elections will involve a choice among responsible politicians who have provided the voters with the information they think is most relevant to the majority. Voters will then be able to make informed choices using no more than the information made available to them. Of course, this second-best model may fail to achieve majoritarian results if a politician fails to perceive the voters' preferences correctly and so provides them with a package of information that does not effectively convey the true relation between the electorate's concerns and the politician's program.

If, however, politicians are insightful as well as responsible, then I

---

[26] Of course, money itself will not assure reelection, and politicians must choose how to use the funds they collect, e.g., they may use them to finance television appearances or to buy votes directly.

have begun to build a second-best model of democracy. It should be emphasized, however, that even here the general electorate must possess some weak forms of political virtue. For they must both believe that they have a duty to vote and be smart enough to evaluate the information provided by political candidates. Nonetheless, this simple example suffices to make the main methodological point: Decreasing the moral burden on one set of actors, increases it for another. Thus it is not obvious that a world of responsible and insightful legislators is any easier to attain than a world of ideal citizens.

Moreover, when these conditions are not met, the resulting picture may easily degenerate into an empty parody of democratic ideals. If politicians are willing to accept money for personal enrichment, as well as for an election campaign that preys on voter ignorance, then the scruples and organizing ability of wealthy interest groups become important. Even if group members have strong scruples against paying bribes, however, the system will not produce majoritarian results so long as they can make legal campaign contributions. Under these conditions, the democratic virtue of a devoted, honest bureaucracy is no longer self-evident. Corruption might then further majority interests more effectively than honest administration. The fundamental lesson to be learned from this degenerate case, however, is not that corruption may be a good way of achieving the majoritarian principle, but that the personal moral beliefs of voters, politicians and bureaucrats play an essential role in a modern democracy.

BIBLIOGRAPHY

Aaron, Henry. "A New View of Property Tax Incidence." *American Economic Review: Papers and Proceedings* 64 (May 1974): 212–221.

Ackerman, Bruce. *Private Property and the Constitution*. New Haven: Yale University Press, 1977.

Ackerman, Bruce; Rose-Ackerman, Susan; Henderson, Dale W.; and Sawyer, James, Jr. *The Uncertain Search for Environmental Quality*. New York: Free Press, 1974.

Adamany, David. *Campaign Finance in America*. North Scituate, Mass.: Duxbury Press, 1972.

Adamany, David. *Financing Politics: Recent Wisconsin Elections*. Madison: University of Wisconsin Press, 1969.

Adamany, David. "Money, Politics, and Democracy: A Review Essay." *American Political Science Review* 71 (March 1977): 289–304.

Akerlof, George A. "The Market for Lemons." *Quarterly Journal of Economics* 84 (August 1970): 488–500.

Albright, Joseph. "How to Get a New Plane (and Its Maker) off the Ground." *New York Times*, February 8, 1976.

Alchian, Armer, and Demsetz, Harold. "Production, Information Costs, and Economic Organization," *American Economic Review* 62 (December 1972): 777–795.

Alexander, Herbert. *Financing the 1968 Election*. Lexington, Mass.: D. C. Heath, 1971.

Alexander, Herbert. *Financing the 1972 Election,* Lexington, Mass.: D. C. Heath, 1976.

Alexander, Herbert. *Money in Politics,* Washington, D.C.: Public Affairs Press, 1972.

Allen, Robert, ed. *Our Sovereign State*. New York: Vanguard Press, 1949.

Amick, George. *The American Way of Graft*. Princeton, N.J.: Center for Analysis of Public Issues, 1976.

Andreski, Stanislav. "Kleptocracy or Corruption as a System of Government." In *The African Predicament*. New York: Atherton, 1968. Reprinted in Heidenheimer (1970): 346–357.

Anonymous. "Note: Control of Non-governmental Corruption by Criminal Legislation." *University of Pennsylvania Law Review* 108 (April 1960): 848–867.

Aranson, Peter H.; Hinich, Melvin J.; and Ordeshook, Peter C. "Election Goals and Strategies: Equivalent and Nonequivalent Candidate Objectives." *American Political Sciences Review* 68 (March 1974): 135–152.

Arrow, Kenneth. "Extended Sympathy and the Possibility of Social Choice." Cambridge: Harvard Institute of Economic Research, Discussion Paper No. 484, June 1976.

Arrow, Kenneth. *Social Choice and Individual Values.* 2d ed. New Haven: Yale University Press, 1963.

Bain, Joe. *Industrial Organization.* 2d ed. New York: John Wiley & Sons, 1968.

Balk, Alfred. "Invitation to Bribery." *Harper's* 233 (October 1966): 18–24.

Banfield, Edward. "Corruption as a Feature of Governmental Organization." *Journal of Law and Economics* 18 (December 1975): 587–605.

Banfield, Edward; and Wilson, James Q. *City Politics.* Cambridge: Harvard University Press and the MIT Press, 1963.

Barro, Robert J. "The Control of Politicians: An Economic Model." *Public Choice* 14 (Spring 1973): 19–42.

Barry, Brian. *Sociologists, Economists and Democracy.* London: Collier-MacMillan, 1970.

Bartlett, Randall. *Economic Foundations of Political Power.* New York: Free Press, 1973.

Barzel, Yoram. "A Theory of Rationing by Waiting." *Journal of Law and Economics* 17 (April 1974): 73–96.

Basche, James R., Jr. *Unusual Foreign Payments: A Survey of the Policies of U.S. Companies.* New York: The Conference Board, 1976.

Bauer, Raymond; de Sola Pool, Ithiel; and Dexter, Lewis. *American Business and Public Policy.* New York: Atherton Press, 1962.

Bayley, David. "The Effects of Corruption in a Developing Nation." *Western Political Quarterly* 19 (December 1966): 719–732. Reprinted in Heidenheimer (1970): 521–533.

Beard, Edmund; and Horn, Stephen. *Congressional Ethics: the View from the House.* Washington, D.C.: Brookings Institution, 1975.

Becker, Gary. "Crime and Punishment: An Economic Approach." *Journal of Political Economy* 76 (January/February 1968): 169–217.

Becker, Gary, and Stigler, George. "Law Enforcement, Malfeasance, and Compensation of Enforcers." *Journal of Legal Studies* 3 (January 1974): 1–19.

Bentley, Arthur. *The Process of Government.* Chicago: University of Chicago Press, 1908.

Ben-Zion, Uri, and Eytan, Zeev. "On Money, Votes and Policy in a Democratic Society," *Public Choice* 17 (Spring 1974): 1–10.

Bergstrom, Theodore C., and Goodman, Robert P. "Private Demands for Public Goods." *American Economic Review* 63 (June 1973): 280–296.

Berle, Adolf, and Means, Gardiner. *The Modern Corporation and Private Property.* New York: MacMillan, 1932.

Berliner, Joseph S. "The Informal Organization of the Soviet Firm." *Quarterly Journal of Economics* 66 (August 1952): 342–365. Reprinted in *Readings on the Soviet Economy,* edited by Franklyn Holzman. Chicago: Rand McNally, 1962.

Berliner, Joseph S. "Managerial Incentives and Decisionmaking: A Comparison of the United States and the Soviet Union." In U.S., Congress, Joint Economic Committee, Subcommittee on Economic Statistics, *Comparisons of the United States and the Soviet Economies* (1959) Pt. I, pp. 349–376. Reprinted in *Readings on the Soviet Economy,* edited by Franklyn Holzman. Chicago: Rand McNally, 1962.

Bhagwati, Jagdish, N., ed. *Illegal Transactions in International Trade.* Amsterdam and New York: North-Holland–American Elsevier, 1974.

Black, Duncan. *The Theory of Committees and Elections*. Cambridge: At the University Press, 1958.

Blau, Peter M. *The Dynamics of Bureaucracy*. Chicago: University of Chicago Press, 1963.

Bonin, John. "On the Design of Managerial Incentive Structures in a Decentralized Planning Environment." *American Economic Review* 65 (March 1975): 226–230.

Bonin, John, and Marcus, Alan. "Information, Motivation and Control in Decentralized Planning." Middletown: Wesleyan University. Mimeographed. June 1976.

Borcherding, Thomas E., and Deacon, Robert. "The Demand for the Services of Non-Federal Governments." *American Economic Review* 62 (December 1972): 891–901.

Boyd, James. *Above the Law*. New York: New American Library, 1968.

Bradford, David, and Oates, Wallace. "Suburban Exploitation of Central Cities and Government Structure." In *Redistribution through Public Choice*, edited by Harold Hochman and George Peterson. New York: Columbia University Press, 1974.

Brandfon, Robert. "Political Impact: A Case Study of a Railroad Monopoly in Mississippi." In *The Railroad and the Space Program: An Exploration in Historical Analysis*, edited by Bruce Mazlish, pp. 182–201. Cambridge: MIT Press, 1965.

Breton, Albert. *The Economic Theory of Representative Government*. Chicago: Aldine, 1974.

Breton, Albert, and Wintrobe, Ronald. "The Equilibrium Size of a Budget-Maximizing Bureau: A Note on Niskanen's Theory of Bureaucracy." *Journal of Political Economy* 83 (February 1975): 195–207.

Broadus, James. *The Economics of Corruption*. Ph.D. dissertation, New Haven: Yale University, 1976.

Brock, William, and Magee, Stephen. "Equilibrium in Political Markets on Pork-Barrel Issues: The Case of the Tariff." Chicago: University of Chicago, Center for Mathematical Studies in Business and Economics, Report 7545, October 1975.

Buchanan, James. "Why Does Government Grow?" In *Budgets and Bureaucrats: The Sources of Government Growth*, edited by T. Borcherding, pp. 3–18. Durham, N.C.: Duke University Press, 1977.

Buchanan, James and Tullock, Gordon. *The Calculus of Consent*. Ann Arbor: University of Michigan Press, 1962.

Buchanan, James, and Tullock, Gordon. "Polluter's Profits and Political Response: Direct Controls versus Taxes." *American Economic Review* 65 (March 1975): 139–147.

Calabresi, Guido, and Melamed, A. Douglas. "Property Rules, Liability Rules and Inalienability: One View of the Cathedral." *Harvard Law Review* 85 (1972): 1089–1128.

Campbell, Angus; Converse, Phillip E.; Miller, Warren E.; and Stokes, Donald. *The American Voter*. New York: John Wiley & Sons, 1964.

Caro, Robert A. *The Power Broker*. New York: Alfred A. Knopf, 1974.

Caves, Richard. "Economic Models of Political Choice: Canada's Tariff Structure." *Canadian Journal of Economics* 9 (May 1976): 278–300.

Clark, Robert. "The Soundness of Financial Intermediaries." *Yale Law Journal* 86 (November 1976): 1–104.

Clark, Robert. "Market Controls." New Haven: Yale University, 1977. Manuscript.

Cochran, Thomas C. *Railroad Leaders*. Cambridge: Harvard University Press, 1953.

Common Cause Campaign Finance Monitoring Project. *1972 Congressional Campaign Finances*. 10 vols. Washington, D.C.: Common Cause, 1974a.

Common Cause Campaign Finance Monitoring Project. *1972 Federal Campaign Finances: Interest Groups & Political Parties*. 3 vols. Washington, D.C.: Common Cause, 1974b.

Common Cause Campaign Finance Monitoring Project. *1974 Congressional Campaign Finances*. 5 vols. Washington, D.C.: Common Cause, 1976.

Coulter, E. Merton. *A Short History of Georgia*. Chapel Hill: University of North Carolina Press, 1933.

Crain, W. Mark. "On the Structure and Stability of Political Markets." *Journal of Political Economy* 85 (August 1977): 829–842.

Crawford, Kenneth G. *The Pressure Boys*. New York: Julian Messner, Inc., 1939.

Cross, John G. *The Economics of Bargaining*. New York: Basic Books, 1969.

Dahl, Robert. *A Preface to Democratic Theory*. Chicago: University of Chicago Press, 1956.

Dahl, Robert. "Pluralism Revisited." New Haven: Yale University, September 1976.

Dahl, Robert. *Polyarchy: Participation and Opposition*. New Haven: Yale University Press, 1971.

Dahl, Robert. *Who Governs?* New Haven: Yale University Press, 1961.

Darby, Michael R., and Karni, Edi. "Free Competition and the Optimal Amount of Fraud." *Journal of Law and Economics* 16 (April 1973): 67–88.

Daughen, Joseph R., and Binzen, Peter. *The Wreck of the Penn Central*, Boston: Little, Brown and Co., 1971.

Deakin, James. *The Lobbyists*. Washington, D.C.: Public Affairs Press, 1966.

Downs, Anthony. *An Economic Theory of Democracy*. New York: Harper and Row, 1957.

Downs, Anthony. *Inside Bureaucracy*. Boston: Little, Brown, 1967.

Dunn, Delmer. *Financing Presidential Campaigns*. Washington, D.C.: Brookings Institution, 1972.

Edelson, Noel M. "Congestion Tolls under Monopoly." *American Economic Review* 59 (December 1971): 873–882.

Edelson, Noel M., and Hildebrand, David. "Congestion Tolls for Poisson Queuing Processes." *Econometrica* 43 (January 1975): 81–92.

Edsall, Thomas B. "State Politics and Public Interests: Money and Morality in Maryland." *Society* 11 (4) (May/June 1974): 74–81.

Eisenberg, Melvin. "Legal Roles of Shareholders and Management in Modern Corporate Decisionmaking." *California Law Review* 57 (January 1969): 1–181.

Farnham, Wallace D. "The Weakened Spring of Government: A Study in Nineteenth Century American History." *American Historical Review* 68 (April 1963): 662–680.

Feldstein, Martin. "The Income Tax and Charitable Contributions: Part I—Aggregate and Distributional Effects." *National Tax Journal* 28 (March 1975): 81–100.

Fenno, Richard F. *Committees in Congress*. Boston: Little, Brown and Co., 1973.

Fenno, Richard T. "U.S. Representatives in their Constituencies: An Exploration." *American Political Science Review* 71 (September 1977): 883–917.

Ferejohn, John. *Pork Barrel Politics: River and Harbor Legislation, 1947–1968*. Stanford, Calif.: Stanford University Press, 1974.

Fischer, Elizabeth. "Altruism and Rationality: A Conceptual Scheme with Implications for Social Change." Chapel Hill: University of North Carolina, 1976. Mimeographed.

Fogel, Robert W. *The Union Pacific Railroad: A Case in Premature Enterprise*. Baltimore: Johns Hopkins Press, 1960.

Ford, Henry Jones. "Municipal Corruption." *Political Science Quarterly* 19 (December 1904): 673–686.

Frey, Bruno S. "The Politico-Economic System: A Simulation Model." *Kyklos* 27 (1974): 227–254.

Fulbright, James W. *The Pentagon Propaganda Machine*. New York: Liveright Publishing Corporation, 1970.

Gardiner, John. *The Politics of Corruption: Organized Crime in an American City*. New York: Russell Sage Foundation, 1970.

Gardiner, John A.; Balch, George I.; and Lyman, Theodore R. "Corruption in Local Land-Use Regulation." Paper delivered at the annual meeting of the American Political Science Association, 1977.

Gardiner, John A., and Lyman, Theodore R. *Decisions for Sale: Corruption in Local Land-Use Regulation*, New York: Praeger, 1978.

Gardiner, John A., and Olson, David J., eds. *Theft of the City*. Bloomington: Indiana University Press, 1974.

Gelfand, Mathew D. "Aspects of the Political Economy of Influence." New Haven: Yale University, departmental essay in economics, January 1977. Manuscript.

Goldberg, Victor. "Institutional Change and the Quasi-Invisible Hand." *Journal of Law and Economics* 17 (October 1974): 461–492.

Gramlich, Edward. "The New York City Fiscal Crisis—What Happened and What Is to Be Done?" *American Economic Review—Papers and Proceedings* 66 (May 1976): 415–429.

Granick, David. *Enterprise Guidance in Eastern Europe: A Comparison of Four Socialist Economies*. Princeton: Princeton University Press, 1975.

Groves, Theodore. "Incentives in Teams." *Econometrica* 41 (July 1973): 617–632.

Hacker, Andrew. "Pressure Politics in Pennsylvania," in *The Uses of Power*, edited by Alan Weston. New York: Harcourt, Brace and World, 1962.

Hammond, Peter J. "Equity, Arrow's Conditions, and Rawls' Difference Principle." *Econometrica* 44 (July 1976): 793–804.

Harris, Frank E. "Annals of Politics (Campaign Expenses)." *New Yorker* 47 (August 7, 1971): 37–64.

Harrison, Paul. "Rule by Thieves." *New Society* 25 (August 1973): 289.

Heidenheimer, Arnold J., ed. *Political Corruption: Readings in Comparative Analysis*. New York: Holt, Rinehart and Winston, 1970.

Henderson, James M., and Quandt, Richard. *Microeconomic Theory: A Mathematical Approach*. New York: McGraw-Hill Book Company, 1971.

Henn, Harry. *Handbook of the Law of Corporations*. 2d ed. St. Paul, Minn.: West Publishing Co., 1970.

Herling, John. *The Great Price Conspiracy: The Story of the Antitrust Violations in the Electrical Industry*. Washington: R. B. Luce, 1962.

Huntington, Samuel. "Political Development and Political Decay." In *Political Modernization: A Reader in Comparative Political Change*, edited by Claude Welch, Jr., pp. 207–241. Belmont, Calif.: Wadsworth Publishing Co., 1967.

Hutchinson, John. *The Imperfect Union*. New York: E. P. Dutton and Co., 1970.

Jacobson, Gary C. "The Electoral Consequences of Public Subsidies for Congressional Campaigns," Paper delivered at the annual meeting of the American Political Science Association, 1977.

Jacoby, Neil; Nehemkis, Peter; and Eells, Richard. *Bribery and Extortion in World Business*. New York: MacMillan Publishing Co., 1977.

Janowitz, Morris. *The Professional Soldier*. Glencoe, Ill.: Free Press, 1960.

Johnson, Omotunde E. G. "An Economic Analysis of Corrupt Government with Special Application to Less Developed Countries." *Kyklos* 28 (1975): 47–61.

Josephson, Matthew. *The Robber Barons: The Great American Capitalists 1861–1901*. New York: Harcourt, Brace and Co., 1934.

Kagen, Robert Allen. "The Wage–Price Freeze: A Study in Administrative Justice." Ph.D. dissertation, New Haven: Yale University, 1975.

Kampelman, Max. "Congress, the Media and the President." In *Congress against the President: Proceedings of the Academy of Political Science* 32 (1975): 85–97.

Kaufman, Herbert. *Are Government Organizations Immortal?* Washington, D.C.: Brookings Institution, 1976.

Kaufmann, Arnold. *Methods and Models of Operations Research.* Englewood Cliffs, N.J.: Prentice-Hall, 1963.

Key, V. O., Jr. *The Techniques of Political Graft in the United States.* Chicago: University of Chicago Libraries, 1936.

Key, V.O., Jr. *The Responsible Electorate.* Cambridge: Harvard University Press, 1966.

Kingdon, John. *Candidates for Office: Beliefs and Strategies.* New York: Random House, 1966.

Kitch, Edmund; Isaacson, Marc; and Kasper, Daniel. "The Regulation of Taxicabs in Chicago." *Journal of Law & Economics* 14 (October 1971): 285–350.

Knapp Commission (Commission to Investigate Allegations of Police Corruption and the City's Anti-Corruption Procedures). *Commission Report.* Excerpted in Gardiner and Olson (1974): 175–191.

Kornblum, Allan N. *The Moral Hazards.* Lexington, Mass.: D. C. Heath, 1976.

Kramer, Gerald. "On a Class of Equilibrium Conditions for Majority Rule." *Econometrica* 41 (March 1973): 285–298.

Kramer, Gerald. "A Dynamical Model of Political Equilibrium." New Haven, Conn.: Cowles Foundation, Discussion Paper No. 396, June 1975.

Kriesberg, Simon. "Decisionmaking Models and the Control of Corporate Crime." *Yale Law Journal* 85 (July 1976): 1091–1128.

Krueger, Anne O. "The Political Economy of the Rent-Seeking Society." *American Economic Review* 64 (June 1974): 271–303.

Lambin, Jean Jacques. *Advertising Competition and Market Conduct in Oligopoly over Time: An Econometric Investigation in Western European Countries.* Amsterdam and New York: North-Holland–Oxford–American Elsevier, 1976.

Leff, Nathaniel. "Economic Development through Bureaucratic Corruption." *American Behavioral Scientist* 8 (November 1964): 8–14. Reprinted in Heidenheimer (1970): 510–520.

Leibenstein, Harvey. "Allocative Efficiency vs. 'X-Efficiency.' " *American Economic Review* 56 (June 1966): 392–415.

Levhari, David, and Sheshinski, Eytan. "The Economics of Queues: A Brief Survey." In *Essays on Economic Behavior under Uncertainty,* edited by M. Balch, D. McFadden and S. Wu, pp. 195–212. Amsterdam: North-Holland, 1974.

Levine, Michael E. "Regulating Airmail Transportation." *Journal of Law and Economics* 18 (October 1975): 317–359.

LeVine, Victor T. *Political Corruption: The Ghana Case.* Stanford, Calif.: Hoover Institution Press, 1975.

Lindblom, Charles E. *The Policy-Making Process.* Englewood Cliffs, N.J.: Prentice-Hall, 1968.

Lindblom, Charles E. *Politics and Markets: The World's Political-Economic Systems.* New York: Basic Books, 1977.

Lindsey, Cotton. "A Theory of Government Enterprise." *Journal of Political Economy* 84 (October 1976): 1061–1078.

Loveman, Brian. "The Logic of Political Corruption." Bloomington: Indiana University Studies in Political Theory and Policy Analysis, 1972.

Machlup, Fritz, and Taber, Martha. "Bilateral Monopoly, Successive Monopoly, and Vertical Integration." *Economica N.S.* 27 (May 1960): 101–119.

Magee, Stepen P., and Brock, William A. "The Campaign Contribution Specialization Theorem." Chicago: University of Chicago, February 1976. Mimeographed.

Manning, Bayless. Review of *The American Stockholder* by J. A. Livingston. *Yale Law Journal* 67 (July 1958): 1477–1496.

Mansfield, E. *Microeconomics.* New York: W. W. Norton, 1970.

Marchand, Maurice G. "Priority Pricing." Leuven: Katholieke Universiteit Te Leuven, CORE Discussion Paper No. 7124, Center of Operations Research and Econometrics, August 1971.

Margolis, Julius. "Public Policies for Private Profits: Urban Government." In *Redistribution through Public Choice,* edited by H. Hochman and G. Peterson. New York: Columbia University Press, 1974.

Matthews, Donald R. *U.S. Senators and Their World.* New York: Random House, Vintage Books, 1960.

May, Kenneth O. "A Set of Independent, Necessary and Sufficient Conditions for Simple Majority Decision." *Econometrica* 20 (October 1952): 680–684.

Mayhew, David. *Congress: The Electoral Connection.* New Haven: Yale University Press, 1974.

McCloy, John; Pearson, Nathan; and Matthews, Beverley. *The Great Oil Spill: The Inside Report: Gulf Oil's Bribery and Political Chicanery.* New York: Chelsea House, 1976. (The report was originally entitled "Report of the Special Review Committee of the Board of Directors of Gulf Oil Corporation.")

McMullan, M. "A Theory of Corruption." In Heidenheimer (1970): 317–330.

McNeill, Robert J. *Democratic Campaign Financing in Indiana, 1964.* Bloomington and Princeton: Institute of Public Administration and Citizens Research Foundation, 1966.

Mendelson, Mary Adelaide. *Tender Loving Greed.* New York: Alfred A. Knopf, 1974.

Merton, Robert K. *Social Theory and Social Structure.* New York: The Free Press, 1968.

Migué, Jean-Luc, and Bélanger, Gérard. "Toward a General Theory of Managerial Discretion." And comments. *Public Choice* 17 (Spring 1974): 27–47.

Milbrath, Lester. *The Washington Lobbyists.* Chicago: Rand McNally and Co., 1963.

Miller, Arthur; Miller, Warren E.; Raine, Alden S.; and Brown, Thad A. "A Majority Party in Disarray: Policy Polarization in the 1972 Election." *American Political Science Review* 70 (September 1976): 753–778.

Monteiro, John B. *Corruption.* Bombay: Manaktalas, 1966.

Montias, John Michael. *The Structure of Economic Systems.* New Haven: Yale University Press, 1976.

Mood, Alexander, and Graybill, Franklin. *Introduction to the Theory of Statistics.* New York: McGraw-Hill, 1963.

Moore, Mark Harrison. *Buy and Bust.* Lexington, Mass.: D. C. Heath, 1977.

Musgrave, Richard, and Musgrave, Peggy. *Public Finance in Theory and Practice.* New York: McGraw-Hill, 1974.

Nadel, Mark V. *The Politics of Consumer Protection.* Indianapolis: Bobbs-Merrill, 1971.

Nadel, Mark V., and Rourke, Francis E. "Bureaucracies." In *Government Institutions and Processes: Handbook of Political Science,* edited by F. Greenstein and N. Polsby, 5:373–440. Reading, Mass.: Addison-Wesley, 1975.

Naor, P. "The Regulation of Queue Size by Levying Tolls." *Econometrica* 37 (January 1969): 15–24.

Nichols, Donald; Smolensky, Eugene, and Tideman, T. Nicolaus. "Discrimination by Waiting Time in Merit Goods." *American Economic Review* 61 (June 1971): 312–323.

Niskanen, William. *Bureaucracy and Representative Government.* Chicago: Aldine-Atherton, 1971.

Niskanen, William. "Bureaucrats and Politicians." *Journal of Law and Economics* 18 (December 1975): 617–644.

Noll, Roger. *Reforming Regulation: An Evaluation of the Ash Council Proposals.* Washington, D.C.: Brookings Institution, 1971.

Noll, Roger; Peck, Merton J.; and McGowan, John. *Economic Aspects of Television Regulation.* Washington, D.C.: Brookings Institution, 1973.

Nordhaus, William. "The Political Business Cycle." *The Review of Economic Studies* 42 (April 1975): 169–190.

North, Douglas C. "Entrepreneurial Policy and Internal Organization in the Large Life Insurance Companies at the Time of the Armstrong Investigation of Life Insurance." *Explorations in Entrepreneurial History* 15 (March 1953): 138–161.

Nozick, Robert. *Anarchy, State and Utopia.* New York: Basic Books, 1974.

Nye, J. S. "Corruption and Political Development: A Cost–Benefit Analysis." *American Political Science Review* 61 (June 1967): 417–427. Reprinted in Heidenheimer (1970): 564–578.

Olson, Mancur. *The Logic of Collective Action.* Cambridge: Harvard University Press, 1965.

Page, Benjamin I. "The Theory of Political Ambiguity." *American Political Science Review* 70 (September 1976): 742–752.

Palda, Kristian S. "The Effect of Expenditure on Political Success," *Journal of Law and Economics* 18 (December 1975): 745–774.

Palmier, Leslie. "Corruption in India." *New Society* 32 (June 5, 1975): 577–579.

Pashigian, B. Peter. "On the Control of Crime and Bribery." *Journal of Legal Studies* 4 (June 1975): 311–327.

Pateman, Carole. *Participation and Democratic Theory.* Cambridge: At the University Press, 1970.

Peltzman, Samuel. "Toward a More General Theory of Regulation." *Journal of Law and Economics* 19 (August 1976): 211–240.

Pennsylvania Crime Commission. *Report on Police Corruption and the Quality of Law Enforcement in Philadelphia.* Saint Davids, Pa.: The Commission, 1974.

Phelps, Edmund S., ed. *Altruism, Morality and Economic Theory.* New York: Russell Sage Foundation, 1975.

Pincus, Jonathan J. "Pressure Groups and the Pattern of Tariffs." *Journal of Political Economy* 83 (August 1975): 757–778.

Pinto-Duschinsky, Michael. "Theories of Corruption in American Politics." Paper delivered at the annual meeting of the American Political Science Association, September 5, 1976.

Pitkin, Hanna Fenichel. *The Concept of Representation.* Berkeley and Los Angeles: University of California Press, 1967.

Plott, Charles R. "A Notion of Equilibrium and Its Possibility under Majority Rule." *American Economic Review* 62 (September 1967): 787–806.

Popkin, Samuel; Gorman, John; Phillips, Charles; and Smith, Jeffrey. "Comment: What Have You Done for Me Lately? Toward an Investment Theory of Voting." *American Political Science Review* 70 (September 1976): 779–805.

Posner, Richard. "Theories of Economic Regulation." *Bell Journal of Economics and Management Science* 5 (Autumn 1974): 335–358.

Rhodes, James Ford. *History of the United States.* vol. 7. New York: Macmillan Co., 1906.

Riggs, Fred W. "Bureaucrats and Political Development: A Paradoxical View." In *Bureaucracy and Political Development,* edited by J. La Palombara, pp. 120–167. Princeton: Princeton University Press, 1963.

Riker, William H. "Federalism." In *Government Institutions and Processes, Handbook of Political Science,* edited by F. Greenstein and N. Polsby, 5:93–172. Reading, Mass.: Addison-Wesley, 1975.

Riker, William H. *The Theory of Political Coalitions.* New Haven: Yale University Press, 1962.

Riker, William H., and Ordeshook, Peter C. *An Introduction to Positive Political Theory.* Englewood Cliffs, N.J.: Prentice Hall, Inc., 1973.

Riker, William H., and Ordeshook, Peter C. "A Theory of the Calculus of Voting." *American Political Science Review* 62 (March 1968): 25–42.

Ritt, Leonard. "Committee Position, Seniority, and the Distribution of Government Expenditures." *Public Policy* 24 (Fall 1976): 463–489.

Roberts, Marc. "Environmental Protection: The Complexities of Real Policy Choice." In *Managing the Water Environment,* edited by Neil Swainson, pp. 157–234. Vancouver: University of British Columbia Press, 1976.

Roberts, Marc. "An Evolutionary and Institutional View of the Behavior of Public and Private Companies." *American Economic Review Papers and Proceedings* 65 (May 1975): 415–427.

Robinson, Frank S. *Machine Politics: A Study of Albany's O'Connells.* New Brunswick, N.J.: Transaction Books, 1977.

Rose-Ackerman, Susan. "Effluent Charges: A Critique." *Canadian Journal of Economics* 6 (November 1973): 512–528.

Rose-Ackerman, Susan. "The Economics of Corruption." *Journal of Public Economics* 4 (February 1975): 187–203.

Rosenblum, Victor. "How to Get into TV: The Federal Communications Commission and Miami's Channel 10." In *The Uses of Power,* edited by Alan Westin, pp. 173–228. New York: Harcourt, Brace & World, 1962.

Ross, Stephen. "The Economic Theory of Agency: The Principal's Problem." *American Economic Review Papers and Proceedings* 63 (May 1973): 134–139.

Ross, Stephen. "On the Economic Theory of Agency and the Principle of Similarity." In *Essays on Economic Behavior under Uncertainty,* edited by M. Balch, D. McFadden and S. Wu. Amsterdam: North-Holland, 1974.

Rossiter, Clinton, ed. *The Federalist Papers,* New York: New American Library, 1961.

Rottenberg, Simon. "A Theory of Corruption in Trade Unions." In *Series Studies in Social and Economic Sciences.* Symposium Studies Series No. 31. Washington, D.C.: National Institute of Social and Behavioral Science, January 1960.

Rubinstein, Jonathan. *City Police.* New York: Farrar, Straus, Giroux, 1973.

Rubinstein, Jonathan, and Reuter, Peter. "Numbers: The Routine Racket." New York: Policy Sciences Center, April 1977. Manuscript.

Rundquist, Barry S.; Strom, Gerald S.; and Peters, John G. "Corrupt Politicians and Their Electoral Support: Some Experimental Observations." *American Political Science Review* 71 (September 1977): 954–963.

Salerno, Ralph, and Tompkins, John. "Protecting Organized Crime." In *The Crime Confederation.* Garden City, N.Y.: Doubleday, 1969. Reprinted in Gardiner and Olson (1974): 144–151.

Schelling, Thomas C. "Economics and Criminal Enterprise." *The Public Interest* 7 (Spring 1967): 61–78.

Schelling, Thomas C. *The Strategy of Conflict.* Cambridge: Harvard University Press, 1963.

Schmidt, Kurt. "Zür Ökonomik der Korruption." *Schmollers Jahrbuch* 9 (1969): 130–149.

Schuck, Peter. "The Curious Case of the Indicted Meat Inspectors." *Harper's* 245 (September 1972): 81–88.

Schumpeter, Joseph A. *Capitalism, Socialism and Democracy.* 3rd ed., New York: Harper and Brothers, 1950.

Scott, James C. *Comparative Political Corruption.* Englewood Cliffs, N.J.: Prentice-Hall, 1972.

Sen, Amartya. *Collective Choice and Social Welfare.* San Francisco: Holden-Day, 1970.

Sen, Amartya K., and Pattainaik, P. K. "Necessary and Sufficient Conditions for Rational Choice under Majority Decision," *Journal of Economic Theory* 1 (August 1969): 178–202.

Shannon, William, "Massachusetts: Prisoner of the Past," in Allen (1949): 23–68.

Shepsle, Kenneth. "The Strategy of Ambiguity: Uncertainty and Electoral Competition." *American Political Science Review* 66 (June 1972): 555–568.

Sherman, Lawrence, ed. *Police Corruption.* Garden City, N.Y.: Doubleday, Anchor Books, 1974, (a)

Sherman, Lawrence. "Becoming Bent: Moral Careers of Corrupt Policemen." In Sherman (1974: 191–208), (b).

Slutsky, Steven. "A Characterization of Societies with Consistent Majority Decision." *Review of Economic Studies* 64 (January 1977): 211–226.

Smith, Hedrick. *The Russians.* New York: Ballantine Books, 1976.

Smith, Howard R. *Government and Business.* New York: The Ronald Press, 1958.

Smith, Richard. *Corporations in Crisis.* Garden City, N.J.: Doubleday, 1963.

Steiner, Gilbert Y. *The State of Welfare.* Washington, D.C.: The Brookings Institution, 1971.

Stigler, George. "Economic Competition and Political Competition." *Public Choice* 13 (Fall 1972): 91–106.

Stigler, George J. "Free Riders and Collective Action: An Appendix to Theories of Economic Regulation." *Bell Journal of Economics and Management Science* 5 (Autumn 1974): 359–365.

Stigler, George J. "The Optimum Enforcement of Laws." *Journal of Political Economy* 78 (May/June 1970): 526–536.

Stigler, George J. "The Theory of Economic Regulation." *Bell Journal of Economics and Management Science,* 2 (Spring 1971): 1103–1121.

Stigler, George J., and Becker, Gary. "De Gustibus Non Est Disputandum." *American Economic Review* 67 (March 1977): 76–90.

Strasnick, Steven. "The Problem of Social Choice: Arrow to Rawls." *Philosophy and Public Affairs* 5 (Spring 1976): 241–273, (a).

Strasnick, Steven. "Social Choice and the Derivation of Rawls' Difference Principle." *Journal of Philosophy* 73 (February 1976): 85–99, (b).

Swaan, Abram de. *Coalition Theories and Cabinet Formations.* San Francisco: Jossey-Bass, 1973.

Swart, Koenraad W. "The Sale of Public Offices." In Heidenheimer (1970: 82–90).

Thompson, Earl. "Book Review." *Journal of Economic Literature* 11 (September 1973): 950.

Truman, David. *The Governmental Process.* New York: Alfred A. Knopf, 1951.

Tufte, Edward R. *Political Control of the Economy.* Princeton: Princeton University Press, 1978.

Tullock, Gordon. *Toward a Mathematics of Politics.* Ann Arbor: University of Michigan Press, 1967.

Tullock, Gordon. "The Purchase of Politicians," *Western Economic Journal.* 10 (September 1972): 354–355.

U.S. Congress, Senate. Committee on Foreign Relations, Subcommittee on Multinational Corporations. *Multinational Corporations and United States Foreign Policy Hearings*. Washington, D.C.: U.S. Government Printing Office, March and April 1973.

U.S. Congress, Senate. Committee on Government Operations. *Reforming the Regulatory Appointments Process*. Washington, D.C.: U.S. Government Printing Office, Volume 1. January 1977.

U.S. Congress, Senate, Special Committee on Aging, Subcommittee on Long-Term Care, *Nursing Home Care in the United States: Failure in Public Policy*. Supporting Paper No. 2, "Drugs in Nursing Homes: Misuse, High Costs, and Kickbacks. Washington, D.C.: U.S. Government Printing Office, 1975.

U.S. Department of Housing and Urban Development. *Housing in the Seventies*. Washington, D.C.: Mimeographed, October 1973.

Von Roy, Edward. "On the Theory of Corruption." *Economic Development and Cultural Change* 19 (October 1970): 86–110.

Ward, Benjamin. *The Socialist Economy*. New York: Random House, 1967.

Warwick, Donald. *A Theory of Public Bureaucracy*. Cambridge: Harvard University Press, 1975.

Waterbury, John. "Endemic and Planned Corruption in a Monarchical Regime." *World Politics* 25 (July 1973): 534–555.

Weber, Max. *The Theory of Social and Economic Organization*. Translated by A. M. Henderson and Talcott Parsons, edited by Talcott Parsons. Glencoe, Ill.: Free Press, 1947.

Weisbrod, Burton. "What is the Non-Profit Sector?" Institution for Social and Policy Studies Working Paper. New Haven: Yale University, 1977.

Weiss, Elliott. *The Corporate Watergate*. Special Report 1975-D. Washington, D.C.: Investor Research Center, 1975.

Weitzman, Martin. "The New Soviet Incentive Model." *Bell Journal of Economics and Management Science* 7 (Spring 1976): 251–258.

Weitzman, Martin. "Prices vs. Quantities." *Review of Economic Studies* 61 (October 1974): 477–492.

Welch, William P. "The Economics of Campaign Funds." *Public Choice* 20 (Winter 1974): 83–97.

White, Henry Kirk. *History of the Union Pacific Railway*. Chicago: University of Chicago Press, 1895.

Williamson, Oliver. *The Economics of Discretionary Behavior: Managerial Objectives in a Theory of the Firm*. Englewood Cliffs, N.J.: Prentice-Hall, 1967.

Williamson, Oliver. *Markets and Hierarchies*. New York: Free Press, 1975.

Williamson, Oliver. "The Vertical Integration of Production: Market Failure Considerations." *American Economic Review Papers and Proceedings* 61 (May 1971): 112–123.

Wilson, James. "The Politics of Regulation." In *Social Responsibility and the Business Predicament*, edited by James McKie, pp. 135–168. Washington, D.C.: Brookings Institution, 1974.

Wilson, Robert. "On the Theory of Syndicates." *Econometrica* 36 (January 1968): 119–132.

Wolfinger, Raymond. "Why Political Machines Have Not Withered Away and Other Revisionist Thoughts." *Journal of Politics* 34 (May 1972): 365–398.

Wraith, Ronald, and Simkins, Edgar. *Corruption in Developing Countries*. London: George Allen and Unwin, 1963.

Yarmolinsky, Adam. *The Military Establishment*. New York: Harper and Row, 1971.

AUTHOR INDEX

SUBJECT INDEX

A

Africa
  Ghana, 138n
  Morocco, 185n
  Nigeria, 50n, 110n, 184n
Agency relationship, 6, 112n, 190
Agent, *see* Expediter
Agriculture, 49n, *see also* Dairy industry
  Department of Agriculture, U.S., 76n
Airlines, 53n, *see also* Civil Aeronautics
  Board
Allende, Salvador, 81n
Antitrust litigation, 50n, 192n, 201
Army Corps of Engineers, U.S., 77
Asia, *see* India, Indonesia, Philippines,
  South Korea, Thailand

B

Banking industry, 49n, 52, 199n, 200
Bankruptcy, 196, 198, 199n, 200, 208
Bargaining, 166, 219
  among bureaucrats, 179, 224
  bureaucrats versus legislators, 82
  bureaucrats versus regulated firms, 176
  competitive bureaucrats versus clients,
    154, 158, 166
  dynamic model of, 129–132
  government agent versus client cartel,
    163–165
  government agent versus monopolistic
    firm, 119–120, 129–132
  interest groups versus legislators, 31–32,
    46–48
  monopolistic bureaucrat versus client,
    160–163, 166–179
  strategies, 130n, 160n
Barriers to entry, *see* Entry barriers
Bilateral monopoly, 46, 119, 129–135, 164n,
  165n, 171, *see also* Bargaining
Board of directors, *see* Firm, board of
  directors
Brasco, Frank, 21n, 75n
Bribery, *see* Corruption
Bureaucracy, *see also* Coercive programs,
  Contracting, Franchising, Licensing pro-
  grams, Qualification programs, Queuing,
  Regulation
  allocation rules, 87, 89